Cultivating Spirituality in Leadership
Synergizing Heart and Mind

Nancy Doetzel, PhD

Detselig Enterprises Ltd.

Calgary, Alberta, Canada

Cultivating Spirituality in Leadership: Synergizing Heart and Mind

©2006 Nancy Doetzel

Canadian Cataloguing in Publication Data

Doetzel, Nancy, 1953-
  Cultivating spirituality in leadership : synergizing heart and mind / Nancy Doetzel.

Includes bibliographical references.
ISBN-10: 1-55059-315-3
ISBN-13: 978-1-55059-315-0

  1. Educational leadership – Moral and ethical aspects.
  2. Spirituality – Study and teaching. 3. Educators – Attitudes.
  I. Title.
LC268.D58 2006   370.11'4   C2006-902017-5

Detselig Enterprises Ltd.
210, 1220 Kensington Road NW
Calgary, Alberta T2N 3P5

Phone: (403) 283-0900
Fax: (403) 283-0900
email: temeron@telusplanet.net
web: www.temerondetselig.com

All rights reserved. No part of this book may be reproduced in any form or by any means without permission in writing from the publisher.

We acknowledge the financial support of the Government of Canada through the Book Publishing Industry Development Program (BPIDP) for our publishing activities. We also acknowledge the financial support for our publishing program from the Alberta Foundation for the Arts.

Cover Design by Alvin Choong
ISBN 1-55059-315-3 and 978-1-55059-315-0
SAN 115-0324
Printed in Canada

This book is dedicated to my late father, Frederick George Gould, and late brother, Robert James Gould, both whom taught me invaluable lessons about spirituality, and left imprints on my heart before they were called from this world.

Introduction

The new millennium is a possible time of synthesis, of bringing together multiple ways of knowing. Many educators are challenging the dualism of a disconnected mind and heart approach to leadership and making space for spirituality within leadership practices. More dialog about the changes that help cultivate a spiritual sensibility are taking place within some public school educational systems. By more openly dialoguing about spirituality at work, educational leaders can rediscover their heart's wisdom, enabling them to view their roles through a fresh lens.

In this book, spirituality is defined as a latent inherent truth awakened by contemplation, rituals, peak life experiences and caring acts of kindness; when awakened, spirituality is a sensation of the sacred, a sentiment of hope, a feeling of enthusiasm and excitement, and a heart-felt sense of interconnection with others. Further, the term "heart" is used metaphorically in both analysis of literature and data base, as a symbolism of the tacit and visceral nature of spirituality that makes it difficult to articulate in words or encompass in religious organizations.

The literature reviewed within this book sets the context for and frames a scholarly study titled: *Cultivating Spirituality in Leadership: Synergizing Heart and Mind.* The purpose of this study was to understand the spiritual insights of ten educational leaders, and to explore how an educational leader behaves spiritually. Appreciative inquiry was applied to the research questions: 1. How are the spiritual experiences of educational leaders understood and articulated by educators? 2. In what ways would this articulation of spirituality best contribute to the development of effective leadership? Appreciative inquiry is a constructive approach to research that creates space for new voices and expands circles of dialog to include discourses about spirituality. It encourages leaders to establish systems that nurture educators within the workplace.

Recollections of study participants' personal and professional spiritual experiences were gathered from on-line interviews, two web-page private discussion forums, and follow-up telephone conversations. Exploring spirituality through electronic communication enabled participants to dialog freely and anonymously on-line within their own selected time frames and locations. They had opportunities to share personal and professional insights about spirituality which moved them beyond muted discourses about spirituality. However, this method of data collection was limited to ten participants and excluded non-verbal cues that could have been observed in a face-to-face interview.

Data were analysed using a triangulated phenomenological, feminist and cooperative inquiry research design. An application of a triangulated approach encourages the application of three different lenses when examining responses to a research question. Qualitative inquirers triangulate among different data sources to enhance the accuracy of a study. The three key concepts found within the literature set the foundation for a synergism: 1. muting discourses about spirituality within educational systems 2. exploring moral issues within educational values, and 3. shifting paradigms affecting educational leadership. These key concepts led to discoveries of threads within the data. After the threads were woven into patterns, they evolved into emergent themes and phases of spiritual leadership development. The phases of spiritual development include 1. awakening spirituality within self, 2. signifying spirituality within the workplace, and 3. cultivating spirituality within leadership practices.

A schemata of cultivation of spirituality within self, and a schemata of cultivation of spirit within the workplace were outcomes of these phases. Both schemata framed ways that participants have cultivated spirituality within self and spirit within leadership, after their innate spirituality had been awakened. The findings were analysed to identify key concepts, threads and themes. The overarching key concepts set a foundation for the questions; the data collected from the questions evolved from threads into emergent themes. Then, the emergent themes enfolded into two heart-centred schemata. Working as a team, treating everyone as equals and "walking the talk" are three elements of spiritual leadership shared by all participants.

Research implications included applying the findings to better understand how to cultivate spirit within educational leadership practices. Articulation of the findings could assist leaders who are working on personal growth and educators who want to initiate effective leadership training programs. Additionally, answering the research questions provided an original contribution to knowledge that encourages more open communication about the spiritual elements of leadership amongst educators and leaders in other walks of life thus, assisting them to introduce discourses about spirituality. Research inquiries, such as this one, move beyond heart and head dualisms within educational systems and encourage the revision of a narrow bureaucratic leadership style into one that is based upon a more spiritual model. Such practices would assist educators to be more adept at dealing with impressionable children and diverse youth and perhaps avoid professional burnout.

Acknowledgments

This book has truly been a team effort. At this time, I express my deep appreciation to my husband, Ken Doetzel, for supporting me throughout my academic career and keeping faith in me during my challenging spiritual journey. I am also grateful for the prayerful and moral support I received from valued friends: Don Costucci, Gisela Engels, Laurie Hill, Roberta Jackson, Margot McKinnon, Neil Meyers, John Ramanaukas, Marilyn Tobin and Mohamed Zayed.

I am also indebted to my mother, Clara Gould-McDonald, who was my first spiritual mentor and my sister Gail Johnson, who reflected spirituality within her professional and personal clowning roles.

I would like to express a deep appreciation to my research supervisor, Dr. E. Lisbeth Donaldson, for her enduring support and invaluable guidance throughout the doctorate scholarly process. I would also like to thank my other major supporters of my academic journey: Dr. Jeff Jacobs, Dr. David Jones, Dr. J. Tim Goddard, Dr. Tim Pyrch and Dr. Ian Winchestor for their insightful contributions and on-going faith in me. Additionally, I would like to express my gratitude to other staff members of the Graduate Division of Educational Research for their ongoing support during my academic journey.

Contents

ONE: Introduction to Exploring "Spirituality" 13
    Setting the Context of the Issue 13
        Proposing Conceptual Definitions of Spirituality 17
        Introducing Paradigm Shifts Within Approaches to
          Educational Research 18
        Outlining Chapter Content 21
    Exploring the Scope of the Research Problem................. 21
        Postulating Standpoints About the Nature of Spirituality...... 24
        Connecting Science with Spirituality and Heart Intelligence.... 27
        Exploring Resurgence of Spiritual Values: School Reform..... 30
    Acknowledging Spiritual Evolution Within Educational
        Leadership... 32
        Introducing Discourses About Spirituality Within Educational
          Leadership... 33
        Reviewing Moral Issues Within Education Systems........... 34
        Examining Paradigms Affecting Educational Leadership 36
    Research Questions and Methodology 39
    Objectives 40
    Overview of Following Chapters............................. 41

TWO: Related Resources: Spirituality Matters 43
    Reviewing Multiple Perspectives of Spirituality 44
        Sensing and Expressing Spirituality......................... 45
        Exploring Discourses About Spirituality 45
        Articulating Aspects of Spirituality Within Leadership 49
        Confusing Spirituality With Relgion: Spiritual Dissonance 51
        Muting Discourses About Spirituality Within Educational
          Systems 55
    Examining Moral Issues Within Educational Values 56
        Reviewing Relationships Between Morals and Spirituality...... 57
        Examining Links Between Morals and Religious Beliefs....... 59
        Silencing Moral Discourses Amongst Educational Leaders 61
    Shifting Paradigms Affecting Educational Leadership 63
        Evolving Educational Leadership and Teaching Models....... 65
        Reviewing Power Relations of Ruling Which Excluded Female
          Leaders 70
        Religious Paradigms: Shifting Toward Articulating Spirituality .. 74

    University Teaching Paradigms: Shifting Toward Addressing
        Spirituality 76
    On-line Dialog: Shifting Towardes Discussing Spirituality in
        Education 77
    Calgary Public School Policies: Shifting Towards Including
        spirituality 77
    Summary of Chapter 78

THREE: Theoretical Framework 79
    Rationale for Utilizing Qualittative Research. 79
        Characteristics of Qualitative Research. 80
        Epistemological Paradigm Shifts Noted in Research Methods . . 85
    Triangulated Paradigms Applied to Research Methodology. 92
        Participants Selected. 93
        Data Collection Process for this Inquiry 95
        Methods of Data Collection 96
    Summary of Chapter 105
s
FOUR: Results: Dialoguing About Spirituality. 107
    Profiles of Participants. 107
    How Are the Spiritual Experiences of Educational Leaders
        Understood and Articulated by Educators? 109
        Not Clear by Words 109
        Articulate Primarily by Action. 111
    Beliefs and Life Experiences Affect Understanding of
        Spirituality. 111
        Summary of Responses 114
    What Was It About This Peak Experience That Would be Defined
        As Spiritual? 114
        Professional and Personal Experiences. 115
        Connection: Others, Community, World 117
        Connection: God, Self, Nature 117
        Summary of Responses 119
    What Are Some Spiritual Values and Moral Beliefs That Influence
        the Effectiveness of Your Leadership Practises? 120
        Viewing Others as Equals 120
        Practising Servant Leadership 121
        Having Personal Accountability and Positive Mentoring. 122
        Summary of Responses 124
        Results From Participant Involvement 125
    In What Ways Would This Articulation Best Contribute to the
        Development of Effective Leadership? 131

What Are Some Changes in Leaderhip Practices That Have
  Added Enthusiasm and Spirit to Your Leadership? 131
  Affirming Self and Others. 131
  Applying Faith 133
  Sharing Leadership, Increasing Accountability, Having
    a Vision and Mission 134
  Summary of Responses 135
What Effective Leadership Practices Would You Recommend to
  Other Educational Leaders?. 136
  Engaging in Team Work 136
  Believing in Self and Others 137
  Mentoring and Continuous Learning 139
  Being True to Self, Connecting With Others, Having
    Clear Goals 139
  Summary of Responses 140
Results From Participants in Discussion 140
Researcher Follow-up 142
Spirituality: Unconventional Means of Articulation 143
Summary of Chapter 145

FIVE: Discussion: Connecting the Concepts, Threads and Themes . . 147
  Examining Participants' Spiritual experiences Through a
    Trangulated Lens 147
  Reasons for Attrition. 151
  Analyzing Key Concepts Guiding Resechar Questions 152
  Emerging Themes From Data Base. 153
    Awakening Spirituality Within Self 154
    Signifying Spirituality Within the Workplace 158
    Cultivating Spirituality Within Leadership Practices at Work . . 160
  Summary of Chapter 166

SIX: Implications and Conclusions: Expresssing Spirituality. 167
  Revisiting Scope of Study. 167
  Summarizing Findings. 168
  Noting Limitations of Study 169
  Understanding and Articulating Spiritual Experiences 170
  Articulating Spirituality Contributes to Developing Effective
    Leadership. 170
  Implications for Further Research 171
  Study Implications for Education, Practice and Policy
    Development. 172
    Personal and Professional Implications for the Researchers . . . 173

Summary of Chapter 174

References 177
Author Information 192

Heart graph no. 1: Synergistic relationship between spirit, spiritual,
    spirituality. 27
Heart graph no. 2: Triangulated perspectives of knowledge domains .. 38
Heart graph no. 3: Triangulated theoretical framework 93
Heart graph no. 4: Triangulated key concepts derived from literature .. 97
Heart graph no. 5: Triangulated "lines of sight" applied to data
    analysis 103
Heart graph no. 6: Triangulated emergent themes from data analysis . 154
Heart graph no. 7: Cultivation of spirituality within self 161
Heart graph no. 8: Cultivation of spirit within the educational
    workplace. 164
All Hearts 176

1
Introduction to Exploring "Spirituality"

Setting the Context of the Issue

An inquiry into spirituality within educational leadership was a timely one because "there is a renaissance of interest in paths of the heart and spirit, and this resurgence of spiritual values crosses racial, ethnic, political, cultural, and class lines" (Glazer, 1999, p. 3). Some leaders crave a "spiritual sense of work" (Fox, 1995, p. 15) which is . . . "to find life-giving forces and sources in the midst of an enterprise which is too often death dealing. Too often we go to schools where learning is made so dull that, once we get out, we don't want to learn again" (Palmer, 1999a, pp. 16-17). These schools lack "spiritualized" learning that could have a positive effect on educators, students, communities and society. Jones, D. (1995) states that "the pride of 'unspiritualized' learning is a treacherous thing in human experience" (p. x). Alternatively, spiritualized learning creates a wakefulness of the sacred aspects of education.

Ideally, learning should be "an ecstasy, a spiritual experience . . . a climax of existence" (Fox, 1995, p. 176) resulting from overcoming challenges that arise when absorbing knowledge that confronts habitual ways of thinking and acting. Acknowledging the value of spirituality within learning is a major step towards moving beyond the sense of meaninglessness and disconnection felt by many educators who appear to have lost touch with the sacredness of their responsibilities (Glazer, 1999; Palmer, 1999a). Impersonal bureaucracies have discouraged spirituality within leadership by focussing more on policy-making and red tape than on the needs of individuals who make up systems. Although bureaucratic structures may be "inherent in man's nature [or] inevitable organizational structures . . . entire countries sometimes break down under the weight of their own bureaucracies"(Thom, 1993, p. 35). Therefore, introducing spirituality into leadership within bureaucratic systems may assist hierarchies of authority to function more synergistically.

Guzi (1999) and Thom (1993) suggested the idea that educators must conform to a secular society lead to the assumption that leaders within schools should not have a firm set of spiritual beliefs and moral values. As stated by Guzi:

> secularism is a fruit of hard-core empiricism. It does not recognize the powers of the human spirit to transcend purely rational and scientific ways of knowing human experience. Secularism denies legitimacy to the trans-rational or spiritual dimensions of life that have been explored for many millennia . . . throughout the world. . . . Secularism reduces the vast, fertile, multi-coloured and multi-textured domain of spiritual experience to a one-dimensional flatland. (p. 244)

For at least a century, an absence of spiritual direction and accountability has resulted in a closed-mindedness coupled with faulty suppositions about educational leadership (Myss, 2001; Nouwen, 1975). Denying spirituality within oneself and others is upholding "blindness of man and woman to an essential part of [their] own reality" (Nouwen, 1975, p. 38). Disclaiming spirituality within educational systems also ignores the reality that people have multiple intelligences and therefore learn in a variety of ways (Gardner, 1999). "Spirituality is one of the ways people construct knowledge and meaning" (Tisdell, 2003, p. 3). Therefore, excluding spirituality from inquiries and curriculum is ignoring intra-subjective ways of knowing.

Spiritual evolution is a process that involves mind and heart. When people lose touch with their hearts, they become disconnected from their spirituality (Curtis & Eldredge, 1997). "Spiritual divorce" is a consequence of people distancing themselves from sacred ways of thinking and reverent ways of acting (Morrisseau, 1998). The danger is that a dualism of mind and heart keeps individuals alienated, resulting in cognitive states of heartlessness and lack of compassion for others. As noted by Curtis and Eldredge (1997), ignoring messages of the heart leads to a loss of passion for life, immoral acts and a deadening of spirituality:

> We make sure to maintain enough distance between ourselves and others and even between ourselves and our own heart, to keep hidden the practical agnosticism we are living now that our inner life had been divorced from our outer life. Having thus appeased our heart, we nonetheless are forced to give up our spiritual journey because our heart will no longer come with us. It is bound up in the little indulgences we feed it to keep it at bay. (p. 3)

A sense of boredom results in addiction to "a consumerism of the spirit" (Bateson, 1994, p. 113). People rush to nightclubs to drink or exhaust themselves by working long hours to silence their hearts' cries for connection with self and others. Vaill (1998) states, a major impediment to experiencing spirituality is "workaholism or hurry sickness" (p. 236), which ultimately tires the mind, hardens the heart, and deadens the spirit.

Many twenty-first century leaders are in revolt against routine bureaucratic systems that promote silence about spiritual experiences, threaten to diminish educational leaders' human character and "deaden" their spirits (Sennett, 1998). Some educational leaders work towards removing "layers of bureaucracy, to become flatter and more flexible organizations . . . more readily . . . redefinable than fixed assets of hierarchies" (p. 23). They aim to treat staff with integrity, rather than as objects within workplaces.

The ideal educator of the new millennium is viewed as an inspirational leader who integrates the intelligence of mind and spirit, and leads from the heart (Hawley, 1995; Secretan, 1999). "Followers are currently seeking leaders who will build their spiritual muscles" (Secretan, 1999, p. 8). To help build their spiritual muscles, leaders and followers need the freedom to express spirituality within their workplaces. Thom (1993) suggests that "firstly a leader in education should be a spiritual moral person" (p. 159), who has a holistic outlook, sound values, a sense of hope and of courage and gratitude for being an educator.

Educators are coming to a juncture in an evolutionary path where they are challenging the dualism of a disconnected mind and heart approach to leadership and alternatively are taking the progressive path of spiritual leadership (Helliwell, 1999). "The spiritual dimension of our lives is an important source of . . . learning and is often represented through art form, music or story telling" (Tisdell, 2003, p. 22). When considering spirituality within the educational process, educators extend the theoretical acknowledgement of multiple intelligences, including the heart, and multiple ways in which people construct knowledge. For example, latent knowledge can be awakened within people's hearts through story telling (Vanier, 1998). In Sacred Scripture, spiritual masters introduced narratives to reveal truths and awaken people's hearts. Vanier (1998) notes:

> to speak of the heart is not to speak of vaguely defined emotions but to speak of the very core of our being. At the core we know we can be strengthened and rendered more truthful and more alive. Our hearts can become hard like stone or tender like flesh. We have to create situations where our hearts can be fortified and nourished. In this way, we can become more sensitive to others, to their needs, their cries, their inner pain, their tenderness, and their gifts of love. (p. 87)

Heart knowledge enables leaders to cultivate spirit, bond with peers, and create community within their workplaces.

Reviewing educational leadership practices entails acknowledging spiritual components that promotes a synergistic and caring approach to leading (Creighton, 1999). A leading corporate executive, Max DePree, who built his company into one of the top 25 in the world, states "love and the awareness of the human spirit are more important than structure or policy" (Hoyle, 2002, p. 11). He asks "without understanding the cares, yearnings, and struggles of the human spirit, how could anyone presume to lead a group of people across the street" (p. 11)? People need to get in touch with their own spirituality to enable them to reach others' hearts and spirits (Hoyle, 2002).

At the beginning of the twenty-first century, a shift with respect to the ways in which educators understand education, leadership, and research is occurring (Begley & Leonard, 1999; Creighton, 1999; Hollaar, 2000; Spears, 1998). Many educators demonstrate a hunger for something beyond the traditional scientific paradigms and are mapping out new territories of spirituality despite tensions created by misunderstandings of the term "spirituality" (Holmes, 2003; Ornish, 1998). As noted by Tisdell (2003), "spirituality is not about pushing a religious agenda" (p. xi); spirituality is about honoring the sacredness and wholeness of life and moving past a dichotomization that results in oppression of people. According to Moffett (1994), even if some educators do not "accept any metaphysical meanings of spirituality" (p. 19), a rallying call for school reform alone "warrants spiritualising education" (p. 19). A spiritual approach to educational leadership involves moving beyond cynicism and rediscovering heart wisdom.

Misunderstandings about the roles of educational leaders have bred cynicism in workplaces. They are confused about the difference between being a manager and being a leader. Thus, followers are not clear about their missions and goals within their workplaces. "You cannot talk about leaders to anyone until you agree on what you are talking about" (Leithwood & Duke, 1998, p. 45). To arrive at a point of agreement about spirituality within leadership, more reflection and dialog about changes taking place in intellectual perspectives needs to be encouraged and a spiritual sensibility cultivated. "We cannot afford the luxury of silence about the spiritual condition of our leaders" (Vaill, 1998, p. 216). As noted by Lambert (2003), leadership is a process, a culturally embedded notion that occurs in the minds of individuals before it is put into practice.

Beyond the domain of scholarly literature, the number of spiritual books and workshops available during the last few decades, as well as an introduction of spirituality into a wide range of different organizations, indicate that some heart and head dualisms of the past are being challenged (Helliwell, 1999). Throughout North America, conference sessions and workshops devoted to spirituality are being developed within and outside educational workplaces. For example, at The University of Calgary, the Faculty of Social Work and the Faculty of Medicine have worked cooperatively with other universities to present conferences addressing the need to introduce discourses about spirituality within their programs. Consequently, educators who have acknowledged a "spiritual crisis" in society attempt to "sacralize" their workplaces by introducing a spirit of significance and meaning (Purpel, 1989). "Sacralizing" suggests that leaders envision their workplaces as sites to be reverent, respectful and service oriented. A spiritual process of sacralizing within workplaces such as health organizations is underway.

Proposing Conceptual Definitions of Spirituality

Kinjerski and Skrypnek (2003) acknowledge that although spirituality is increasingly being addressed within workplaces, an agreed-upon conceptual definition of "spirit" in the context of leadership continues to be in the developmental stages. "Spirituality" is a higher state of consciousness that promotes a feeling of being fully alive and elicits an awakening of awe, resulting in creativity, acts of passion, a connection with others and a celebration of the meaningfulness of one's life (Fox, 1991). Spirituality within pedagogy is "the transformation of consciousness that takes place in the intersection of three agencies, the teacher, the learner, and the knowledge they produce together" (Lusted, 1986, p. 3). Spirituality in educational leadership is about connecting with the experience of re-awakening the sacred spark within oneself and others (Fox, 1995; Glazer, 1999). "Out of connection, grows compassion and passion – passion for people, for students' goals and dreams, for life itself" (Kessler, 1998, p. 52). Therefore, encouraging expressions of spirituality within leadership practices could be compared to a Hawthorne effect that results in workers becoming more passionate about their work when they sense they are valued.

Spirituality is associated with renewed sensitivity to life, inner peace, connection, enlightenment, enthusiasm, patience and awe; further, the term characterizes an abiding human search for a connection with something greater and more trustworthy than our egos, and is viewed as a transformed state of consciousness towards connection, compassion, kindness, passion, and love (Fox, 1991; MacDonald, 2000). Because it is inherent and latent, spirituality may not be able to be defined or taught in traditional ways; thus, it needs to be uncovered, evoked, found, or recovered because it is like a light switch that needs to be turned on (Fox, 1991; Kessler, 1998). Through the process of contemplation, inquiry, and dialog, one's spirituality can be recovered, which results in embracing the concept of oneness, while advocating service to others.

For the purpose of this study, spirituality is defined as a latent inherent truth awakened by contemplation, rituals, peak life experiences and caring acts of kindness; when awakened, spirituality is a sensation of the sacred, a sentiment of hope, a feeling of enthusiasm and excitement, and a heart-felt sense of interconnection with others. The term "heart" is used metaphorically throughout this study to symbolize an awareness of the tacit and visceral nature of spirituality that makes it difficult to articulate in words or encompass in religious organizations. This image is also used graphically at times to frame key concepts.

Within an educational leadership model, "heart" could metaphorically represent spirit, while "mind" would depict intellect. A holistic integration of mind and heart within leadership practices could result in leaders being more effective in their work. One goal of this research is to explore how educational leaders could integrate spirituality into leadership practices to become more effective leaders.

Introducing Paradigm Shifts Within Approaches to Educational Research

A reductionist approach to educational research has resulted in overlooking latent essences, such as a butterfly within a caterpillar or a tree within an acorn, which are metaphors for spirituality within a person. Descartes built the foundation for the construction of reductionism and the objective sciences (Abram, 1996). However, as noted by Abram (1996), "the tree bending in the wind, [a] cliff wall, the cloud drifting overhead: these are not merely subjective [or objective]; they are inter-subjective phenomena – phenomena experienced by a multiplicity of sensing subjects" (p. 38). Abram suggested that an evolving higher consciousness within humankind is resulting in a movement away from reductionism towards holistic perspectives within inquiry paradigms. Some educators question the assumptions of scientific enlightenment and "are re-discovering the realm of the sacred. Scientists and visionaries alike are identifying a spiritual hunger. . . . On every side we hear calls to reinvent the sacred" (Albright & Ashbrook, 2001, p. xv). Reinventing the sacred means moving away from exclusively embracing a reductionist worldview that excludes recognition of higher states of consciousness or a dynamic that cannot be encapsulated by experimental research (Lather, 1991; Wilber, 1996).

A shift towards "consciousness-raising" perspectives over-rides notions that an objective world exclusively defines reality (Lather, 1991; Wilber, 1996). "Within educational research, while positivism retains its hegemony over practice, its long-lost theoretical hegemony has been disrupted and displaced by newly hegemonic discourses of paradigm shifts" (Lather, 1991, p. 2). Changes are informed by new methods of collecting and interpreting data, which are not explainable within the Cartesian worldview of what is and what is not "real" (Albright & Ashbrook, 2001; Morse, 2000; Wilber, 1996). Such changes enable educators to "get outside of the imprisoning framework of assumptions" (Bateson, 1994, p. 43) learned within reductionist positivist hegemonies.

Quantum physics and holographic inquiries make people aware that there is more to the invisible world than they ever believed, and their five senses cannot be totally relied upon for insights about reality (Drouin & Rivard, 1997; Talbot, 1991). As noted by Abbott (1984), spiritual realities are comparable to a fourth dimension, everywhere accessible, but not always visible. Because invisible phenomena cannot be empirically explained within a dualistic model, their presence is commonly overlooked. For example, a Cartesian worldview cannot explain the holographic phantom limb phenomenon, "a sensation experienced by amputees that a missing arm or leg is still present" (Talbot, 1991, p. 26). However, not being able to explain scientifically this phenomenon does not stop amputees from encountering the reality of the sensation they feel.

Examining shifts from Cartesian models to post-modernist paradigms

An inquiry into spirituality within educational leadership is part of a broader movement, associated with post-modernist paradigm shifts towards acknowledging Cartesian tensions, related to a "flatland" worldview (Lather, 1991; Wilber, 1996); "flatland . . . is the ideal that the sensory, empirical and material world is the only world there is" (Wilber, 1996, p. 11). Influenced by Descartes' theories in the early seventeenth century, Cartesian scientific traditions have gradually devalued the sacredness and wholeness of individuals and of life (Albright & Ashbrook, 2001; Drouin & Rivard, 1997). However, as Wilber (1996) states, to deny the pre-existence of a former worldview because of its "inherent limitations" is to fall into another "dualistic trap" (p. 11). When educators attempt to convert from one leadership model to another, they discover that there are overlapping sections associated with former paradigms (Bateson, 1994).

If educators focus on merely trying to amend Cartesian approaches to research, they may miss the ways that both critical and appreciative inquiry "are equally expressions of spirit" (Wilber, 1996, p. 66). Most new paradigm approaches to inquiry have hidden subtle Cartesian dualisms. "As . . . higher stages of consciousness emerge and develop, they . . . include . . . components of the earlier worldview, then add their own new and more differentiated perceptions. They transcend and include. Because they are more inclusive, they are more adequate" (Wilber, 1996, p. 67). Therefore, acknowledging, complementing and balancing multiple worldviews are major goals of post-modernist inquiries.

As suggested by Bateson (1994), if we learned to read Descartes' cogito beyond the first person concealed in the Latin verb, it could be expressed as "we think; therefore we are." In different languages the terms "I" and "we" can have different meanings. Varying cultural meanings of what it is to be human and to be spiritual beings cannot "free us from the need to bring one another into being [because] I am only real and only have value as long as you are real and have value" (Bateson, 1994, p. 63). Reflective of sacred interdependence, human community becomes "reality" when people move beyond dualisms towards shared holistic visions. Although spirituality is not necessary for the realization of community, incorporating spirituality within leadership would encourage a synergistic approach to leading.

Lather (1991) states that post-modernism is the initiation of shifts associated with a post-industrial, post-colonial flux that challenges the concept of disinterested knowledge and confronts Cartesian anxieties. Postmodernism is thinking differently about how we think and becoming "multi-voiced;" it is weaving "varied voices together as opposed to putting forth a singular authoritative voice" (p. 9). Wilber (1996) refers to post-modernism as a continuous process of self-transcendence, "spirit-in-action," "God-in-the-making," and a balancing of male and female-orientated spirituality; it involves spirit unfolding itself, "an infinite process that is completely present at every stage" (p. ten). Morse (2000) takes the stand that "we are exploring a new paradigm, one in which science and spirituality join hands to help people on all sides of the mind-body argument find common ground" (p. 26). Similarly, Abbott (1984) promotes a view of reality "in which the natural and supernatural worlds exist together in the harmony of a multidimensional framework" (p. 14). Wilber, Morse and Abbot's perspectives suggest that post-modernists support a holistic, balanced worldview.

Emergent scholarly inquiries about spirituality within educational leadership coincide with post-modernist paradigm shifts towards appreciative inquiry, a constructive mode of research that is "a shift from vocabularies of deficit to conversations of possibility" (Park, 2001, p. 196). Different than most critical modes of research, appreciative enquiry promotes transformative dialog and action by presenting positive questions. Spirituality is evident within this approach to inquiry when research participants "begin to feel a sense of hope, excitement, co-operation and ownership about the future" (p. 196). Such a paradigm shift in scholarly inquiry requires rethinking former ideologies that shaped reality, and formulating new ways to discover truth; latent truths can be unearthed when Cartesian ideologies that separate head from heart are transcended by new ways of knowing (Vanier, 1998). This evolution in thought can mean "formulating new words and new ways" (p. 16). Such a shift in ideologies can create tensions within educational systems.

An acknowledgement of post-modernist paradigm shifts and a need for school leaders to transform schools from their apparent states of anomie and mediocrity indicate that there is a vocational calling for a current language, research methodology, and a means of cultivating spirituality within educational leadership (Begley & Leonard, 1999). If the dynamic of spirituality is ignored within educational systems, students will limp into the future, ignorant of how their higher essence can be activated (Wilber, 1996). Such an acknowledgment supports exploring the spiritual behavior of an ideal educational leader and suggests applying a modern technological means to collect data for an inquiry about spirituality. This research involves examining spirituality through the voices of ten educational leaders who had the opportunity using the web page to dialog with one another.

Outlining Chapter Content

This chapter began with an outline of the context of the study. The research is introduced by addressing the scope of the problem and presenting literature related to moving beyond muted discourses about spirituality within educational leadership. The two main sections of the chapter include an exploration of the scope of the research problem and the acknowledgement of spiritual evolution within educational leadership. The first sub-sections introduce explanations of the scope of problem and postulate standpoints about the nature of spirituality. Section two has three sub-sections: 1. introducing discourses about spirituality within educational leadership; 2. reviewing morals within educational systems; and 3. shifting paradigms affecting educational leadership. Research questions, methodology, and objectives of the study are presented, followed by a summary of subsequent chapters. The objective of this inquiry was to understand how spiritual experiences of ten educational leaders were understood and articulated, and in what ways this articulation of spirituality would best contribute to the development of effective leadership.

Exploring the Scope of the Research Problem

Muting discourses about spirituality within educational systems could lead to a generation of spiritually deaf, blind and illiterate youth, who are morally confused and suffering from spiritual amnesia (Fox, 1995; Griffin, 1998; Myss, 2002; Rolheiser, 1999; Simington, 2003; Vaill, 1998; Wilber, 1996). Conversely, acknowledging the value of introducing discourses about spirituality into educational systems could result in educator and student understandings about the importance of cultivating spirituality within their lives. Educator attitudes towards spirituality are influenced by how they perceive this dynamic of life fitting into school culture (Griffin, 1998; Vaill, 1998).

According to Creighton (1999) spiritual leaders "have a deep sense of values and beliefs, and willingness to expose those values and beliefs for inspection and dialog with others" (p. 7). However, because faith and morals have become associated with personal conviction and values, public educators are becoming mostly silent believers who "no longer talk about their faith in public settings" (Banks, 2000, p. 6). Also, the Charter of Rights and Freedoms has led to secularization and muting of discourses about spirituality within educational systems.

> The Section 15 clause on quality rights is particularly relevant. . . . Every individual is equal before and under the law and has the right to the equal protection and equal benefit of the law . . . without discrimination based on race, national or ethnic origin, colour, religion, sex, age or mental or physical disability." (as cited in Thom, 1993, p. 16-17)

The danger of silencing spirituality when attempting to honor the Charter is that muting spirituality affects the styles and goals of educators' leadership practices, which influence how they mentor students. On the other hand, if leadership mentors feel free to discuss their spirituality, they will be motivated to assist their protégés to "develop spiritual and leadership potential" (Emmerich, 2000, p. 109). Developing their spiritual and leadership potential might generate a positive ripple effect among the next generation. Excluding spirituality from leadership practices could result in educators mentoring a fragmented style of leadership that mirrors reductionism. Alternatively, by connecting spirituality with leadership, educators would reflect a synergistic approach to leadership that would help them to mentor a holistic way of leading.

In public educational systems, the notion of spirituality having both a transcendent and an ever-present domain is emerging as important phenomenon associated with core values and ethics (Wilber, 1996). Some educators are starting to break the silence about spirituality (Tisdell, 2003) and are initiating a "spiritual process" of creating community within their workplaces, which fosters "compassion, loyalty, a desire for hard work, [and] a sense of trust" (Drouin & Rivard, 1997, p. 39). Vaill (1998) points out that if educators exclude spirituality from education and training for leadership, they truly are "just re-arranging the deck chairs on the Titanic" (p. 114) while it sinks, or creating permanent "white water" conditions of unhealthy structures within leadership models unequipped to address unanticipated problems. White water is the confusion and tension educators face when they encounter competing leadership models that lack a clear vision and mission statements (Vaill, 1998).

As influential mentors who work with one of the major shaping institutions of a secular society, public school educators have been applying a

Cartesian dualistic paradigm that excludes spiritual phenomena (Graham, 1990). The secularisation of Canada "by industrialization, urbanization, science and technology, mass communication and pluralism" (p. 12) has framed educational leadership models and compelled public school educators to mute discourses about spirituality within their workplaces. Consequently, there has been a lack of spiritual "moral glue" that helps unify people and a crisis of spirit has resulted (Vaill, 1996). Many educators have been sensing a "paralyzing purposelessness" within their workplaces, when at the same time facing secular individualism, violence amongst students, and critical approaches to scholarship.

Although scholarly critiques of accepted truths promote quality research, this assessment tool can also become detrimental to educators when not combined with an appreciative critique that also affirms organizational strengths. "Scholars and practitioners alike are becoming increasingly disillusioned with the destructive consequences of a critical approach to scholarship" (Ludema, Cooperrider & Barrett, 2001, p. 190) that may judge peers and students harshly and exclude affirmations of an individual's and organizational strengths. The rhetorical impact of select approaches to exclusively critical inquiry has been known to erect artificial boundaries that exclude exploring new knowledge, erode community and preserve patterns of social hierarchy. Schools commonly have become "dispiriting places, and . . . have dispiriting leaders . . . . whose impact blocks the spirit of others, setting people against each other and souring the climate of the organization" (Vaill, 1998, p. 220). As educators become expert critics and problem solvers, educators may weaken their collective ability to see and build upon personal and organizational strengths which are more tacit.

On the other hand, "appreciative inquiry distinguishes itself from critical modes of research by its deliberately affirmative assumptions about people, organizations and relationships" (Ludema, Cooperrider & Barrett, 2001, p. 191). Appreciative inquiry is a constructive approach to research that creates space for new voices and expands circles of dialog to include discourses about spirituality. This approach invites organizational members to "co-create a future for the system that nurtures and supports . . . enthusiasm " (p. 191). It highlights and illuminates organizational strengths by commencing with an unconditional positive question. Appreciative inquiry is assumed to be a spiritual approach to conducting research that moves beyond the limitations of Cartesian dualistic models by initiating positive questions within an inquiry (Ludema, Cooperrider & Barrett, 2001).

Postulating Standpoints About the Nature of Spirituality

Musical compositions have a primary theme with variations, which is comparable to spiritual development in that it usually has a primary theme with improvisational variations (Bateson, 1994; Tisdell, 2003). "Life is not made up of separate pieces. A composer creates patterns across time with ongoing themes and variations, different movements all integrated into a whole, while a visual artist combines and balances elements that may seem disparate" (Bateson, 1994, p. 109). Moving forward and spiralling back is a common primary theme when using the ongoing development of spirituality as one important variation of its evolution.

Noting this theme and the variations, Tisdell (2003) articulated seven assumptions about the nature of spirituality in relation to education. Spiritual experiences, which are about meaning-making and honor the interconnection of all things, usually happen unexpectedly. Such experiences are a means of constructing knowledge through an unconscious process made concrete through art forms and ritual. Becoming more spiritually attuned leads to emergence into a more authentic self. Although spirituality is always present within workplaces, it is usually unacknowledged, and despite the fact that spirituality and religion are different, many people perceive them as inter-related (Tisdell, 2003).

Tisdell's (2003) seven assumptions about spirituality are based on interviews with adult educators, who engaged in discussions about a "spirited epistemology (a view of knowledge that incorporates the spiritual)" (p. 31). The interviews focussed on how participants' spirituality altered with time; how it was associated with their childhood religious traditions, their culture, and gender; and how it directed their teaching. During the interviews, participants referred to significant life experiences that awakened their spirituality. Tisdell noted the educators' shared experiences commonly signified hope, healing, or affirmation during "meaning-making moments," and times of "significant learning." These incidents of significant learning contributed to the cultivation of spirit and moving beyond muted discourses about spirituality within their workplaces.

Chopra (1994), Rolheiser (1999) and Simington (2003) suggested humans are spiritual beings having human experiences, rather than human beings seeking spiritual insights. Similarly, Holmes (2003) indicated that humans are both physical and spiritual, but not in a dualistic way, "rather having two aspects to one nature" (p. 4). The Urantia Foundation (1999) further states that people are "divine in heritage as well as human in heritage" (p. 1215), and Vaill (1998) claims that "spirituality is an aspect of our existence that is truly undiscussable in objectivist science" (p. 28). After acknowledging her divine heritage in her midlife years, Simington (2003) questions whether or not her education was "rooted in a philosophy of disempowerment to keep [her] subservient by blinding her to her birthright" (p. 90), by ignoring her innate spirituality and its connection to her own heart, mind, and all of creation.

Morrisseau (1998) stated that there is no difference between the spiritual and physical worlds within Aboriginal culture. Spirituality is people's connection to the Creator, whose voice can be heard through a quiet stream or seen in the glory of a sunrise. Humans have spiritual, emotional, physical, and mental aspects to their holistic nature. To live a balanced spiritual life, a person must function with head and heart synergistically. The sacred circle of the Medicine Wheel is a spiritual symbol that represents the four directions and four elements of nature: fire, earth, air and water. Additionally, the wheel symbolizes that the four races: red, yellow, black and white are part of the same human family (Morrisseau, 1998).

The Medicine Wheel helps people to better understand spirituality and its relationship to morals (Morrisseau, 1998). A vital part of the Aboriginal spiritual value system promotes a belief in interconnection between all things which promotes a reverence towards one another and nature. When people are dispirited and act immorally they bring shame upon themselves, their families and community. Conversely, when they embrace their spiritual values, they foster a mutual respect for one another and exist cooperatively. Thus in Aboriginal communities spiritual leadership is crucial (Morriseau, 1998).

Like expressions of love, spirituality is often tacit because language cannot always communicate what is experienced within the heart or one's higher state of consciousness (L'Engle, 1997). "Words are merely utterances: noises that stand for feelings, thoughts, and experience. They are symbols, signs, insignias. They are not truth. They are not the real thing. Words help you to understand something. Experience allows you to know" (Walsch, 1995, p. 4). Experience may come before or after an idea. For example, a pre-meditated act suggests the intent preceded the experienced act.

Words are only maps or models that represent something, but are not the thing they represent (Albright & Ashbrook, 2001). Alternatively, "nonverbal vocabularies are limitless sources of spiritual insight if we simply assume the artist's spirit is present in the work" (Vaill, 1998, p. 231) and feel personally touched by that spirit. Similarly, people who are given the space to engage "spiritually" on-line may sense "spirit" within and beyond words, which could be described as a "spiritual" transmission.

Although three related terms may be used within different contexts, "the words 'spirit,' 'spiritual,' and 'spirituality' originally referred to breath and wind and first appeared in the thirteenth and fourteenth centuries respectively"

(Janis, 2000, p. 12). Used interchangeably, the three terms can symbolize a triangulated expression of spirituality within leadership. Triangulation has been symbolized by the three-leafed shamrock, as Ireland's national emblem and in Catholicism to symbolize three aspects of God: the Trinity of Father, Son, and Holy Ghost (Handy, 1989). "The lens of three windows helps you ignite 'spiritual alchemy,' the process through which we convert physical perceptions from their 'leaden' manifestation into their highest expression, the spiritual or 'golden' level" (Myss, 2001, p. 103). Myss (2001) used a three-column model: tribal external necessity, individual internal choice and symbolic archetypal compassion to demonstrate the physical, internal and symbolic dimensions of triple vision. "In essence, triple vision is the ability to remain centred in any situation, whether it be joyous, disturbing, or neutral. It will give you poise and perspective" (p. 192).

Introducing metaphoric and triangulated heart graphs

Using a heart-shaped image to demonstrate an inter-relationship between "spirit," "spiritual" and "spirituality" complements the triangulated research design applied to this study and metaphorically represents the relationship between heart and spirit. "Triangulation [is] a strategy for increasing the validity of evaluation and research findings. A triangulated, three-pronged approach to inquiry helps the researcher obtain more valid and credible research findings. "Qualitative inquirers triangulate among different data sources to enhance the accuracy of a study" (Creswell, 2002, p. 280). Collection and analysis of data for this study involved a triangulated approach to "making sense of the . . . lessons learned" (p. 277) from ten participants' spiritual experiences. Their shared spiritual experiences indicated that a heart-centred leadership model could help them to cultivate spirit within their workplaces.

Aside from the synergistic relationship between the three terms "spirit," "spiritual" and "spirituality," the term "spirit" may be expressed in a varied context. When differentiating between the terms "spirit" and "spirituality" Vaill (1998) states that "spirit is where you find it and spirituality is finding it. . . . Expressions of human spirit are constantly running though the thoughts, feelings and actions of human beings. "The present is where the spirit is most naturally found" (Vaill, pp. 232, 237). Guzie (1995) further states "spirituality . . . is a word that describes our yearning for more spirit" (p. 184). There is spirit in serving others, being creative or being meditative; and, after sensing the spirit in oneself, a person can recognize spirituality reverberating from others (Vaill, 1996). "When we say we genuinely 'feel the spirit' in or of some entity . . . we are making a statement about a presence of a current of energy . . . an intrinsic characteristic that has become manifest to us" (p. 183-4). Guzie

(1995) suggested that "the invention of language was a great 'spiritual' break through. . . . Language was 'more spirit,' an expansion of our consciousness" (p. 184). When conducting this inquiry, I sensed "spirit" while connecting with participants and reviewing the literature. This sensation was a "spiritual" experience that cultivated "spirituality" within me.

Heart graph no. 1 is a metaphoric conceptual framework to symbolize the synergistic relationship between spirit, spiritual and spirituality that is embedded within this study. The flow lines on the graph indicate the three terms spirit, spiritual and spirituality can be used interchangeably, within varying contexts. Although the image of a heart applied to graph no. 1 is metaphoric, later applications of the heart within the text are organizing frameworks representing triangulation and heart graphs no. 7 and no. 8 are depicting heart-centred schemata.

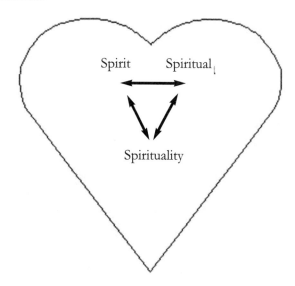

Heart graph no. 1: Synergistic relationship between spirit, spiritual, spirituality

Connecting Science With Spirituality and Heart Intelligence

Collingwood (1940) argued that science and spirituality are "inextricably united, and stand or fall together" (p. 41). Further, Lerner (2000) noted "the divorce of scientific knowledge . . . from an ethical and spiritual foundation made it possible for some of the most . . . brilliant people to serve very evil ends" (p. 62). For example, German scientists, doctors and engineers used their brilliance to exterminate Jews, and those who developed gases for concentration camps did not question if their efficiency was ethically appropriate or spiritually acceptable (Lerner, 2000).

Because the metaphysics of spirituality is a "science of absolute presuppositions" (Collingwood, 1940, p. 41), it is immeasurable and commonly ignored by scientists. "Spiritual oneness cannot be objectively verified, but our literature, our music, and our current yearning for spiritual connection" (Lerner, 2000, p. 49) verify its authenticity. Also, a transformed state of consciousness associated with spiritual experiences is "biologically observable and scientifically real" (Newburg, D'Aquili & Rause, 2001, p. 7). As a higher state of consciousness, a spiritual experience may have a neurological nature that alters the brain.

Prayer enhances people's conscious awareness of their spirituality, which promotes a sense of well-being (Vaill, 1998). Research on intercessory prayer conducted in a controlled double blind study with 406 individuals found that both the subjects being prayed for and the agents doing the praying improved their measures of self-esteem (Dossey, 1999). Other studies "reveal healing can be achieved at a distance by directing loving and compassionate thoughts, intentions, and prayers to others" (Dossey, 1999, p. 25). Thus, prayers may help cultivate spirituality within educational leaders.

Spiritual experiences such as the peace of mind attained during meditation are evident in "both automatic shifts and hormonal changes observed during such states" (Newburg, D'Aquili & Rause, 2001, p. 44); experiments conducted with Tibetan meditators and Franciscan nuns demonstrated their spiritual experiences "were in fact associated with observable neurological activity" (p. 36). Other studies have demonstrated that people participating in spiritual behaviors such as prayer and meditation have experienced decreased heart rates and improved immune systems, and individuals involved with ritualized dancing, singing or chanting have experienced ineffable pleasurable feelings, by stimulating the brain's cortical rhythms. Dyer (2001) noted that "just being in the energy field of those who meditate raises the serotonin levels of the observers" (p. 58); serotonin is a neurotransmitter in the brain that affects how peaceful and harmonious a person feels. Conversely, one might suppose being in the presence of those who are negative could have an adverse affect on others.

Research (Newburg, D'Aquili & Rause, 2001) suggests that whatever the nature of a spiritual experience, meaningful of the neurological functional change, takes place within both the brain and heart. This insight suggests that human nature has mental, physical and spiritual dimensions that are interconnected (Bateson, 1994). According to Pearce (2002), people's hearts maintain a holographic electromagnetic connection with the mental, physical and spiritual dimensions of their being, which is why heart transplants have been successful. Hearts carry universal cellular memories that are transferred to heart transplant recipients. The heart also has a universal function of mediating between "our individual self and a universal process, while being representative of that universal process" (Pearce, 2002, p. 65). Thus, the heart and mind need to function cooperatively to enable leaders to cultivate spirituality within their personal and professional lives.

Ideally, head intelligence and heart wisdom should function as an interdependent dynamic; however, "the heart's latent capacity for deep universal intelligence [and wisdom] must, like the mind, be provided with models for its full growth and development. . . . If no nurturing or modelling is given, the powers of the heart can't unfold [and] they lie dormant for life" (Pearce, 2002, p. 54). Keeping spirituality out of schools may result in a student's heart wisdom remaining dormant. However, incorporating spiritual rituals, such as meditation, into curriculum could help awaken a student's heart intelligence. Incorporating specific rituals within school curriculum may violate some students' Charter rights; therefore educators need to discern what is acceptable within their systems.

Acknowledging key benefits of spiritual exercises

Acknowledging all dimensions of a person as part of the whole often takes place during rituals that awaken spirituality within individuals. The primary function of spiritual rituals is to connect spiritual stories with spiritual experiences,"to turn something in which you believe into something you can feel" (Newburg, D'Aquili & Rause, 2001, p. 91). For example, rituals practised in various religions turn people's beliefs into felt experiences, into mind-body, sensory, and cognitive events. "It is an awakening of the mystical intelligence . . . [and] strengthening of buddhi, spiritual intelligence" (Kiely, 1996, p. 28). Therefore, a taste of spirituality through rituals provides believers with satisfying proof their beliefs are real. As Bateson (1994) noted:

> more often ritual is a sort of metaphysical housework, intended to sustain some continuity in the world. Many people perform their rituals and ceremonies again and again in the conviction that the sun rises, the tides ebb, seasons come and go . . . because they are doing their part, in dance and song and prayer to sustain these rhythms. (p. 114)

No human culture has been discovered in which the individuals did not engage in some kind of ritualistic behavior to support spiritual belief systems (Thurston, 1998). "Many rituals seem moribund, but the death of ritual might also be the death of delight – or rather the loss of form and courtesy as entry ways of learning and participation" (Bateson, 1994, p. 113). Like exercising regularly at a gym to build physical muscles, frequent mindful engagements in rituals can result in a person becoming more spiritually fit.

The Islamic ritual of praying five times daily increases a Muslim devotee's sense of well-being and social stability; this ritual "emphasizes selflessness, healthy altruism, perfection of self and giving happiness to others" (Al-Krenawi & Graham, 2000, p. 293). Collective group prayer, which is considered more effective than individual prayer, helps reinforce a sense of connection and equality with a worldwide community of believers. "The individual achieves balance between thought and action (internal), while caring for the collective welfare of society (external)" (p. 293). Thus, praying five times daily enables Muslims to become spiritually fit, which would assist them to be effective leaders.

The language of the spirit is mainly experiential (Janis, 2000). "All spiritual practices and exercises, such as prayer, meditation, contemplation, yoga . . . and devotional rituals are part of the process of purifying your heart" (p. 13). Spiritual and devotional rituals such as prayers and chanting assist people in clarifying their highest goals, by opening their hearts to divine guidance. Additionally, acts of kindness and compassion towards others can help "our emotional and spiritual hearts like the muscle of our physical heart grow stronger with practice" (Ornish, 1998, p. 136); studies of volunteers have indicated they not only tend to live longer and healthier lives, but also show "a sudden burst of endorphins similar to a runner's high, while helping others" (p. 131). Thus, the ontology of spirituality can be experienced and expressed ritualistically and in heart-felt service.

Exploring Resurgence of Spiritual Values: School Reform

A new trend to make life more spiritual and meaningful is leading some Canadian activists towards "integrating the transcendent with the immanent, the male with the female, the heart with the head, [and] authority with conscience" (Graham, 1990, p. 394). This trend toward unity within a spiritual paradigm is inspiring fresh approaches to educational leadership. Rather than viewed exclusively as an "institutional activity," in the learning context, leadership is being acknowledged as "a way of being" (Vaill, 1996, p. 55), and "a process of expressing it" (p. 45), which implies life-long learning. Lambert (2003) suggests the term "leadership" is being re-framed and re-invented to change its assumed qualities and move its definition more towards stewardship and the conjoining of head and heart.

To accommodate a shift in understanding of leadership competencies as they are evolving in the twenty-first century, more dialog should be encouraged about both the organizational and cognitive contexts of a leader's decision-making process (Leithwood & Steinbach, 1995; Spears, 1998). A shifting focus on educational requirements has resulted in pressure for educators to "transcend the hierarchical functionalism implied by administration in pursuit of a more socially palatable and dynamic leadership role" (Richmon & Allison, 2000, p.2). Educators need to question and communicate about how to nurture school improvements and to offer hopeful visions that inspire others. As Vaill (1998) noted:

> without a willingness to try to lead a more spiritual life, we cannot understand what is going on in a human organization, we will not be able to see very clearly how to be personally effective there, and we won't get much personal pleasure out of being there. (p. 203)

Therefore, to appreciate their roles as leaders, educators need to have the freedom to communicate about spiritual experiences within the workplace. Establishing discourses about spirituality in educational leadership could assist them in rediscovering their latent heart wisdom, thus empowering them to view their roles through a fresh lens (Pearsall, 1998). "If one wants to educate, it is incumbent upon educators to examine the variety of ways in which people construct knowledge" (Tisdell, 2003, p. xi). Knowledge can be constructed from heart wisdom, in addition to other means of formation.

Currently, the notion of leadership is in transition and characteristics of leaders are being re-defined with a more purposeful profile (Lambert, 2003). Some negative contexts associated with the term "leadership" are being clarified by new attitudes about leading that are being introduced within school systems. On the topic of educational reform, spiritual approaches to leadership have been credited for the development of vibrant school communities (Bohac Clark, 2002); on the other hand, toxic school cultures have been associated with a lack of spiritual leadership, and are described as being "spiritually fractured negative places where rituals, traditions, and values have gone sour and threaten the very soul of the school" (Deal & Peterson, 1999, p.xii). In spiritually fractured schools, there is a loss of hope that breeds a cynicism and nihilism, which corrodes the human spirit (Somerville, 2000).

Real transformation in schools involves a "paradigm shift towards a spiritual expedition" (Hawley 1995, p.vii). Purpel (1989) refers to this paradigm shift as a "reillumination" of the dimension of human "be-ings" that has been repressed and rejected; this is a time of "heightened consciousness . . . when more people are aware than perhaps at any other time in history" (p. 2). Although still a minor movement, this fresh insight within educational systems introduces "hope, [which] is the oxygen of the human spirit" (Somerville, 2000, p.xvi) that helps transform school systems. Infusing spirit into educational systems would have a ripple effect of awakening spirituality within educators and students.

Acknowledging Spiritual Evolution Within Educational Leadership

"The search for spirituality is like the man who searched for the fire with a lighted candle. Fire was in front of his face all the time, he was just looking beyond it" (Morse, 2000, p. 9). Spirituality is often tacit knowledge and therefore, it needs to be understood more deeply through articulated discourses. As Chopra (1994), Rolheiser (1999), and Simington (2003) suggested, because we are spiritual beings, we have a right to acknowledge and express spirituality within our workplaces. Ideally, spiritual evolution is a spiral process that involves considering fresh ideas and learning to view life from multiple perspectives (Janis, 2001; Tisdell, 2003). Because all thinking takes place within a framework, these insights indicate that educators' work involves awakening more fully their own and their students' real spiritual identity, "to make finite the infinite, to give personalized expression to the Divine" (Thurston, 1998, p. 13), as their "spiritual birthright" (p. 15). Thus, educators should be free to introduce discourses that address spirituality within educational leadership.

As Dyer (2001) noted, many choices within leadership practices remain unexplored because of a closed mindedness, preserved by hierarchies within systems; "having a mind that is open to everything and attached to nothing sounds easy until you think about how much conditioning has taken place in your life" (p. 3). Most educators have been conditioned not to address spirituality within their workplace. They hold their beliefs unconsciously because they absorbed them throughout their lives, without consciously exploring them (Bohac Clark, 2002).

Therefore, outdated leadership paradigms that exclude discussing spirituality within the workplace have been preserved (Vaill, 1998). A major consequence of preserving reductionist models is expressed by Vaill (1998): "then dies the person in you, if you deny spirit" (p. 28). To bring spirit into the workplace, he proposes an organizational transformation (OT) model with a "spiritual condition" that progressively changes educators' thoughts and actions surrounding leadership.

Spiritual conditions relate to leaders' capacities to be moral agents by re-thinking and re-examining basic values within themselves and their workplaces (Vaill, 1998). According to Vaill, when he applies the phrase "spiritual condition" he is addressing "the feelings individuals have about the fundamental meaning of who they are, what they are doing, and the contributions they are making" (p. 218). When the OT model is adapted to leadership development, having a clear vision and establishing a personal credo become a call of the spiritual condition. "The vision is glue, binding people together in common effort and common values" (Vaill, 1998, p. 69). Therefore, having vision within the workplace helps to cultivate spirit. However, the visioning process is not necessarily connected to spirituality.

Vaill's (1998) processes related to having a clear vision and establishing credos include creating fruitful interaction that gives a sense of team. Retaining a clear perspective on organizational issues by working through conflicts is also part of the process. Lastly, to cultivate spirit within the workplace, leaders need to uncover and highlight feelings; determine the steps for re-entry of spirit; and "institutionalise the process for creating and re-creating vision" (p. 89). With the OT model, the leader facilitates an emerging vision to infuse progress within an organization by encouraging dialog related to spiritual conditions. An encouragement to bringing the spiritual condition into conversation is very important because it affects a leader's own desires to act correctly and responsively.

Introducing Discourses About Spirituality Within Educational Leadership

Research conducted during the 1990s indicates there is an overwhelming need for more understanding and articulation about spirituality within educational leadership (Creighton, 1999; Moffett, 1994; Noddings, 1992; Palmer, 1998; Spears, 1998; Sweet, 1997; Thom, 1993). A lack of understanding about this component of leadership in the public educational system has resulted from a secular ideology that discourages dialog about spirituality (Begley & Leonard, 1999). Repressing dialog about spirituality can stunt personal and systemic growth because as words are representations of tacit meanings. "When our language changes, behaviours will not be far behind" (Handy, 1989, p. 13). However, as Moffett (1994) states, if possible he "would avoid the word 'spirituality', because it makes red flags pop up in many minds" (p. 17). Vaill (1998) further states that:

> it is not cool in some circles to interpret experiences in spiritual terms, and many will err on the side of keeping silent or of rephrasing their ideas in right-sounding psycholinguistics rather than risk being perceived as having got religion. (p. 230)

Teachers do not feel free to apply the term "spirituality" to anything that appears to be associated with being spiritual (Stewart, 2000). Fox (1998) attributes this lack of a clear understanding of spirituality to the ineffability of some spiritual experiences, which involve "letting go and letting be." Educators' tendency to over-dissect discourses has resulted in an under-articulation of a more emotive spiritual context (Fox, 1998). Even during times of deep need to speak about spirituality, some educators find it is difficult to articulate spiritual matters so close to their souls (Jones, D., 1995). "It is as if we were all heretics, punished long ago by an inquisition of political correction we have no relish for again" (Jones, D., 1995, p. ix). Conversely, for some educators expressing spirituality by their actions is more important than communicating it verbally. Thus, actions expressing spirituality may represent a major issue that affects how moral concerns are addressed within school systems.

Reviewing Moral Issues Within Education Systems

Major historical phenomena observed within different educational systems suggest that Christianity has had an impact on moral issues within Canadian education systems (Graham, 1990). Until the late nineteenth century, moral issues within Western World educational systems were assumed part of a universal moral consciousness shaped by strong Christian beliefs (Ryan, 1999). Most people simply believed life was the result of divine creation and thus morality was divinely ascertained (Ryan, 1999; Yob, 1994). As noted by Gadamer (1994), "all attempts of human beings to understand themselves from themselves and from the world . . . are ill-fated. Indeed, it appears that the word and concept of 'self understanding' owes its first formulation to the Christian experience" (p. 37).

Plato's theories about the nature of humankind were associated with a belief that people are composed of two basic elements, matter and spirit, with the spiritual element in the position of superiority (Dupuis, 1966). This viewpoint was congruent with Plato's belief that happiness is the highest good and "only in being like God, can man attain true happiness" (Dupuis, 1966, p. 37). Such a belief in the unity between man and God was expressed further in the teachings of Jesus, who taught that all wisdom lies in a person's willingness to immerse himself or herself totally into the grace and care of one Supreme Being (Ulich, 1945). In his Sermon on the Mount, Jesus preached the moral value of having faith, hope, love, charity, and humility, which influenced other cultural beliefs, such as "Greek-Roman ideals of wisdom, courage, self discipline, and justice" (p. 66).

In other cultures, spiritual masters of different religions taught "divine states of mind" (Vanier, 1998, p. 127) that shaped a person's moral conduct. For example, as Vanier (1998) points out:

> Buddhism teaches that there are four different . . . divine states of mind. The first, metta, is loving kindness, a love that seeks to give and serve, rather than take and demand. The second, keruna, is compassion, a quivering heart in response to another's suffering, the wish to remove that which is painful from the lives of others. The third, mudita, is a sympathetic joy, a joyfulness in the heart as we perceive the weak, the poor, and the oppressed rising up in freedom. The Fourth, pekka, is a peace of heart. (p. 126)

Expressing these divine states of mind would promote moral conduct within school systems.

Cultural teachings such as the Buddhist divine states of mind were ignored by school leaders during the last quarter of the nineteenth century; most Canadian educational leaders spoke with "virtual unanimity" when stating that an immediate goal of schooling was the "inculcation of Christian values . . . and the prevention of deviant behaviour and crime" (Stamp, 1982, p. 10). In addition to training the mind to be accurate and logical, teaching the moral value of mental discipline and self-control was a priority. In Ontario schools, "between 1871 and 1875, Christian morals appeared on the curriculum as a separate subject for Fourth and Fifth Class pupils" (p. 10). Schools were considered places where youth were under a "wholesome discipline, and a humanizing and elevating influence" (p. 10). However, as educators acknowledged the corruption and cynicism of many Christian leaders, Christianity became less influential in moral teachings.

An information explosion, an influx of immigrants and a modernization of technology also led to challenging Christian values embraced within educational systems (Henslin & Nelson, 1996). When educators needed to deal with school violence, they had to exercise caution in modelling values associated with any specific religion (Begley & Leonard, 1999; Shakotko & Walker, 1999). Immigration and development of secular ideologies further altered attitudes about morality and resulted in shifts towards various fundamentalist religious groups, such as Christian sects, claiming their own truths and making value choices accordingly (Ryan, 1999). According to Fox (1995), these shifts in values lead to assumptions that the spiritual and academic world did not blend. Thus, "spiritual dryness [,] soul dehydration" (Fox, 1999, p. 86) and "ungrace awareness" (Yancey, 1997, p. 36) began plaguing schools.

Despite some educational leaders' good intentions to mentor moral and spiritual judgments, they fear being misunderstood within their workplaces. Thus, many educational leaders feel like refugees existing in hostile environments. Begley & Leonard (1999) observed, "when they speak of virtue, they must do so privately, in whispers, lest they be charged with the grievous crime of being unsophisticated" (p. xiv). However, educators continue to hold the difficult but strong position of being major role models to students (Young & Levin, 1998).

If students are to reflect being human "vessels of goodness," they need to acknowledge their abilities to act spiritually "by constantly embracing the virtues of humanity and righteousness in life, just as they could not for a moment dispense with food and clothing" (Chow, Ng & Henderson, 1999, p. 170). Nevertheless, as pointed out by Noddings (1992), within educational systems "little attention [is] given to the spiritual life in education" (p. 49). Spirituality has become "de-historicized" and ignored in some historical works as if it had never existed (Purpel, 1989). However, "the way of nature is the root of moral principles [and] nature is embodied in the mind-heart" (Chow, Ng, & Henderson, 1999, p. 175). Therefore, moving towards a rebirth of heart-centred education is a crucial turning point towards a holistic and moralistic paradigm shift in education (Ocker, 1999).

Examining Paradigms Affecting Educational Leadership

By acknowledging that "education will play the greatest part in the rebirth of the world" (Stamp, 1982, p. 97), educators can work towards elevating schooling to a more holistic spiritual level that supports a more synergistic hierarchy (Moffett, 1994). Spiritual elevation involves connecting more with others and life and living a holistic healthy lifestyle. More than most agencies, schools are depended on to "heal and guard the past and stabilize progress in the future" (Stamp, 1982, p. 97). Therefore, to encourage future progress, educators need to acknowledge the value of spiritual wisdom and adopt a heart-centred approach to their leadership practices.

A paradigm shift towards educators seeking a more spiritual approach to leadership is gaining momentum in the twenty-first century (Dallarie, 2001). Many educators have acknowledged that only though a "reconstruction of a spirituality as communal and political can ways be found to reverse the damage of social and economic decline" (p. 34). They are recognizing their innate need to reconnect to the divine spirit, and become more socially active in mentoring moral values (Simington, 2003).

A new epistemology that distinguishes spiritual wisdom from knowledge and associates "conscientization" with morals is emerging (Purpel, 1989). As "paradigm pioneers," some educators are revisiting "assumptions about the meaning, purpose, and function of education, [to] come to a new awareness" (Ocker, 1999, p.75). This new awareness can guide educators to help students discover their own truths, abilities and skills. Introducing a heart-centred approach to education "will take care of the body, soul, and spirit . . . [and] renew the educational system for the betterment of humanity" (p.76). Such a holistic approach to leadership will result in transitions within educational systems that could encourage a "natural hierarchy" perspective.

To destroy hierarchies and bureaucracies altogether is impossible. They have provided a valid arrangement for human development and preservation of systems. "Denying hierarchy itself is a hierarchy" (Wilber, 1996, p. 29); hierarchy becomes unconscious when it is hidden or denied. Renewing educational systems involves replacing former dualistic hierarchical paradigms with a "natural hierarchy" perspective, which is "simply an order of increasing wholeness, such as particles to atoms to cells to organisms, or letters to words to sentences to paragraphs" (p. 28); it is acknowledging that the "whole is greater than the sum of its parts . . . [which] means the whole is at a higher or deeper level of organization than the parts alone" (p. 28). Although "wholes" are dependent upon parts, segments can exist independently, while lacking the effectiveness of functioning as part of a whole. In educational systems, where leaders treat peers with dignity and respect and share leadership, the effectiveness of functioning as a whole in the workplace would support a natural hierarchy perspective.

Park (2001) suggests that educators need to broaden "the existing epistemological horizons to include . . . representational, relational and reflective knowledge" (p. 82). One sub-type of representational knowledge comprises portrayals of people, events or experiences that predict "antecedent events leading to probable consequences" (p. 82); predictions make it possible to "produce desirable events or to prevent undesirable ones" (p. 82). Another sub-type, interpretive knowledge, is "representational in the sense that we as knowers re-describe or re-present the object of knowing" (p. 83). Relational knowledge is "mind/heart knowledge" (p. 85), which means knowing with the head and heart simultaneously. Reciprocal interaction, such as story telling, conversing or hugging is an integral part of relational knowledge; it constitutes bringing people together and providing opportunities for them to strengthen community by connecting with one another.

An integral part of reflective knowledge is social action, which aims to change the world (Park, 2001). People engaging in political activities can feel empowered and experience changes within themselves that exceed their intellectual comprehension. "Through action, we learn how the world works . . . ; we learn from the mind/heart" (p. 87). Park suggested that by broadening epistemological frameworks to include a triangulated perspective of knowledge, educators can gain competence from representational knowledge, connection from relational knowledge, and confidence from reflective knowledge. Thus, a triangulated perspective of knowledge may empower educators to engage in a holistic process of awakening, signifying, and cultivating spirituality within their workplaces. By cultivating all three forms of knowledge, they may feel liberated to work towards becoming more human and enriching both themselves and their workplaces.

In heart graph no. 2, the heart is used as an organizing framework to demonstrate a triangulated relationship between representational, relational and reflective knowledge claims. Applying a heart-shaped image to the relationship between these three forms of knowledge is congruent with the triangulated research design applied to this study. The flow lines show this is an equilateral triangle, where representational, relational and reflective knowledge are interrelated and interchangeable and could appear in any order within the heart graph. In association with heart graph no. 1, representational knowledge could be connected with the term "spirit," relational with "spiritual" and reflective with "spirituality." After having their spirit awakened and connecting with peers to re-describe and signify the spiritual experience, leaders may actively cultivate spirituality within their personal and professional lives.

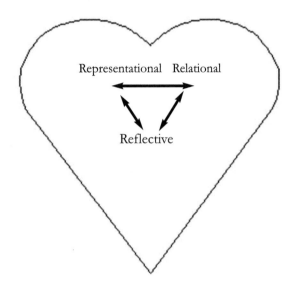

Heart graph no. 2: Triangulated perspectives of knowledge domains

Connecting mind and heart with educational leadership practices

Major positive social changes taking place within the world commence inside the minds and hearts of each student, one at a time (Carroll & Tober, 1999). Thus, educators can elevate schooling to a more spiritual level, by tuning into students' heart wisdom more effectively. Although the "human brain wants to know, the human heart wants to believe" (Arieti & Wilson, 2003, p. 3). As suggested by Coelho (1998), "you will never be able to escape from the heart, so it's better to listen to what it is has to say" (p. 129). Curtis and Eldredge (1997) think that living a life without heart leads to a sense of worthlessness. In addition to Coelho, Curtis and Eldredge's insights, Kant (as cited in Arieti & Wilson, 2003) reminds us, that if we mute our hearts and refuse to believe in something greater than ourselves, "we are likely to go mad" (p. 233). These outlooks suggest research related to spirituality and heart wisdom within educational systems would make an illuminating contribution. A problem noted in the literature is a muting of discourses about spirituality within the workplace. In my research, I focus upon educational leaders and the quality of their spiritual experiences. My research questions were formulated from the literature introduced in this chapter and Chapter 2.

Research Questions and Methodology

Studies conducted about educational leadership in the late 20th century asked questions about why certain principals were such effective school leaders (Leithwood & Steinbach, 1995). The major criteria used to judge these leaders related to the social skills and behavior patterns that enabled them to practise leadership effectively. As suggested by Handy (1989), effective leadership is "like beauty, or love, we know it when we see it, but cannot easily define or produce it on demand" (p. 105). Thus, effective leadership is often demonstrated in actions.

Leithwood and Steinbach (1995) questioned how one school principal in their study could appear to be the "Wayne Gretzky of principals" (p. 4) who knew all the correct moves to reach his goals. While they "frankly marvelled at his repertoire of behaviour" (p. 4), they were in wonder about its source. Thus, they asked if "differences in the nature of thinking or problem solving of principals offer an explanation for variations in principals' practices," and they questioned "the nature of these differences" (p. 18). Their questions suggest that more studies should be conducted on belief systems, values and thought processes that educational leaders experience before selecting certain behaviors that reflect effective leadership. For this study, I used interview data to examine relationships between ten educators' spiritual experiences and effective leadership.

This inquiry was inspired by Leithwood, Begley and Cousins' (1992) question: "how can the experiences of future school leaders be constructed so as to contribute best to the development of effective orientations to that role" (p. 27). Additionally, they suggest that "productive answers to these questions . . . are rooted in a better understanding of the principal's mental processes and states" (p. 27). In my research, I adapted this question to understand better one aspect of the processes and states of educational leaders. I built on the above question by giving it a "spiritual focus" that reflects major themes located in the literature. Within the questions, I connected spiritual development with morals and paradigm shifts. Beck (1993) suggested spiritual and moral values are synergisticand interrelated to major human needs including endurance, quality of life and survival. Good habits of the mind, influenced by spiritual beliefs and moral values began degenerating when the Charter of Rights forbid spiritual exercises, associated with a particular religion.

Ludema, Cooperrider and Barrett (2001) point out that organizations tend to move in whatever direction their research is focussed. "When groups study high human ideals and achievements, such as peak experiences . . . these phenomena . . . tend to flourish" (p. 192). Thus, they suggest asking participants positive questions to mobilize the inquiry into moments of enthusiasm. The positive core questions guiding this research about spirituality support an "appreciative inquiry" approach to research. Appreciative inquiry focuses on asking positive questions to "ignite transformative dialog and action within human systems" (p. 191).

Chapter Two provides more explanation of what resulted in the core questions. The core questions were:

1. How are the spiritual experiences of educational leaders understood and articulated by educators?
2. In what ways would this articulation of spirituality best contribute to the development of effective leadership?

The methodology applied to the study triangulated a phenomenological, feminist and action research approaches. The research was conducted on-line with ten participants, using e-mail for one-to-one interviews and a web-page discussion format for dialog amongst participants.

Study Objectives

This study was built upon Dallaire (2001), Kinjerski and Skryneki's (2002) and Thom's (1993) research findings that helped create a better understanding of the perception of the spiritual component of leadership within Canadian public education systems. The inquiry does not address spirituality within Catholic School systems. The expected outcomes of the research were to encourage a more open dialog about spirituality within public educational systems and, also to make a contribution to the development of a fresh spiritual leadership model by identifying participants' practices.

This model could approximate the "spirit at work" model designed by Kinjerski and Skrypneki (2003), who undertook a qualitative study with fourteen professionals who experienced and promoted spirit at work. Their data indicated that spirit at work is "a distinctive state that is characterized by physical, affective, cognitive, interpersonal, spiritual and mystical dimensions" (p. 4). Additionally, the leadership model could be compared with Kass' (2003) "essence of spirituality" model, which presents key experiences that demonstrate whether spirituality is central in a person's life. Five spiritual experiences connected with this model include: "1. a sense of profound inner peace; 2. a sense of overwhelming love; 3. a feeling of unity with the earth and all living beings; 4. complete joy and ecstasy; [and] 5. sensing God's energy or presence"

(p. 58). Both models (Kass, 2003; Kinjerski & Skrypneki, 2003) suggest there is a movement towards acknowledging and articulating the essence of spirituality personally and professionally.

The primary purpose of answering my research questions was to make an original contribution to knowledge that encourages more open communication about the spiritual elements of leadership among educators. To make this contribution, I facilitated and examined ten educational leaders' articulation about the spiritual component of leadership. During the study, five female leaders and five male leaders had the opportunity to dialog about spirituality within their lives and workplaces.

Overview of Following Chapters

Chapter One is an introduction that addresses the scope of the larger societal problem related to silencing "spirituality" within workplaces and presents literature related to moving beyond muted discourses about spirituality within educational leadership. Chapter Two is an interdisciplinary literature review organized according to key concepts introduced in Chapter One. In Chapter Three, the theoretical framework and the methodology applied to the study are explained. Chapter Four presents the findings of the study, identified by connecting common threads in the data and Chapter Five is a discussion of the findings. Chapter Six presents the conclusions and implications from the data analysis and states the limitations of the study.

2
Related Resources: Spirituality Matters

An exploration of the literature presented in this chapter indicates that a spiritual approach to educational leadership can assist educators to re-discover their heart-felt connection to one another and to life and therefore enable them to act morally. Muting discourses about spirituality can result in silenced discourses about morals and discourage educational leaders from signifying both spirituality and morality. Literature reviewed within this chapter expands upon three key concepts, identified in the previous chapter: 1. muting discourses about spirituality within educational systems; 2. examining moral issues within educational values; and 3. shifting paradigms affecting educational leadership.

In connection with the first key concept, "muting discourses about spirituality within educational systems," the chapter opens with a review of multiple perspectives of spirituality within educational systems, followed by a section addressing how a confusion between the terms "spirituality" and "religion" has resulted in "spiritual dissonance" and muted discourses about spirituality within school systems. Silencing discourses about spirituality has also led to spiritual poverty and blindness. Conversely, leading with heart awakens and nurtures spirituality.

In association with the second key concept "examining moral issues within educational values," the relationship between morals and spirituality is explored, followed by sections outlining the links between morals and religious beliefs, and addressing the effects of silencing moral discourses amongst educators. Teachers are moral instructors. Therefore, if educators do not signify morality within schools, moral values may be neglected by students.

In conjunction with the third key concept, "shifting paradigms affecting educational leadership," the literature further provides insight into how spiritual sensibility within leadership practices can be cultivated when individual actions and discourses signify spirituality. Leadership paradigms start shifting towards challenging power relations of ruling, introducing servant leadership and decentralizing school policies. Shifting paradigms within educational systems has resulted in the acknowledgement of feminist contributions and inquiries about bio-neurological aspects of spiritual intelligence

Chapter Two also provides evidence that there is a simultaneous resurgence of spiritual values and some leadership reform incentives within public school systems indicated by university courses and public board of education policy changes. For example, by offering courses about spirituality, holding an international People's Group of Six Billion (G6B) Summit, and providing opportunities for on-line interactive communication about spiritual issues within an educational institution, the University of Calgary has encouraged paradigm shifts toward dialoguing about spirituality. This chapter concludes after a brief review of the Calgary Board of Education recommendations to introduce new policies addressing spirituality and religion within public school systems. The context of the chapter is introduced by a review of literature that expands on multi-perspectives of spirituality.

Reviewing Multiple Perspectives of Spirituality

In the context of educational leadership, "spirituality" could be viewed as "intercultural visioning" (Vaill, 1998, p. 92), "heightened awareness of something of profound significance beyond what is taken as normal everyday reality" (Woods & Woods, 2002, p. 10), and a way of existence that moves beyond the self and the ego (Chee, 2002). According to the Urantia Foundation (1999), spirituality can help people to monitor and adjust their thoughts which enables them to feel more hopeful about life situations. Janis (2000) suggests spirituality is "beyond mere outer appearances and the five senses and is an intuitive perception" (p. 10). Vaill (1998) further states that spirituality is "wholeheartedness and wholeheadedness." Thus, spirituality signifies wholeness, immanence and transcendence.

Bohac Clark (2002) and Donaldson (1997) express spirituality as a recognition of the spark of divinity within oneself and others. Simington (2003) describes her spirituality as " a journey of . . . rediscovering and reclaiming our . . . true essence . . . a process . . . that takes us . . . deeper into our hearts and minds . . . an infinite and circular process of expanding love and consciousness" (pp. 14-15). Despite all the different insights about spirituality, a common observation is that spirituality is pre-conscious to a person's own free will, which means people can tune into or tune out their spirituality (Urantia Foundation, 1999).

Regardless of the foregoing perspectives presented about spirituality, a universal definition of spirituality has not been established. As noted by Holmes (2003), "spirituality is a domain without a definition; . . . spirituality is still inchoate, not yet having a developed language" (pp. 2-3). Therefore, many educational leaders tend to equate spiritual with "religiosity" and view it as esoteric and inclusive (Yob, 1994), rather than having any connection to conjoining head and heart or revising previously held beliefs or shifting paradigms of thought.

Sensing and Expressing Spirituality

The way a person's spirituality finds a path to his or her heart and mind may exceed a person's understanding, but spirit can be sensed by people in revelations, a communal urge, Inner peace (Ulich, 1945) and in creative expressions, such as songs (Keeney, 1996) or patient acts such as polishing a dissertation. Passionate and compassionate expressions of love are a universal spiritual language people can comprehend within their hearts (Coelho, 1998). Therefore, such expressions may not require explanation, "just as the universe needs none as it travels through endless time" (p. 93). When expressed from mind and heart, spirituality is evident.

The word "spirit" comes from the Latin term "spiritus" which means breath. To some indigenous peoples, "such as the Klamath Indians, spirit is also a word for song" (Keeney, 1996, p. 85). Arends (2000) views spirituality as a "God-shaped" vacuum and "aching chasm" within people, giving them evidence that they are in need of something beyond themselves; encountering God and becoming spiritually attuned fills the emptiness in one's soul. Coelho (1998) associates spirituality with a voice speaking from a person's heart; "even if you pretend not to have heard what it tells you, it will always be there inside you, repeating to you what you're thinking about life" (p. 129). If educators tuned into this spiritual voice, they could attend to sacred callings.

Curtis and Eldredge (1997) take a similar stand to Coelho (1998), claiming that spirituality is an inner voice informing us that "there is something missing in all this. . . . There is something more" (p. 1). Because discourse about spirituality has been muted within public educational systems, spiritual illiteracy has become an issue in schools. As examples of spoken and written language, "discourses are of central importance of how people understand their own identities and place in society" (Foley, 1999, p. 15). Additionally, discourses are central to the construction of ideologies and hegemonies.

Exploring Discourses About Spirituality

Articulating aspects of spirituality in educational leadership introduces "secular sacred" discourses that do not endorse a particular religion, but that promote teaching from both the head and heart (Beck, 1986). The term "spirituality" should be retained, rather than substituted by other terms because it can be the juncture for both religious and secular people. "It introduces an element of depth that has been lacking in discourse about public education. . . .

It would be possible to gain acceptance for the word, the concept and the goal in the realm of public education; and the advantages of such an acceptance would be considerable" (Beck, 1986, p. 154). By using the term "spirituality," both religious and secular educators would be encouraged to grapple with the interior and exterior spiritual aspects of life. As stated by Park (2001), "it is through dialog that personal conversations evolve into organizational discourse and individual ideals become co-operative or shared visions for the future" (p. 192). Conversely, an absence of personal conversations results in a lack of shared visions within workplaces.

Discourses about spirituality could challenge the traditional Cartesian inquiries, act as a compass placed alongside intellectual maps that guide educators' methods of teaching, and give deeper insights into students' needs (Roels, 2000). Introducing rhetoric about spirituality in public schools could encourage educators to improve theirs and other's lives by validating leaders' and students' cognitive processes and feelings (Moffett, 1994), as "the unspoken is easy to miss" (Goding, 1995, p. 115). Spoken words often can be recalled and act as a prompt. However, spiritual truths may also be discovered and expressed within the inexplicable, ineffable silence between words (Parker, 2000).

Experiencing spiritual poverty and spiritual blindness

An evident silence amongst educators surrounding the issue of leading with spirit in the public school system mirrors a lack of any "agreed or publicly acknowledged discourse of spirituality . . . and shows teachers' fear of being politically incorrect, offending others or meddling in the personal lives and beliefs of children . . . if they address spirituality" (Stewart, 2000, p. 3). Therefore, many educational leaders tend to resist becoming "spiritually attuned" (Stewart, 2000) while remaining pragmatically and unreflectively focused on procedural matters (Begley & Leonard, 1999). "This kind of administration can lead to a meaningless existence" (Thom, 1993, p. 5), as meaning in leadership arises from a nurturing that transcends the self and reaches to others (Frankl, 1963; Moffett, 1994; Thom, 1993). "The human spirit is the 'yes' that repeatedly drives out egocentrism . . . toward higher levels of meaning and purpose" (Loder, 1998, p. 104). Spirituality transcends ego and gives people a sense of purpose.

A major cause of this sense of meaningless in one's leadership is "spiritual poverty" and spiritual blindness resulting in an "existential vacuum" (Frankl, 1963). The lack of discourses about spirituality in educational leadership have played a strong role in creating an existential/spiritual vacuum and moral erosion (Hawley, 1995; Thom,1993). Myss (2001) refers to this vacuum as "spiritual panic . . . a desperation that we will never accomplish what we were meant to do in life" (p. 272). Discouraging discourses that arouse others to feel spiritually uplifted is like ignoring the human ability to move the heart to work by a force of love stirred up when sharing spiritual experiences (Fox, 1995). "Genuine spirituality must be the willingness to enter into the process of dialog within oneself and with others" (Vaill, 1998, p. 180). Without freely conversing about spirituality in the workplace, educators tend to become blind to their spirituality and thus view their leadership roles through a smeared lens (Myss, 2001).

Awakening and nurturing spirituality: Leading with heart

Single words, stories, actions and art addressing spirituality can move people's hearts with forces of love, hope, faith and compassion (Fox, 1995). "We want to tell . . . the divine story, the story bigger than ourselves that we have been graced to breathe in" (p. 121). Sharing such stories could induce spiritual clarity through the experience of an epiphany, which is a sudden recognition of a person's intimate connection with the divine (Chopra, 2000, Myss, 2001). Myss suggests that an epiphany can be "a sudden ending of the inner chaos and lack of direction of significance. . . . Through a sudden infusion of charisma, your inability to make sense of life's challenges, coupled with the emotional weight of feeling as if you are living without purpose or direction, is transformed into the knowledge that each moment in you life is divinely ordered" (p. 27). Conversely, the silencing of discourses about spirituality may prevent educators and students from experiencing epiphanies that could awaken their spiritual essence and help them re-discover their heartfelt connection to one another and life.

Such a re-discovery has been known to make a difference between someone "living to die and someone dying to live" (Bender, 2001, p. 48). A genuine spiritual awakening manifests itself as a desire to be of service to others (Myss, 2001) and to follow the path of one's personal calling (Coelho, 1998). Thus, freely articulating spiritual experiences would connect "head with the heart" (Myss, 2001, p. 20) and empower leaders to be servants of a holistic dynamic.

A spiritual approach to educational leadership involves self-reflection, kindness towards peers, and a working environment conducive to spiritual activity, to assist teachers to discover their hearts wisdom and pass this revelation on to their students (Palmer, 1998). Such a leadership style must take up the feminist challenge to be relational, have a pluralistic, global-village perspective, and take on a mind/heart connection (Dallaire, 2001). Leading without a conscious awareness of spirit keeps the mind and heart divided, which is like having "two battle encampments within, each one fighting for authority over our power and choice" (Myss, 2001, p. 25). Typically within educational systems, the mind wins over the heart.

"We have to talk with ourselves and others if we are going to understand and improve our spiritual condition" (Vaill, 1998, p. 229). As examples of one's spoken and written language, discourses can be like gentle winds that fan the sparks of spirituality within leaders and illuminate their integrity (Fairclough, 1992; Fox, 1995). "Dialogue is meant to illuminate both the parallels and the divergences of belief in order to dispel the dark forces of delusion, fear, anger and pride" (Kiely, 1998, p. 20). For example, using the Buddhist term "metta" to conceptualise loving kindness, compassion and equanimity within a leadership framework could introduce rhetoric that encourages spiritual awareness and moral conduct within school systems (Salzberg, 1995).

How educators view their leadership roles is influenced by ideologies, constructed from established discourses within their workplaces (Foley, 1999). "But whether it takes a millennium to admit, the spirit of teaching excellence must be about the spirituality of teaching excellence" (Jones, D.,1995, p. ix).When educators lead with excellence, their labor becomes sacred prayerful work, because their efforts are driven by their hearts, which awaken and move others' hearts. Their work has a positive spiritual ripple effect.

Because "everyone embodies a spirituality" (Griffin, 1988, p. 2), it is important for educators to recognize and articulate how different aspects of spirituality are related to spiritual inclinations of diverse cultures (Kiely, 1998). For example, epiphanies are given various names in different religious traditions: "enlightenment, God realization, illumination, awakening, self-knowledge, gnosis, ecstatic communion" (Fisher, 1999, p. 24). Regardless of the vocabulary applied to describing a spiritual awakening, experiences of enlightenment are common amongst all cultures and religions. Therefore, a person does not have to belong to a particular religious group or endorse certain beliefs, to experience enlightenment.

An acknowledgement of diversity in beliefs is like a person choosing a certain food and not claiming that everyone must eat it. People should consume suitable foods for the best physical health, according to their physical constitution (Loder, 1998). Similarly, religions can awaken and nurture the heart and spirit; therefore, from a smorgasbord of ideological positions, educators and students should be free to articulate aspects of religion or secularism that are most suited to their spiritual disposition and moral development.

Articulating Aspects of Spirituality Within Leadership

The lives of some great spiritual masters such as Buddha, Muhammad, and Jesus, have provided roadmaps that can assist educational leaders to evolve spiritually. "Without a guru, the spiritual path is like trying to walk in quicksand when there is a paved highway nearby, going in the same direction" (Walters, 1990, p. 94). Although these three leaders all shared a common fate of abandonment and separation from their own communities in their early missions to serve mankind (Myss, 2001), they each enlightened the world by articulating different aspects of spirituality. However, within most Western educational systems, Christian celebrations such as Christmas and Easter are acknowledged on school calendars and declared as national holidays. This suggests Christian beliefs are very influential in decision-making within most Western school systems.

Christian teachings suggest Jesus' leadership mission was to give sight to people spiritually blind and demonstrate to individuals who thought they could see that they were blind (Jampolsky, 1983). Stories about Jesus proclaim that He came into the world as light to awaken the fruits of the spirit: love, joy, peace, patience, kindness, gentleness, fidelity and self control within his followers (as cited in Kiely, 1996). Some Christians believe that parables about Jesus' leadership awakened them to their divine nature (Loder, 1998) and that an "ontological change occurred in human nature as a result of the birth, life, death and ascension of Jesus" (Kiely 1996, p. 148). Followers became more grateful, compassionate, and heart-centred in their treatment of others, which demonstrated their hearts had become "faith-filled" (Jones, L., 1995).

Although Christianity was based on the original teachings of Christ, "Churchianity" is the result of institutionalizing His spiritual messages; "Jesus Christ was crucified once, but his teachings have been crucified daily" (Walters, 1990, p. 47). Thus, the meanings of his spiritual teachings have often been misconstrued within and outside churches. If the Christian religious context of Jesus was dropped, His life story could simply symbolize a death of primitive belief systems and a transcendence beyond cultural limitations for people (Pearce, 2002). Within this framework, the story of His death and resurrection helps cultivate faith within people's hearts and gives them hope about personal and professional spiritual evolution.

Like Buddha and Muhammad, Jesus was judged harshly for frequently speaking loudly against injustice, courageously standing up for women's rights and confidently encouraging new ways of thinking (Jones, L., 1995). Although Jesus articulated and mentored many divine aspects of leading, spiritual leadership is not restricted to a belief in the Christian God and "belief in God does not constitute spirituality" (Solomon, 2002, p. xii). Buddha, Muhammad and other spiritual leaders who perceived transcendence in non-personal terms also modeled inner peace, social justice and spirituality (Yob, 1994). Additionally, there are many charitable, caring leaders who do not believe in God (Bierle, 1992), but their active expressions of the divine gives them a sense of joy, wonder, and awe. As noted by Keen (2004),

> no matter whether the holy appears to us in an encounter with a rock, a bush, a flower . . . or in the words or presence of a teacher or prophet such as Jesus or Mohammed, we find ourselves in the presence of power that is luminous and revelatory. To encounter the holy is to live in the presence of what is real rather than illusory, lasting rather than ephemeral, power. The moment we pass through the looking glass into the realm of the sacred, everything changes, turns upside down, is transvalued. (p. 30)

Transvaluing leadership in the context of spirituality supports a holistic worldview that encourages interconnection, interaction, interbeing, interfeeling and interpower within the workplace (Keen, 2004).

The most common of all spiritual leadership experiences reveals the "nature of the Divine without a God label. . . . Though the experience is a gift, it is the opposite of anything that enhances ego or makes one feel superior" (Van Dusen, 1996, p. 18). For example, when a radiant Buddhist monk walked peacefully and silently across a battlefield, the "blood-thirsty emperor" Ashoka experienced an epiphany that resulted in him altering from a tyrant to a highly respected benevolent ruler. "The radiance of that one Buddhist monk is still affecting the world today; one person's serenity changed the course of history, and delivered to us the Buddhist path to happiness" (Salzberg, 1995, p. 11). As a spiritual leader, Buddha taught that regular experiences of the Divine produce humility that enables a person to feel equal to others and all creatures. "In this humility it is not unreasonable to think that any creature that comes for your help may be the Buddha or Christ" (Van Dusen, 1996, p. 22).

Comparable to Christians and Buddhists, the Islamic followers had a spiritual leader who articulated the faith system of his particular belief. "Islam is an Arabic word which means peace, purity, acceptance, and commitment" (Fisher, 1999, p. 354). In the Islamic faith, Muhammad's character, like Jesus' and Buddha's in their own religions, was considered a model of the teachings of the Holy Book (Fisher, 1999). According to the Qur'anic revelations, Muhammad promoted brotherhood amongst people of various faiths. Similarly to Jesus, He presented himself as God's slave and a vehicle for God's message. Muslims are to adhere to the five pillars which involve professing their faith, praying five times daily, paying alms to the needy, fasting during Ramadan, and making a pilgrimage to Mecca.

According to the Islamic Holy Book, the mission of Islamic followers is to feed the hungry and spread peace among people (Fisher, 1999). However, like Jesus, Muhammad was ridiculed for his prophet-hood by people in his own community but he continued to present the central teachings of Islam - there is "no God but God" and all people's thoughts and actions should "spring from a heart and mind intimately integrated with the divine" (p. 354). Unity and connection with others as a global family with a direct relationship with God is part of the central teachings of Islam.

Having a direct relationship with God and a mind-heart connection within self were also major teachings of Mother Teresa, who believed "it was in actions not words that faith was at its most universally articulate," (Spink, 1997, p. 159); actions, not words, can speak to individuals who do not subscribe to any religious viewpoint. Her spirituality exceeded religious beliefs, and transcended thought, rationality, logic and words. As Spink (1997) observed:

> it was possible for some to find in her spirituality elements of both Buddhist and Hindu mysticism, to detect for example in her desire for continual 'oneness with Christ,' the path which Buddhist mystic treads towards 'nirvana,' the real of enlightenment where he becomes one with the One; to find in Mother Teresa's self detachment – the process of emptying herself of self – a parallel with the Buddhist 'samadhi' with its emphasis on silence, emptiness, the void and cessation of desire. . . . Christians referred to her as a saint. Some more accustomed to the Hindu mode of thinking chose to see in her the 'reincarnation of Jesus,' Muslims acclaimed her as an 'evolved spirit' and people of all religious beliefs and denominations were prepared to recognize her as a 'holy person.' . . . Mother Theresa is among those emancipated souls who have transcended all barriers of race, religion, creed and nation. (p. 158)

Her expressions of unconditional love reflected Christlikeness, Muhammad-likeness, Buddhistlikeness.

Mother Teresa demonstrated that there is a place for spirituality inside the individual soul, which is outside church buildings and the walls of organized religions (Solomon, 2002). Her articulation of her beliefs and her servant leadership promoted a spiritual evolution towards inter-religious and inter-cultural dialog and a movement of the spirit, rather than a spiritual movement (Spink (1997). Therefore, some of her leadership practices may have induced spiritual dissonance amongst some traditional religious leaders.

Confusing Spirituality With Religion: Spiritual Dissonance

As stated by Janis (2000), "spirituality is beyond all religions yet containing all religions" (p. 18). Further, Kiely (1996) suggested spirituality within all religions is the "realization of a good heart, a human being's innate qualities of compassion and tolerance" (p. 6). Arriving at a comprehensive and universal meaning of "spirituality" is difficult (Dallaire, 2001; Griffin, 1988), as "spirituality may be described, but not easily defined" (Cully & Cully, 1971, p. 607). Thus, the term "spirituality" is commonly misunderstood and tends to be exclusively associated with "religion" (Dallaire, 2001; Guzie, 1995; Hawley, 1995; Mathews & Clark, 1998; Moffett, 1994; Rolheiser, 1999). Although both terms address a search for the sacred, spirituality is different than religion (Guzie, 1999); religion is an outer path some individuals follow to nurture their inner inherent spirituality and is a form of institutionalized spirituality (Hawley, 1995).

Spirituality is not something that comes from the outside in, but is "something individuals already possess and are able to access when in relationship with their creator" (Grimbol, 2000, p. xvii). Griffin (1988) boldly asserted "spirituality is not an optional quality which we might elect not to have" (p. 2); in agreement, Parker (2000) stated that denying the ontology of spirituality is like claiming that an ocean is separate from water. Thus, as noted by Ulich (1945), "the definition of spirituality should be that which is its own evidence" (p. 45). While religion codifies and institutionalises the spiritual experiences in communities, spirituality is associated with the lively, enthusiastic qualities inside a person (Guzie, 1995, 1999, 2000).

There was an enforced separation between religion and spirituality among Aboriginal people with the introduction of missionaries to this continent (Armstrong, 2004). Even in the new millennium, many Aboriginal communities experience tension between those who follow Christianity and those who practice traditional native spiritual ways. Spirituality, within the definition of missionaries who preached among the Aboriginal people, was equated with paganism, yet those same spiritual beliefs guided Aboriginal leaders in their decision-making for the people. The genocide of spiritual cultural practices among Aboriginal people resulted in a vacuum in leadership decision-making for the people. This colonization of the mind continues to be a contemporary Aboriginal issue that reflects spiritual dissonance within their communities (Armstrong, 2004).

Spirituality is primary to religion and is the life-giving impulse to celebrate the transcendental and the immanent awareness of life itself (Donaldson, 1998). Spirituality is embracing faith which will "always mean believing in what cannot be proven, committing to that of which we can never be sure. A person who lives in faith must proceed on incomplete evidence, trusting in advance what will only make sense in reverse" (Yancey, 2000, p. 93). For example, I wrote about my research study with the faith that it would assist me in my own spiritual evolution and help to awaken the latent inherent spirit within its readers.

Seeking spirituality beyond organized religion

People of particular religious beliefs tend to become divided when "they worship a particular shadow in the mosque, in the temple, in the church" (Rajagopal, 1989, p. 81). Therefore, the walls of organized religion can oppress people's spirituality rather than nurture it. As stated by Krishnamurti (cited in Rajagopal, 1989), "most people's minds are asleep. They are drugged by knowledge, by the Scriptures, by what . . . somebody else has said" (p. 154). Religious groups' conceptualisations of God may support their own narcissistic desires and their ethnocentrisms within their own communities, rather than humankind's built-in-need for "God beyond God – beyond narcissism and ethnocentric projection" (Albright & Ashbrook, 2001, p. 46). In some religious sects, God may be created within the image of humankind, rather than humans created within the image of God.

Not grounded in a set belief system, as in religious sects, spirituality is a means of experiencing life, interacting with others, engaging in heart-felt activities and connecting with something greater than oneself (Solomon, 2002). Sometimes, this dynamic is expressed by secular movements. For example, not grounded in any religious doctrine, the Alcoholics Anonymous (AA) recovery program has overlooked sectarian issues, but kept a spiritual focus by using the terms "Higher Power," "Creative Intelligence," or "Spirit of the Universe," to mean "something greater than oneself" (B. Mel [anonymous last name], 1991, pp. 3-4). In the twelfth step of the AA program, the term "spiritual" appears in connection with the word "awakening." Program members insist AA is a spiritual fellowship not a religion; and different than religions in that "the realm of spirit is broad, roomy, all-inclusive; never exclusive or forbidding to those who earnestly seek" (pp. 3-4). This spiritual program assists people to connect with something greater than themselves.

Spirituality is more concerned "with love, compassion, forgiveness and service to others" (MacDonald, 2000, p. 206) than theological arguments and religious doctrines which can be oppressive. Spiritual development is not about adopting a certain ideology or being at a particular stage in life, "but rather the entire process of unfolding itself, an infinite process that is completely present at every stage" (Wilber, 1996, p .10). Spiritual development takes a path towards the inner person, resulting in a deeper sense of connection with others and a resurrection of the heart's wisdom (Fox, 1991).

Fearing articulation of spirituality

The way that spirituality is connected with an individual's heart and mind may exceeds one's understanding. Because spirituality is divine intelligence (Loder, 1998, p. 1), the destructive overshadowing of some educators' view of this intelligence has resulted from a "cognitive confusion" associated with their language (Thom, 1993). The confusion arises when trying to cognitively comprehend clearly what "spiritual" means. Given the inter-disciplinary nature and ineffability of "spirituality," words may be the least effective communicator. "They are most open to misinterpretation, most often misunderstood" (Walsch, 1995, p. 4). The application of language that deals with spirituality often sounds "artificial, stilted, and preachy" (Vaill, 1998, p. 230). The contextual meaning depends on the perspective from which it is being examined. For example, when several blind men were touching different parts of an elephant each one described the animal totally differently, according to where they were standing (Parker, 2000).

"Through confusion of meanings and words, we lose our ability to think clearly, to reason, and to communicate" (Loder, 1998, p. 107) what we believe and who we truly are spiritually. As Goding (1995), a retired teacher, noted, "describing himself as a spiritual intellectual [is] a labour that would no doubt pigeonhole [him] as an oxymoron in some circles" (p. 115). Furthermore, Bohac Clark (2002), a university professor, stated: "really declaring ourselves – what we are, our real values including those in the personal area of spirituality can be akin to disrobing in public . . . what are we really willing to say out loud" (p. 11)? Bohac Clark and Goding suggested some educators' ontological perspectives about spirituality may be ruled by tension and a cognitive intellectual battle that induces fear of being misunderstood if they articulate their true beliefs.

Conversely, some educators may attribute their silencing of spirituality to having a desire to focus upon other intellectual interests in their professional lives or they may believe cognitive intellectual battles are caused from attempting to engage in conversations about spirituality. An example of a cognitive intellectual battle is how the word "servant" prompts an immediate negative connotation "due to the oppression which many workers . . . have historically endured" (Spears, 1998, p. 13). Because fear becomes the accepted ruler that decides how a person interprets and applies the concept of servant to leadership, only individuals such as Mother Teresa, who dig deep enough to understand the inherent spiritual nature of "servant," can understand what is intended by "spiritual leadership" (Spears, 1998).

Often, educators' fears of being "biased, . . . judgmental, and letting . . . prejudices show" encourages them to "use words which are bleached of moral distinctions, neutral, value free, and non-judgmental" (Thom, 1993, p. 107). When this fear takes place, it appears impossible to debate issues surrounding spiritual leadership (Creighton, 1999; Noddings, 1992, Spears, 1998). Therefore, Bohac Clark (2002) questioned "to what extent are teachers willing to resist peer pressure in order to remain true to themselves. . . . What's the payoff for all this sacrifice of personal anonymity" (p. 11)? Furthermore, Postman (1995) pointed out that "without narrative, life has no meaning. Without meaning, learning has no purpose . . . . Without a purpose, schools are houses of detention, not attention" (p. 4). Encouraging more narratives about spirituality could motivate leaders to share their spiritual experiences, which could add more meaning, a sense of purpose and values to their lives.

When there is a gap between leaders' values and the ways they practise leadership, they may encounter "spiritual dissonance" (Snow, 2000), which is a confusion about what their conscience is telling them. Values constitute the main construct of leadership; "if there are no value conflicts then there is no need for leadership" (Hodgkinson, 1991, p. 11). These value conflicts demand open-ended genuine dialog that promotes caring, connects people, guides decision-making and contributes to a good "habit of the mind" (Noddings, 1992, p. 23). The caring component of confirmation, which involves staying connected and affirming the best in others, is an example of responding to a good habit of the mind, and practising spiritual leadership. Muting discourses about spirituality, on the other hand, could discourage connection and affirmation of leaders' strengths.

Muting Discourses About Spirituality Within Educational Systems

When discourses about spirituality are excluded in the school setting, leaders with spirit may be overlooked, connections with others discouraged, and addictions that hide the cosmic loneliness educators and students experience may become issues (Fox, 1995). "Perhaps the prior silence on the topic of spirituality in areas of academic is due not only to the difficulty of defining spirituality, but also to the ambivalence of many who work in an academic world that has emphasized rationality and the scientific model for most of the 20th century" (Tisdell, 2003, p. 25). Such a model has overlooked the value of nurturing spirituality.

Kessler (1998) suggested the moral issues: "drugs. . . violence, and . . . suicide may be both a search for connection and meaning and an escape from the pain of not having a genuine source of spiritual fulfilment" (p. 49). Furthermore, some alcoholics claim their alcohol cravings can be compared to "the spiritual thirst of our being for wholeness (B. Mel, 1991, p. 12). The foregoing perspectives about spiritual impoverishment indicate that inadequacies and gaps existing in public educational systems that exclude spirituality from their discourses should not be ignored (Rolheiser, 1999; Thom, 1993; Yob, 1994). Spiritual rhetoric is required to raise a leader's consciousness and encourage the quality of community within the school system (Thom, 1993).

Introducing or reintroducing spirituality in public schools would familiarize educational leaders and their students with an experience of the sacredness of all life (Fox, 1998, Foxworth, 1998). "An education system that ignores the human search for meaning through spiritual belief is . . . inadequate and does a grave disservice to its students" (Sweet, 1997, p. 11). Because of the synergistic relationship between morals and spirituality, ignoring the force of spirituality can devalue the moral purpose of schools. Alternatively, acknowledging the spiritual dimension of education reform entails elevating a commitment to making a positive difference in the lives of all students by introducing a moral purpose (Fullan, 1991; 1998). However, it is common for researchers and educators committed to highly moral school communities to preclude spirituality as one form of intelligence and thus avoid discourses that would encourage leading with spirit, grounded with a moral purpose (Sergiovanni, 2000).

Educational administrators, who have been excluding any reference to spirituality from their discourses, are promoting forms of learning that can "readily kill awe . . . . Education that ignores awe kills the soul" (Fox, 1998, p. 50). Therefore, school leaders need to encourage peers and students to express spirituality with actions and words. Dialoguing about spirituality and putting spirit into action can foster intellectual rigour, clear one's vision, increase energy, and encourage moral behavior (Spears, 1998). To reconcile attention to spirituality and the Charter of Rights and Freedoms, educators could initiate non-religious activities that could awaken a student's spiritual values and promote moral behavior. For example, students could be given opportunities to commune with nature, volunteer as mentors to younger peers, do creative projects and assist the elderly.

Examining Moral Issues Within Educational Values

Schools are becoming more "demographically heterogeneous and diverse in terms of race, religion, national origin, ethnicity, gender, age, physical ability, and language preference" (Vaill, 1998, p. 91). This pluralistic nature of schools discourages administrators from advocating any universal set of moral principles (Mitchell & Kumar, 2001). "Teachers, students, and parents bring a multitude of moral sensibilities that are derived from various diverse cultures, ethnic groups and socio-economic backgrounds" (p. 48). However, during the twenty-first century, "the core values which differentiate schools, and the ways in which these values are articulated will become one of the defining features of education and the communities in which schools exist" (Walker, 2002, p. 3).

Some researchers (Bates, 1993; Evers & Lakomski, 1991; Greenfield, 1991; Leithwood & Duke, 1998, Noddings, 1992) argue that an individual's values and conscience should guide all educational leadership practices because modelling morality is an important component of the social role played by school leaders. This administrative role is an example of caring, which is a major quality of good leadership in the educational administration field (Leithwood, 1999). From a feminist perspective of caring, Noddings (1992) states that moral education involves four major components: "modelling, dialog, practice and confirmation" (p. 22). Furthermore, Gilligan (1993) suggests a "care-based" approach to morality has been proposed as a compensation for or a supplement to embedded moral systems exclusively established by male administrators.

Leaders become moral by experiencing caring for others and practising caring towards others (Noddings, 1992). Practising caring means moral behavior is not something to be reserved for sudden problems; "it must be a constant companion" (Lashway, 1996, p. 12). In the United States, some studies indicate elementary schools that become more caring, responsive places foster a child's ethical and social development (Walker, 2002). In competitive Japanese elementary schools, "the three R's are underlined by the three C's – connection, content and character" (p. 4).

Despite acknowledgements of connections between morals and caring, many moral codes and practices remain "unarticulated, unquestioned, and therefore untested" (Mitchell & Kumar, 2001, p. 54). Because some values are in constantly being questioned while others are unquestioned and unarticulated, it is difficult to claim that certain absolute values influence particular actions (Beck, 1993). However, "thou shall not kill" and "respect others as yourself" could be considered ideal absolute values endorsed by some cultures. Conversely, there are cultures who believe in holy wars and others that believe killing for freedom of their countries is a moral act.

Reviewing Relationships Between Morals and Spirituality

Beck (1993) suggested both spiritual and moral values relate to major human needs including "survival, health, happiness, friendship [and] . . . freedom" (p. 24). While spiritual values tend to focus on ethereal attributes such as "awareness, breadth of outlook, integration, wonder, gratitude, hope, detachment, humility [and] love" (p. 24), moral values are associated more with trustworthiness, honesty and justice. Applied as guides to people's thoughts and actions, these values have been articulated and acted upon within educational systems. However, many good habits of the mind, spiritual beliefs and moral values began degenerating during the industrial revolution (Ryan, 1999) when education became "secularized and anthropocentrized" (Fox, 1995, p. 175).

Anthropocentrism meant educators interpreted and regarded the world in terms of human values, rather than in the context of sacred laws (Fox, 1995). Before secularism and anthropocentrism influenced educational systems, many outstanding leaders took for granted that the spiritual, moral and intellectual aspects of life were connected; but their viewpoints about connection were challenged when science began replacing religion as the basis of social morality and design (Fox, 1995). In response to a public degeneration of spirituality and morality, a "discourse of fear" (Ryan, 1999, p. 77), along with "moral scepticism" (Mitchell & Kumar, 2001) was being circulated within educational systems. Consequently, some educators attempted to control the situation by legislating morality. When establishing laws, they interpreted morality as exclusively meaning "thou shall nots" rather than "aiming to do good" (Duke, 1999, p. 9), which is associated with spiritual principles. Inquiries such as this study aim to challenge the legislating of morality and encourage the introducing of ways that students can learn to act morally.

In Baden-Powell's Boy Scout/Girl Guide Oath, which is grounded by spiritual principles, a youth is not governed by do not, but is led on by "do" (Baden-Powell, 1945). The oath's stated promise to carry out in God's honor was devised as a moral guide to a person's actions, rather than as a repressive approach to dealing with their faults. "It is the spirit within, not the veneer without that does it. And the spirit is in every boy [and girl] . . . only it has to be brought to light" (p. 22). The underlying feature of the awakening of the youth's spirit is the romance of communing with nature and observing the wonders of the universe. Furthermore, to teach active citizenship, Scout and Guide leaders work towards inculcating character, health and strength, and service to others from within the youth, rather than from the exterior. With its honored oath to do a good turn daily, Scoutcraft is a way by which even wayward, immoral youth have been brought to a higher consciousness and an awareness of their spirituality when serving others (Baden-Powell, 1945).

Another example is Lickona's character education program which demonstrates a relationship between "aiming to do good," and moral/spiritual development (Goodman & Lesnick, 2001). Some of its principles are based on the belief the human spirit needs participation in a common "task of public value, and it has need of personal initiative within the participation" (p. 142) to develop good moral conduct. When applying Lickona's program, educators aim to model good moral conduct and reflect pride in their school community while the students engage in different service activities, including assisting teachers, raising funds for their school and helping other students. Celebrations and "good-spirited" fun are a way of emphasizing school values and giving a common sense of purpose to the students and educators. Furthermore, students aim to be moral beings through practising self-control, being kind, acting fair, and depicting self reliance.

Another character program "The Virtues Project," implemented in 85 countries, including Canada, was initiated by the United Nations to support the moral and spiritual development of people of all cultures by assisting them to live by their highest values (Wheatcroft, 2003). The five empowering strategies of this project are: speaking the language of virtues, recognizing teachable moments, setting clear boundaries, honoring their spirituality and offering the art of spiritual companioning. When applying the project principles, educators encourage students to nurture their virtues, viewed as gifts of character.

An application of these project strategies into educational systems is known to have cultivated respect, developed responsibility, built self-esteem, promoted unity, and restored justice (Wheatcroft, 2003). As noted by Hunter (2000), "by restoring a sense of spirituality and morality in learning, the discourses that make up moral education are strengthened and educators feel freer to address important questions" (p. 4). They would also feel more liberated to express their own spirituality within their workplaces.

Examining Links Between Morals and Religious Beliefs

Although the terms "spirituality" and "morals" have been associated with religion, many educators argue that most religions are so stained by violence and bloodshed, they do not reflect spiritual values or moral behavior (Chopra, 2000; Griffin, 1988). Furthermore, educators are "uncomfortable suggesting there is a set of absolute values which must be taught to all students" (Weingarten, 2002, p. 6). However, Henry (2000) suggested that educators need to recognize "the profound relationship between the moral, the religious, and the spiritual" (p. 6). Because religious and spiritual insights provided some of the earliest roots of moral leadership, educators should continue to acknowledge moral principles as central to moral conduct in the new millennium. "Even though new situations not envisioned by the law will always exist, there are certain unchangeable principles of right action which are almost universally held. They form the bedrock of moral action. . . . These principles include do good and avoid evil; do to others as you would have them do to you; live not by lies; love your neighbor as yourself" (Henry, 2000, p. 4). Practicing such principles reflects spiritual values and leads to moral behavior.

Aside from associating morals with religion, Henry (2000) suggested that moral principles do not depend solely on a particular religious belief. There are laws written in the hearts of individuals which are part of their spirituality, and to enable these ordinances to become personal principles of action, leaders need to help educate a student's conscience. Coles (1990) also suggested that children of varied cultural, ethnic and religious backgrounds demonstrate within their individual narrative and artistic revelations that they are spiritual beings with their own interpretations of God. Children are innately spiritual beings on a pilgrimage towards finding peace and a sense of connection with a God of their understanding. Therefore, life-long education of conscience, which takes place through the influence of spiritual leadership within educational systems is essential to students' spiritual maturity. Educators can teach a moral way of life by informing the conscience through proclamation, instruction, public debate, and "particularly by example" (Henry, 2000, p. 5). Therefore, educators need to find ways to introduce discourses about spirituality within their workplaces.

Thom (2001) suggests conscience can be informed by a spiritual framework that assists educators to deal with family, gender, visible minorities, violence and alcohol and drug abuse issues. To establish morals, one's conscience needs to be educated with "concepts such as grace, faith, compassion and forgiveness" (p. xx). Literature indicates spiritual leaders such as Jesus and Buddha reflected "personal conscience" within their actions and words; conscience is an inner voice informing individuals of what is right and wrong and therefore setting a moral base (Thom, 2001).

Like Jesus, Buddha taught that if people learned to love themselves, they would feel connected to one another, sense right from wrong and thus never want to harm another person. As noted by Salzberg (1995), "If the heart is full of love and compassion, which is the inner state, the outer manisfestation is care and connectiveness, which is morality" (p. 172). Honoring the five basic principles of Buddhist tradition could educate the conscience in a similar fashion to Christian principles. The Buddhist precepts of conduct admonish people to refrain from killing, physical violence, stealing, sexual misconduct, lying, harsh speech, idle speech, slander and taking intoxicants. These precepts reflect the Buddha's strong intent to teach his followers to be generous, compassionate, kind and very careful about what they say and do as a cardinal approach to morality (Salzberg, 1995).

A limited context in which educators and students in the public school system can acknowledge or express their own or other's religious views, because of the Charter of Rights and Freedoms, can result in spiritual, religious and moral illiteracy within the public school systems (Sweet, 1997). Conversely, giving young people an awareness of the different religious beliefs of others could encourage them to rediscover their own. Objectors to religion in the classroom may have difficulty understanding that education about spiritual leaders is not value-less.

Although religious education about Christianity enforced within residential schools can indoctrinate, education about religion can illuminate and promote moral literacy (Sweet, 1997). Students can benefit from learning about how different spiritual leaders demonstrated generosity, kindness and compassion. As stated by Watkinson (1999), "schools need to be places that neither inculcate nor inhibit religion. Religious conviction should be treated with respect" (p. 13). However, religious beliefs such as Christianity should not be forced upon students. Sweet (1997) states that:

> we've gone from times when the religious were often intolerant of the non-religious . . . to a day when it is those who hold religious convictions who are subjected to societal intolerance. It's often implied that anyone holding a religious belief system must be either brainwashed, intellectually challenged, or in direct need of a psychological crutch. (p .7)

Consequently, educators are fearful of being misunderstood if they share spiritual experiences that could be interpreted as being religious. They do not want to be perceived by peers as being intellectually challenged or closed minded.

The Latin root word of "religion" means "that which binds us together as people or community" (Williams, 2000, p. 65). As Sweet (1997) states, educational leaders attempting to free children from religious indoctrination by excluding the topic from the public school system may have resulted in "throwing out the baby with the bath water" (p. 12). Keeping religion out of the public system may be why "hundreds of thousands of parents reject public education in favour of schools that ghettoise their children on the basis of religion" (Sweet, 1997, p. ix). Ghettoising students according to their religions keeps them isolated from others with different belief systems. Because educators are responsible for "teaching habits of the mind and habits of the heart" (Sergiovanni, 1996, p. xii), some parents may want their children to learn about morality within a religious and spiritual framework with which they agree and personally endorse. The problem with putting students in separate schools to learn good habits of mind and heart is that they may be inculcated with religious or cultural beliefs that encourage violence or intolerance against their neighboring peers.

Silencing Moral Discourses Amongst Educational Leaders

The sideling discourses about morals among educational leaders has had a "silencing effect on other members of the moral community: teachers, parents, students and others" (Mitchell & Kumar, 2001, p. 48). Because the term "moral" carries the potential for excessive misunderstandings, and tends to be put in the context of controversial issues such as "sex" or "piety," the expression "character education" has become a replacement phrase for morals in some schools (Goodman & Lesnick, 2001). "Character education holds that certain core values form the basis of good character – the attitudes, beliefs, and behaviors that the school wants from and is committed to teach to its children" (Walker, 2002). However, Goodman and Lesnick (2001) state their concerns about the "moral anesthesia" they have noted in educational systems. "All too often, the choice between doing what is right and costly and what is advantageous but morally flawed is viewed as . . . choice, with the moral option accorded no obligatory weight" (p. 4). As Fenstermacher (1990) indicates, the effect of teaching is reduced when separated from its basic moral purposes.

If educators do not model or speak about moral qualities, moral values may be neglected and thus never be developed by children (Fenstermacher, 1990). "In the moral wasteland of a technological society, formal education must give moral direction, provoke serious thought about good and evil, and enable young people to discover what is true and good in human experience" (Manzer, 1994, p. 248). A person's moral identity is an aspect of him/her that needs to be developed through a process that takes place in the school, as well as at home and in church.

Because of the interconnection between morality and spirituality, spiritual values should be reflected by educators who hope to instill morals in their students. Teaching is "saturated with morality" (Goodman & Lesnick, 2001, p. 14), so teachers are moral instructors, whether they accept this or not. As Palmer (1998) stated, "ultimately, we teach who we are" (p. 10), so let your life speak; person-to-person interactions between educators and students are at the heart of teaching. Palmer's viewpoint suggests teachers can introduce spirituality and morality into the classroom through their own heart-felt, passionate, and caring approach to pedagogy.

Mitchell and Kumar (2001) stated, "a curriculum for moral discourse can enable administrators to construct an operating environment that reflects the hearts and minds of people whom education serves and that invites fresh perspectives to enrich practices, policies and procedures" (p. 60). Ideally, as one shifting paradigm influencing the educational system, a curriculum for moral discourse could help students build spiritual muscles and become spiritually fit, which would assist and guide them towards moral behavior.

Shifting Paradigms Affecting Educational Leadership

The term "paradigm" refers to value systems and organizational principles that construct a "disciplinary matrix" guiding everyday social thoughts and actions (Vaill, 1998). Toulmin (1990, 1996) refers to the new millennium as an era of "historical discontinuity" and major epistemological changes influenced by an ending of the political supremacy of Europe and hegemony of European ideas. He states that,

> historically, the last time our ideas about knowledge went through such a deep change was the mid-seventeenth century. Between 1630 and 1690, a set of fundamental issues was framed, which, for most of the next 300 years, defined the Received Program of epistemology and human sciences. Contemporary critics of this program refer to it as the "Cartesian" program, and attribute it to the writings of Rene Descartes, notably to his Discourse on Method and Meditations, both of which first appeared in the 1630s. Advocates of the program . . . do the same: In their eyes, the fact that the whole agenda of modern philosophy took complete and convincing shape in the mind of one man is a mark of Descartes' supreme genius: His work seems to supersede all that had gone before, so removing any need for us to inquire into his relations with his forerunners. (Toulmin, 1990, p. ix-x)

Descartes promoted dualism, absolutes and certainty in a positivistic way of knowing (Lather, 1991). After his death, his successors continued to draw upon his main epistemological assumptions, which they believed were beyond question. Until Wittgenstein challenged their Cartesian standpoints, most educators were persuaded that "the true locus of 'knowledge' is personal and individual, not public" (Toulmin, 1995, p. x). Therefore, any account that philosophers gave of the nature of knowledge had to be derived empirically and ideally take the "form of a deductive system, such as the classical Greeks created for geometry" (Toulmin, 1995, p. x). Descartes' ideologies did not encourage exploration of other ways of knowing.

However, in the book *Investigations,* published in 1953, Wittgenstein challenged Descartes' epistemological assumptions; Wittgenstein argued that "all knowledge is socially and culturally situated . . . its primary locus must be collective, not individual" (p. xii). Further, in the 1980s, Hesse (1980) and Reinhartz (1985) indicated that attempts to produce positivistic value-free knowledge is "self-deceptive" and "logically impossible," which is why many explicit ideologies are being replaced by implicit ones. This paradigm shift in epistemological assumptions is reflected in Vaill's (1998) notion that:

> no discipline or school of thought is secure from the winds of revolution . . . partly due to new substantive discoveries about man, partly due to the collapsing faith in positivistic objectivity, and partly to a refreshing . . . new interest in ethics, morality and the spiritual nature of man. (p. 9)

Paradigm shifts demonstrate the continuous invention of fresh ways of interpreting educational leadership. In the late twentieth century, environmental issues and the internet helped create an "Electronic/Ecological Era" where the goal of educators was to act as facilitators to teach students how to learn and care about their environments and (Walker, 2002). As the twenty-first century was approaching, a shift in educators' understanding of education and leadership took place (Begley & Leonard, 1999; Creighton, 1999; Hollaar, 2000; Spears, 1998). They were encouraged to "rethink the boundary between the secular and sacred" (Vaill, 1998, p. 5) and recognize that for decades they had "tried to say the wrong thing better and better" (p. 11) because their rationale was founded on narrow boundaries of values based on Cartesian paradigms.

Walker (2002) referred to the twenty-first century as the "Systems-/Spiritual Era." The concept of systems "recognizes that schools are now hubs of interconnected networks. . . . Here, students are the creators of meaning, and teachers the co-creators. . . . Spiritual here does not refer to religion, but . . . to values that go beyond the mere physical sustenance" (p. 2). Maxcy (2002) further suggested that with the beginning of a techno-culture controlled by computers and the internet, this century may result in one of the most epoch-making shifts that will greatly influence future educational leadership models. "Technology offers us the hope that we can separate ourselves from our God-less past; technology may be seen as a vehicle through which we may come to understand God and the universe . . . as we invent and re-invent ourselves" (p. 8-9). This perspective indicates that computers and the internet enable leaders to become more globally informed and connected with people around the world, which may result in shifts within their leadership practices.

A shifting focus on leadership approaches has resulted in pressure for educators to transcend administrative hierarchical functions and move towards more socially acceptable and dynamic leadership roles implied by shared leadership concepts (Richmon & Allison, 2000). With a shift in leadership approaches in the beginning of the twenty-first century, more dialog should be encouraged about both the organizational and cognitive contexts of a leader's decision-making process (Leithwood & Steinbach, 1995; Spears, 1998).

"Everybody is talking about paradigm shifts and moving from the industrial to the information age, but few are talking about the qualities of mind, body, and spirit that are involved in making those shifts" (Vaill, 1998, p. 217). To execute shifts towards addressing these qualities, educators need to rethink and re-examine basic values and practices within their leadership style that may have been suppressed or politicised to fit some presumed organizational need. Maxcy (2002) claimed that at the beginning of the twenty-first century, the model of educational leadership has shifted from a "knowledge leader to one of inspirational leadership" (p. 2). This variance in models and practices has created misunderstandings of what the role of an educational leader entails.

Like members of an orchestra, leaders and followers have a responsibility to inspire and work with one another; leadership is a "co-created" activity, rather than a dictatorship controlling others through fear tactics, which was encouraged in some Cartesian models (Secretan, 1999). As Porat (1985) asserts, leaders should be willing to grow towards being more effective in the workplace by upgrading their knowledge base with continuous learning, fresh leadership models, and personal accountability.

Evolving Educational Leadership and Teaching Models

Traditional leadership models are male-oriented, with an emphasis on individual ambition rather than connections with family and community (Sergiovanni, 2000). These well-established leadership models have shaped the cognitive process of educators by providing them with scripts of roles to play as administrators and teachers (Sergiovanni, 1996). Instead of questioning or altering the models, many leaders have attempted to fix and preserve them. Senge (2000) referred to them as "mental models" (p. 18) that become ingrained assumptions and generalizations about leadership. For example, three major theories have influenced the way educators have viewed their roles during the past few decades (Sergiovanni, 1996).

According to the "hierarchical pyramid" theory, leaders are responsible for supervising, directing and inspecting staff (Sergiovanni, 1996). The "railroad" theory suggests that leaders should invest their efforts into anticipating questions and problems that will arise and then developing answers and solutions. When applied within school systems, both these theories require that principals be experts in human relations and capable of facilitating high morale amongst staff and students. Nevertheless, the third theory, "high performance," de-emphasizes the hierarchies and scripts that control people's actions; it focuses on de-centralization and on the empowerment of individual workers making their own decisions.

Although the preceding theories about ways to lead embrace valid truths and have strengths, they influence the construction of leadership models that are based on "separation of function by roles" (Sergiovanni, 1996, p. 13); these three theories do not support a synergistic or charismatic approach to leadership. Therefore, administrators, teachers and students may face problems of isolation, fragmentation, and loss of meaning when feeling disconnected from others within educational systems (Sergiovanni, 1996).

Destructive types of charismatic leadership were practised by leaders such as Hitler. However, charismatic leadership is considered by some educators to have a creatively compelling and successful conceptual framework of authority (Weber, 1978). When referring to charismatic leadership, Weber drew upon historical examples of successful spiritual leaders, such as Abraham and Jesus. Faith and a sense of a calling to serve others are the main foundations on which this form of leadership is built. Charismatic dominion has an emphasis on the exceptional spiritual gifts of leaders, rather than their legal or traditional rights to authority based on their roles (Weber, 1978). Those who are charismatic leaders do not necessarily feel a call to serve others. However, servants of others may be considered charismatic leaders and a charismatic approach to leadership could be determined a spiritual way to lead.

By incorporating a charismatic approach to leadership with a high performance style, organizational members could draw from one another's spiritual resources and successfully enact their roles (Senge, 2000). This change may involve experiencing "mentanoia" which means a "shift of mind . . . or an awakening shared intuition and direct knowing of the highest of God" (Senge, 2000, p. 22). Some educators may conclude that "mentanoia" happens as a result of their having peak spiritual experiences, resulting in them signifying and cultivating spirit within their workplaces.

Exploring bio-neurological aspects of spiritual intelligence

Morse (2000) suggested a spiritual awakening means learning how to "activate the right temporal lobe, the place where God lives" in the brain (p. 2); the right temporal lobe gives individuals their ability to heal, to be telepathic, and to communicate with God. Similarly, Gardner (1999) indicated that people have spiritual intelligence, comparable to musical or mathematical or emotional intelligence, that enables them to be skilled at meditating, praying, and being in touch with spiritual phenomena.

Pearsall (1998) claimed the heart has spiritual intelligence and wisdom that enables it to "think in a more type B, gentle, relaxed, connective way" than a type A brain, which is always in a hurry (p. 25). Zohar and Marshall (2000) support Pearsall's research that suggested spiritual intelligence is part of the brain's make-up that facilitates a dialog between "reason and emotion, between mind and body" (p.7). Despite research that suggests spiritual intelligence may exist, an acknowledgment of this existence has not been beneficial for many educators because, like some other intelligences, it cannot be measured.

Introducing an educational model to awaken spirituality

Despite the fact that spirituality cannot be measured, Dallaire (2001) has articulated a method for spiritual education that he frames as a "contemplation-in-action" (p. 45) model. In this model, he embraces holism, a theory that conceives the universe in terms of interacting wholes that are more than the sum of their separate parts. In his model, he acknowledges tradition, pluralism and diversity within schools and demonstrates an appreciation for ontology, the nature of their existence. He believes "an appeal to ontology can be a meeting point for those who espouse secular humanism, feminism, ecologism, holism, and pluralism" (p. 45). Dallaire (2001) explained that as a way of knowing, perceiving and beholding, "contemplation" is an experience of being awakened to life-giving energy and an attentiveness to the wonder and awe of each moment. Contemplation "permits one to see the connection between polarities and to see the unity beyond dualism that exists in reality today" (p. 62). Thus, to acquire balanced spiritual learning, students require both contemplation and action incorporated within their studies (Dallaire, 2001). Contemplation is a concentration on spiritual things as a form of private devotion.

"A contemplative-in-action spirituality strives to integrate the active and contemplative dimensions of life; through such integration, the fruits of one's contemplation are brought to one's active life" (Dallaire, 2001, p. 64). Because some public school systems tend to focus on preparing students for the paid job market and retaining a healthy status quo as indicators of their worth, many education models have centred on active employment rather than contemplation or volunteer work. However, many problems within educational systems can be attributed to "incomplete knowing" perpetuated by muting discourses about spirituality. Thus, adding a contemplative element to a model of spiritual development could lead to a paradigm that corrects such an imbalance (Dallaire, 2001).

Shifting paradigms towards stewardship

There is a need for supporting alternative paradigms for education that put the developmental needs of students as persons ahead of the materialistic concerns of a consumer nation (Cully, 1984; Palmer, 1998, Sweet; 1997; Yob, 1994). As stated by Kuhn (1970), paradigms are accepted models or patterns and when they alter, "the world itself changes with them" (p. 111). For example, when educators believe that they are advocates of stewardship, their leadership roles become student-centred. They have the proper regard for the rights of others and are willing to accept accountability for their own actions, without imposing control over others. Stewardship involves leaders acknowledging their own human faults and limitations instead of hiding behind their power and status.

Manzer (1994) called this ideological position a "person regarding" approach to education. Policies for person-regarding education "shift the argument for accessibility of education from a criterion of equal educational opportunity in order to pursue economic success to a criterion of individual development" (p. 148). Student-centred schools aim to encourage individual development by introducing learning experiences that meet the individual needs of each person in the system. Different than an economic approach to learning that focuses on ranking, competition, and class selection, a student-centred approach may find room for leadership that acknowledges the ontology of spirituality, rather than endorses a traditional bureaucratic approach to leadership that discourages leading with spirit (Manzer, 1994).

"The lighting-a-flame philosophy of education" recognizes the need for spiritual, intellectual and emotional development of a learner" (Bosetti, 1995, p. 34). This philosophy is positioned in the belief "there is something in the learner ready to be set on fire," which supports a caring leadership style, wherein leading and teaching is viewed as "heartwork" (p. 34). While sharing parts of students' journeys, educators focus on caring for and nurturing students to help them to become "self-reliant, responsible, and caring" individuals actively engaged in constructing and making sense of their lives (Bosetti, 1995, p. 34). Thus, spirituality serves as a means through which we might treat one another with dignity and respect.

Wilber's (1996) integrated model of human development also proposes a holistic framework for education that could incorporate heart work. His model places human development into four main categories: 1. the interior of a person, which is the subjective conscious part of individual awareness; 2. the exterior of an individual, which is the objective behavioral aspect influenced by facts; 3. the inside of the collective aspect of the person, which contains cultural values and ethics shared by a group; and 4. the exterior of the collective social self, which involves social systems such as institutions. In addition to the traditional social and behavioral aspects of educational models, Wilber's framework for mapping human development introduces an interior and collective context in which both account for the spiritual development of individuals. Therefore, his framework could be applied to revising some educational leadership models that would promote a more student-centred and spiritual component of learning.

Establishing a spiritual leadership perspective involves honoring the heart and right brain that processes awe and wonder as much as the analytic left brain when engaging in making decisions (Fox, 1995). It means developing a higher consciousness informed by the spirit. Leaders with heart who view the welfare of others as a priority in the workplace, are known to be more productive in their work than managers who lead exclusively with their heads (Hoyle, 2002). Therefore, the term "spirit" has been associated with high-performing schools and other organizations in which results validate the importance of spirituality in the workplace.

Applying both a spiritual and a scientific perspective to decision-making in the educational system could create "wisdom schools, as opposed to knowledge factories" (Fox, 1995, p. 170). From a scientific perspective, knowledge and theories of leadership are derived solely from "empirical sense experiences or observation" (Abercrombie, Hill & Turner, 1984, p. 10); on the other hand, from a spiritual perspective, knowledge claims are based on actual lived experience (Ballou, 1995). These lived experiences can result in transformational leadership practices.

Decentralizing school policies

Decentralizing schools allowed some educational leaders to experience a transformation toward spiritual approaches to leadership. "With the move to site-based management and the decentralization of school management in the 1980s, a new mission for the principal was erected: principal as transformational leader" (Maxcy, 2002, p. 2). Therefore, new leadership theories needed to be crafted and administrative styles reinvented. At the core of the problem of central educational governance are the issues of institutional separation, educational politics, and administration (Manzer, 1994, p. 19). "Centralizing trends encourage a discourse that places great value on control, accountability, and efficiency, whereas decentralizing trends foster a discourse in which empowerment, cooperation, and continuous improvement are strongly valued" (Leithwood, 1999, p. 30). Valuing these aspects of leading reflects a spiritual approach to leadership.

As noted by McKinnon (2004), trends to enrich educational systems resulted in the establishment of site-based management within some Alberta schools to empower educators to use their professional skills in establishing budgets and developing curricula. The goal of this approach to management was to give voice to educators who have been silenced within centralized governance structures. Site-based management resulted in school "re-culturing" because teachers and administrators had to collaborate in decision-making practices (McKinnon, 2004). Thus, site-based management reflects a decentralized "person-regarding" approach to educational leadership.

Manzer (1994) points out that person-regarding education implies a decentralization of educational decision-making. It challenges the economic, other-centred view of education which bases a student's value upon a selected occupation within the system. In contrast to a generalized teacher-centred method, which is considered politically conservative, person-regarding education is founded on the liberal principle of "universal human development" (p. 148). Ideally, this approach to education indicated schools would contribute to individual development by introducing learning experiences that de-emphasize competition. However, because of accountability issues and provincial exams, Western schools have been forced to function competitively. Although person-regarding education was envisioned as the future "hegemonic ideology" of Canadian education, rifts inside educational-policy communities reflect criticisms of this approach (Manzer, 1994). These rifts mirror "relations of ruling" standpoints educators have confronted when attempting reform their approaches to leadership.

Reviewing Power Relations of Ruling Which Excluded Female Leaders

Relations of ruling are affairs and structures advocated by texts that rule, guide, organize and dominate societies (Smith, 1992). "Our knowledge, practices of thinking, theorizing, and images of the world are textually grounded ... in the relations of ruling" (p. 6). Therefore, this ruling has an effect on the type of educational research that is conducted and the participants that are chosen. Relations of ruling also influence ways that educators have been taught to lead. A major barrier to women entering educational leadership positions has been relations of ruling standpoints preserved within governing systems (Armstrong & Armstrong, 1994). For example, relations of ruling within educational systems preserved hierarchical models of leadership.

Many female leaders have challenged male-dominated relations of ruling practices and endorse more spiritual approaches to leadership (Lowe & Krahn, 1993). In addition, many male leaders are adopting participatory ways of leading that have been stereotyped as feminine approaches to leadership. Grob (1984) compares a female leader to a midwife in that she cares enough to assist others in the process of giving birth to their own truth and strengths. This approach to helping others to succeed reflects "a distinctive spirituality" within their leadership style (Donaldson, 1997).

Women's leadership practices have supported decentralization of power and encouraged others to develop their own power and self-dependence to effect change. Many female leaders believe that a leader who promotes collective effort is more effective than a leader who attempts to "chart a course alone" (Restine, 1993). Their leadership style, which evokes participation more than representation has influenced some paradigm shifts in educational leadership theory (Lowe & Krahn, 1993).

"One great shift in educational research has been increased publication of feminist literature" (Donaldson, 1998, p. 1). When more women started becoming scholars, feminist literature influenced the minds of academics. A higher quality in methodological designs, theoretical development and academic dialogs has ensued from this shift. "Nevertheless, most feminist research still tends to be published in edited monographs, the chapters of which represent seeds of ideas rather than the full flowering of scholarly maturity" (p. 1). Therefore, as Donaldson (1998) suggested, to make public education more equitable, women's leadership and research abilities need to be more valued within the system. Furthermore,

> to achieve equity, a critical mass of women academics must through their collective effort, sustain a core level. Critical mass . . . is formed when the numbers of people necessary to adopt a new practice, product or belief system also have sufficient awareness to kindle a chain reaction which persuades most people to adopt the change. (Donaldson & Emes, 2000, p. 35)

Ideally, to introduce a spiritual feminist leadership perspective, the proportion of female leadership appointments in education should at least reflect the proportion of female students.

However, women's leadership roles and scholarly involvement with universities has only been during the past century (Donaldson & Emes, 2000). "The monastic values that shaped the evolution of universities from the eleventh to the nineteenth centuries excluded females: women were not considered intellectually capable of academic pursuits" (p. 37). This exclusion of female scholars and administrators involved with post-secondary education resulted in "womanless administration," and therefore a lack of female influences on leadership practices (Hill & Ragland, 1995).

Setting educational policies was a role performed primarily as a male leadership function throughout the mid-twentieth century (Woods, Lentz, & Mitchell, 1993, p. 409). Towards the end of the twentieth century, educational reform policies continued to preserve educational hierarchies that hardened, rather than softened, the division of labor in leadership (Blackmore, 1999). As noted by Blackmore, this division of labor of leadership may partially be the result of women's leadership roles being excluded from history books, dating as far back as Plato's time in ancient Greece when women were not considered worthy of receiving an education.

Although Plato included women as guardians of state, subsequent philosophies did not, a consequence that placed females into an "ontological basement," where they were valued exclusively as leaders of the reproductive process (Martin, 1985, p. 15). Thus, educators and students were denied exposure to historic female intellectual leaders and were led to assume women were incapable of any role outside of reproduction. A shift in how leadership is viewed by educators has involved challenging some traditional sceptical attitudes related to women in leadership and reconstructing discourses of leadership that have been mainly established by male religious leaders (Reynolds & Young, 1995). Adopting leadership discourses that maintain leadership as a male-dominated practice "decontextualize, distort, and depoliticize the issue of gender" (Blackmore, 1999, p. 3) in leadership practices and, therefore, denies women's intellectual capacities and spirituality. Dallaire (2001) cites an example of how relations of ruling established by Christian dogma have deterred many women from leadership roles:

> The minimization of feminine figures in Christian scripture, the inclusion of mainly masculine images in titles of the divine, the organization of religious committees along patriarchal lines, the historical exclusion of women from ministerial leadership, and the presentation of spiritual growth as only linear rather than also cyclical are all aspects of a sexist legacy within Christianity. (p. 20-21)

As noted by Tisdell (2003), spirituality and religion can be synergetic or exist separately. However, Dallaire's example of relations of ruling demonstrates why some educators are reluctant to incorporate religion into curricula and the reason that feminists are enthused about introducing a spiritual approach to leadership.

During the past two decades, discourses created by the women's movement portray women with "a spark of the divine" (Donaldson, 1996, p. 194). As spiritual beings, they are "Goddess-centred . . . [and] not yet ready to be institutionalized, but the sense of women as spiritual beings is global" (p. 203). Therefore, many female leaders have been arguing for a reinstatement of the "feminine aspects of the divine and a recovery of the Goddess image" (Dallaire, 2001, p. 203). A major goal of re-instating spirituality in the postmodern world is to "complement and balance . . . male-oriented spirituality with its 'corrective' female forms" (Wilber, 1996, p. 53). Thus, women's spirituality and ability to be servant leaders can assist in constructing more humane, spiritual and productive workplaces (Helgesen, 1990; Peters, 1990).

Outlining feminist characteristics that reflect servant leadership

Spears (1998) states that "servant-leadership emphasizes increased service to others, a holistic approach to work, a sense of community, and shared decision-making power" (p. 4). Listening, empathizing, healing, conceptualizing, having awareness and foresight, practicing stewardship, and being committed to the growth of people and building community are key characteristics associated with servant leadership. Hesse (1998), who inspired Greenleaf's (1991) work on servant leadership viewed servants as individuals who sang and whistled as they worked, and who were invisible except when needed. He specifically associated the term "servant" with women mothering their children when he stated "it is just the same with mothers. When they have borne their children and given them milk and beauty and strength, they themselves become invisible, and no one asks about them any more" (Hesse, 1998, p. 34). Aside from demonstrating servant leadership by mothering children, the invisibility of women's work has been oppressive to females whose diligent contributions have been overlooked.

Although many feminists may disagree, Hesse (1998) suggested that a mother's approach to servant leadership reflects a natural holistic law. Spears (1995) supported this stand when he pointed out that traditional autocratic and hierarchical models of leadership established by men are dying and being replaced by an emerging approach, more attributed to females, called servant leadership. Many women are currently writing and speaking about servant leadership as a style of leading that is commonly associated with how women naturally lead (Spears, 1995). Spears (1995) stated that "so called (service oriented) feminine characteristics are exactly those which are consonant with the very best qualities of servant leadership" (p.12). Women in many different cultures have been practising servant leadership for a long time. They have been applying a holistic cooperative, spiritual, communal approach to leading, while taking care of their families, building community, and engaging in religious practices but they have no public roles.

Exploring ways religious leaders shaped servant leadership

According to Nair (1994), Gandhi reflected "selfless service" in his leadership practices. His servant life of service was devoted to being active towards "eliminating violence and promoting mutual respect between Hindus and Muslims" (p. 3). Indicating that actions express spirituality more powerfully than words, Gandhi suggested that "if Christians would live their lives according to the teaching of Jesus Christ" they would be accepting of other religions (Spink, 1997, p. 155). Kersten (1999) states that contrary to acting as a political strategist, Jesus mentored servant leadership by demonstrating examples of how "moral purity may be attained" (p. 10). However, Christian churches have portrayed multiple versions of Jesus, which has resulted in misconceptions within different religious sects.

Kersten (1999) claims that when Jesus became "managed, monopolized and codified" by churches, his servant voice became replaced by "narrow minded and rigidly dogmatic beliefs" (p. 4). Consequently, after Jesus' leadership image was narrowed, many public school educators did not view Him as a servant leader who reflected a spiritual element of leadership. Similarly, before the Islamic religion became politicized, Muhammad was viewed by

Muslims as a servant leader, whose mission was to serve God and humankind (Fisher, 1999). In his devotion to God and service to the Muslim community, he endured poverty, hunger and ridicule. As a servant leader, he lived his belief that God did not want his servants to act as if they were superior to anyone. Glimmers of appreciation for Muhammad's modelling of servant leadership are starting to be expressed outside Islam "as sincere Muslims attempt to counteract negative media portrayals of their religion" (Fisher, 1999, p. 344). This negative portrayal of the Muslim religion was evident in the media after the terrorist attacks in New York, September 11, 2001.

Before her death in 1997, Nobel Peace Prize winner Mother Teresa was strongly portrayed by the media as a servant leader and regarded by millions as a contemporary saint for her dedication to serving the poorest of the poor (Spink, 1997). Driven by an absolute faith in God, she consistently claimed she was simply responding to Christ's infinite love, which she saw in every person she encountered. Taking on the role of a servant mother to her young Sisters in the Missionaries of Charity, she advised them that they were loved by God who was using them to "light the light of love in the world" (Spink, 1997, p. 147). Her drive to light love in the world was recognized in one of her many awards that honoured her for her "struggles [that] have shaped something beautiful for God" (p. 160).

Throughout her life, Mother Teresa's sacred work became the "focus of a growing interest on the part of the world's public and media (Spink, 1997). Wanting to remain invisible she struggled with being interviewed by the press, but leaned on the conviction that "God's work should be known . . . and how can it be known if it is not announced" (p. 159). Mother Teresa can be credited for shifting the paradigms within religious leadership in the twentieth century towards a more feminist, empathetic, healing, inter-faith, spiritual approach to leading. She was canonized as a saint by Pope John Paul in the year 2003.

Religious Paradigms: Shifting Toward Articulating Spirituality

At the beginning of a religious paradigm shift, "many people of different religions have the common desire to meet, to share, to enter into dialog, and to pray. . . . This desire for unity. . . is there in the hearts of many all over the world. It is a seed that will grow and bear much fruit" (Vanier, 1998, p. 122). At the beginning of the twenty-first century, spiritual dialog "is more urgent than ever" (Knitter, 2001, p. 1). Spiritual dialog amongst leaders must abandon absolute claims of certain religious beliefs and alternatively make their truth claims in a relative fashion. As noted by Knitter (2001) it means that one can be absolutely committed to one's own truth – ready to share it with others, defend it, die for it – but at the same time, one can be genuinely open to the truth of others – ready to learn from that truth and to clarify and correct one's own truth. (p. 13)

A spiritual gathering held in Calgary demonstrated a readiness for religious leaders to be open to others' truths (Williamson, 2001). Differences were put aside when more than 300 people filled a hotel room to participate in "Calgarians Pulling Together" (Williamson, 2001). Organized by the Council for Canadian Unity, the occasion brought together a variety of cultural and religious leaders. "Muslim sat beside Catholic and Jew, joining each other in prayer. Participants in the event joined in the traditional breaking of bread to end the day's fasting during the Muslim holy month of Ramadan. All had one common thread – a desire to put aside differences and remember together . . . the event was a celebration of unity and offered a way forward after the divisiveness seen immediately after September 11" (p. B4). As noted by Kiely (1996), when "inter-religious" and "inter-cultural" dialog takes place, a universal common spirituality can be experienced by diverse leaders.

At an international Group of Six Billion (G6B) People's Summit, held at the University of Calgary from June 21 to 25, 2002, leaders representing five world religions addressed "Faith in Peace" during a workshop (Doetzel, 2003). From this workshop, the speakers provided eight leaders from the world's most powerful countries, who were attending the G8 Summit in Calgary, with their recommendations to work collectively on perspectives of peace. Representing the Buddhist faith at the workshop, Janet Willis emphasized there is no path to peace, because peace itself is a path and she suggested that with forbearance, humankind can be patient enough to practice non-violence.

Speaking from a Hindu perspective, Prem Kalia called himself a "spiritual humanist" who worships the God of his own heart, but resonates with all religions (Doetzel, 2003). He stated that religion is a human creation, but spiritual truth is eternal law. Jewish Rabbi Lindsay Joseph spoke about justice and peace being the light of wisdom within his faith; the purpose of major religious traditions should not be to construct huge places of worship, but to create temples of caring and compassion within people's hearts.

Rev. Bill Phipps from the United Church said that the Christian "dream of God" is peace, which is communal and begins inside of people's hearts (Doetzel, 2003). The tender-hearted are proactive and acknowledge the embodiment of the peace of their Creator. As the representative of Islam, Dr. Jamai Badawi defended the sacredness of his faith and argued that Muhammad preached about the purity of intention, universal brotherhood, no-force conversation, peaceful co-existence and acceptance of plurality.

Engaging in interfaith dialog to seek a common spiritual ground and recognize differences in perceptions of God is common amongst the Muslims; they are taught to approach everyone with kindness, justice, compassion, love and respect (Doetzel, 2003). In sum, the five religious leaders agreed all their beliefs are subject to misinterpretation. However, peace, not war; compassion, not hatred; collaboration, not conflict are common ideals shared by all religions. For example, peace is a global spiritual language that all religious leaders comprehend and aim to support (Doetzel, 2003).

The power of a fresh vision of leadership, induced by the energy of religious leaders gathered together to dialog about peace initiatives, could generate a major paradigm shift toward a global perspective of spiritual leadership within education (Knitter, 2001). "This power is contained in what Christians call "conversion," Buddhists call "enlightenment" and Muslims, "submission." Through the energy generated by community within the sharing of diverse faiths, religious leaders find themselves able to act differently and able to "do things that previously seemed beyond imagination" (p. 3).

Without realizing it, people re-write their agreement with reality, which means challenging some former conditioning and beliefs (Knitter, 2001). Metaphorically speaking, this global vision of spiritual leadership reflects a form of cultural unity "in which a river of water from the sea (western knowledge) and a river of water from the land (Aboriginal knowledge) mutually engulf each other upon flowing into a common lagoon and becoming one" (Pyrch, 1998a, p. 651); when cultural rivers intersect, "the foam ... created ... represents a new kind of knowledge" (p. 651). This new knowledge gained from conversion, enlightenment and submission experienced by diverse religious leaders could have a ripple effect that would help cultivate spirit within educational leadership practices.

University Teaching Paradigms: Shifting Toward Addressing Spirituality

The University of Calgary Graduate Division of Educational Research offers seven separate graduate courses about aspects of spirituality and education, such as: Spirituality in a Post-Modern Age; Spirituality and Teaching Excellence; Spirituality of Inspired Leadership; Love, Spirituality, and Leadership; and The Spiritual and Moral Dimensions of Spirituality. School administrators and teachers working on Master of Education degrees are the students most commonly registered for these non-required courses. According to a recent presentation, the seminars are encouraging transformative learning (Groen & Jacobs, 2004).

In the "Spiritual and Moral Dimensions of Leadership" students examine necessary changes in consciousness and heart that are prerequisites for the transformation of organizational cultures (Groen & Jacob, 2004). "The course was designed explicitly to engage learners beyond an abstract or conceptual level, to challenge them to learn how to skilfully manage one's own emotions – one's inner life" (p. 3). Thus, the goal of the seminar was to practice spiritual precepts, not just learn about them. "Over the course of the seminar's 13 weeks, many of the seminar members underwent significant transformational experiences" (p. 3). Students reported a "rotation of consciousness," such as experiencing a sudden dramatic re-orientating insight, resulting in significant changes in their lives. These findings suggest that it is possible for students in a particular setting, a graduate university seminar, to have spiritual experiences resulting in personal transformation that is beyond intellectual insights. Groen and Jacob's (2004) research indicates paradigm shifts in curriculum have been taking place within some university programs, addressing spirituality. Thus, educators and students are sometimes given opportunities to move beyond muted discourses about spirituality.

On-line Dialogue: Shifting Towards Discussing Spirituality in Education

In the new millennium, subscribers of the Change Agency (2000-1) initiated at the University of Calgary have been chatting on line about spirituality within school systems. After having attended a "Schools and Spirituality Seminar," several subscribers introduced postings that acknowledged the value of awakening the spiritual essence of students. Other subscribers wrote about the importance of breaking away from a dysfunctional educational vision and establishing new ones that recognize the connection between spirituality and education. The Change Agency on-line dialog indicates that discussions about spirituality in education, community in schools, and morality issues are a response to the school reform movement and loss of meaning pervading modern cultures. The on-line communication amongst educators demonstrates there is a desire to articulate aspects of spirituality related to their work.

Calgary Public School Policies: Shifting Towards Including Spirituality

Calgary Board of Education Trustees approved the creation of a committee to develop a plan for a public participation process to address the question of the role of spirituality and religion within public schools (DeBoice, 2003). The trustee backgrounder titled "Religion and Public Education: Public

Consultation Calgary Board of Education," states that an educator's mission is:

> Educating tomorrow's citizens today . . . includes an ever-increasing diversity of students with a rich variety of needs – including all of the moral, ethical, spiritual, and religious aspects of being human. . . . As a public system, we must accept children of all faiths and creeds, and show tolerance and respect for differences among faiths while at the same time encouraging inquiry and discussion in the continuing search for truth. (p.1)

This trustee backgrounder suggests that Calgary's public school trustees are communicating about spirituality and religion in order to develop new policies guided by the School Act and the Canadian Charter of Rights and Freedoms (DeBoice, 2003). Therefore, they are taking steps towards moving beyond muted discourses about spirituality within educational systems. Such a move could result in fresh curriculum that addresses the whole student by exploring their spirituality in addition to other aspects of their intelligences.

Summary of Chapter

As a point of reference, this chapter outlines literature related to three key concepts identified in chapter one: 1. muting discourses about spirituality within educational systems; 2. examining moral issues within educational values; and 3. shifting paradigms affecting educational leadership. Related to the first key concept of this study, literature that articulated aspects of spirituality was introduced and examples of spiritual dissonance were presented. In association with the second key concept of the study, the synergistic relationships between morals and religion and morals and spirituality were outlined. Additionally, the effects of silencing moral discourses amongst educational leaders were outlined. An examination of the literature related to the first two key concepts demonstrates how muting discourses about spirituality within the workplace has had an adverse effect on educational leaders.

Connected with the third key concept, an extended literature review and summary of various programs provided insight into evolving educational leadership and teaching models. Recent trends of international religious leaders communicating about spirituality and courses about spirituality being offered at the University of Calgary were outlined. Also, the Calgary Public Board of Education Trustees' dialog session that addressed spirituality within school policies was outlined. The literature suggests that the resurgence of spiritual values has occurred in consonance with leadership reform incentives within the public school system. Therefore, this review of the literature and courses about spiritual leadership indicate that paradigm shifts towards breaking the silence about spirituality are taking place within educational systems at the beginning of this new millennium.

3
Theoretical Frameworks

The theoretical frameworks used to shape the methodology and design for this qualitative study are a type of action research, informed by the application of triangulated research paradigms. After the research design for the study evolved, appreciative and cooperative inquiry techniques were applied during the data collection and analysis. In this chapter, the rationale for utilizing qualitative research in this study is outlined and characteristics of an epistemological paradigm shift in research about educational research are identified. Additionally, literature that supports why feminist, phenomenological and action research are exemplary tools for framing the study is presented. Before the research design is introduced, the methods of data collection used to answer the two main research questions are presented: 1. How are the spiritual experiences of educational leaders understood and articulated by educators? and 2. In what way would this articulation best contribute to the development of effective leadership? Selection of participants, the data collection process, methods applied to the study and a summary of collection and storage of data are described prior to the chapter summary.

Rationale for Utilizing Qualitative Research

Qualitative researchers view their data as interpretative rather than objective truths (Bogdan & Bilken, 2003). Therefore, they do not assume findings to be absolute truths. They acknowledge that because truths can be changing and growing commodities or occurrences, researchers can discover "a" truth but not "the" truth. They examine the world as it naturally occurs, without the conventional tools of experimental research, such as surveys. A major characteristic of qualitative research applied during this study was interviewing to obtain descriptive data and to inform the ongoing data analysis (Bogdan & Biklen, 2003; Gay & Airasian, 1992). This approach to research supports Goddard and Foster's (1999) belief that "it is only through the analysis of recorded narrative of those most familiar with the phenomenon that meaning can be elicited and knowledge constructed" (p. 7). In this study, the researcher analyzed ten educational leaders' recorded narratives.

The lived experiences of educational leaders cannot be portrayed and comprehended through analysing responses with reference to a numerical scale (Goddard & Foster, 1999). Furthermore, attempting to apply quantitative research methods to study spiritual elements of educational leadership could be like "trying to figure out if the refrigerator light stays on when the door is closed. If you open the door to look, the experiment is ruined" (Schoemperlen, 2001, p. 235). Because certain types of knowledge are transcendent, experiments to validate their existence may not work.

Educational studies have commonly supported taken-for-granted assumptions about how knowledge is obtained, which have influenced ontological, epistemological and methodological methods (Young, 1999). These assumptions have resulted in historically dominant and contextually shaped approaches to research that exclude alternative approaches to inquiry. Many leadership researchers are moving away from positivistic, "reductionist" behaviorism, toward a "more descriptive, naturalistic phenomena of leaders in action" (Starratt, 1993, p. 5). They are assuming a holistic stance, in which "they look at the overall context to obtain and guide their understanding . . . and focus on individual person-to-person interactions" (Gay & Airasian, 1992, p. 169). In-depth interviews complement or replace survey questionnaires and statistical analyses applied in quantitative research (Maxcy, 1991; Starratt, 1993). This approach to inquiry supports the standpoint that theoretical gains may not be superior to experiences, and that researchers should be permitted to share their own stories (Lazar, 1998). However, theoretical insights may emerge from experiences and reciprocate with further experiences.

Characteristics of Qualitative Research

Data collected in qualitative research are descriptive, which means they take "the form of words or pictures rather than numbers" (Bogdan & Bilken, 2003, p. 5). These data can be descriptive, narrative, or non-written (Rockford, 2003). The process of doing qualitative research is viewed as dialog between researchers and their participants. Doing qualitative research without having a connection with participants is impossible (Shank, 2002). A researcher is an important part of the research process and their influence should be acknowledged (Johnson & Christensen, 2000). The researcher benefits from direct contact with the people, situation, and phenomenon under study; their personal experiences and insights can be a valid part of the inquiry, and critical to understanding the phenomenon being studied (Johnson & Christensen, 2000; Rockford, 2003). Therefore, researchers' standpoints should be acknowledged and reflexively reviewed as data that are examined.

Because researchers are human communicators studying humans communicating, they are inside the context they are studying (Connelly & Clandinin,

1990). However, researchers have "long been silenced in the research relationship" (p. 4). Their silence has prevented them from developing a connective resonance with study participants. Wilber (1996) states that the "mapmaker" of the inquiry is excluded when the researcher is silenced. Sweet (1997) further suggests that sharing one's own experience is the only way to commence understanding how perceptions of each other are developed. Given these assertions, I share some personal experiences that inspired this inquiry.

Researcher's personal experiences related to this inquiry

My father was a public school teacher who asserted that the only true religion in the world is the religion of love and the solely genuine universal language is the language of the heart. He claimed that he had learned this model of religion and standpoint about heart language from studying the life of Jesus, his spiritual mentor. A great yearning for light and sacred wisdom led him to investigate the teachings of Jesus when he was attending college. He did not refer to Jesus as an exclusive religious leader. Instead, he spoke about Jesus' spiritual qualities of unconditional love and how the story of His crucifixion and resurrection had helped him feel hopeful and forgiving during times of tribulation that he faced as an educator.

During his teaching career, my father reflected his spiritual beliefs by giving students novel opportunities for experiential learning. His former students claimed he brought spirit into the classroom when he taught them to sing uplifting songs that he referred to as musical prayers of gratitude. They also spoke about occasions when he took them into the forest during science classes, told them how wind and spirit were comparable and encouraged them to respect the wonders of nature as gifts from their Creator. A common assignment he gave to students was for them to check out sunrises, sunsets, and rainbows and then write about them for an English assignment. One of his students who chose to pursue a teaching career referred to him as a wise, caring "man of heart" who manifested spirit and a love for his students and teaching.

This honorable father taught me about spirituality by his peaceful presence, non-judgmental nature, caring compassionate treatment of others, and by his incredible respect for nature. Before cancer resulted in his becoming bedridden, he took this researcher on a meditative walk through a forest when the wind was whistling, and told me the names of all the trees. As he cautiously removed thorns from the stems, while picking a bouquet of wild roses for me, he asked the Creator for forgiveness for removing these beautiful creations from their source of life to express love to his daughter. Then he stared towards the heavens and whistled a joyful Irish melody. I sensed this would be my final venture hand-in-hand in the forest with a loving father I revered as my greatest mentor of spirituality.

During the final hours of my father's life, I embraced his frail body and squeezed his hand while he sang an Irish farewell love song to me. Although by then, he had lost the ability to speak clearly, somehow, miraculously in a song sung from his heart, he revealed to me that my sacred mission in life was to help awaken the inherent latent spirit within anyone the Creator had put into my life. Metaphorically speaking, I was to assist others to evolve from caterpillars into butterflies. I hope my inquiry about spirituality will assist me to follow such a divine mission.

Like my father, I believe that the only true religion is the religion of love and that a solely universal language comes from the heart. When working within the field of addictions, I acknowledged how successful the universal language of the 12 step Alcoholic Anonymous (AA) program was for helping clients to heal from their addictions. The AA program is based on spiritual principles connected with cultivating self love and love towards others. The twelve steps of AA are comparable to meditative and active spiritual exercises that assist recovering addicts to cultivate spirituality within themselves. When applying the twelve steps to treatment programs that I designed for my clients, I refrained from incorporating any Christian ideologies.

My Christian roots may have resulted in my inquiry being grounded within some Christian and post-Christian ideologies as understood in North America and Western Europe. However, my involvement in Buddhist meditation practices and Aboriginal powwows have broadened my horizons about how other non-Christian religious groups awaken, signify and cultivate spirituality. My sense of spiritual truth is continuously evolving when I acknowledge that the more I learn, the more I realize that I do not know. When I discover "a" fresh truth, this discernment does not indicate that I have found "the" truth. Nevertheless, some literature and data introduced within this inquiry may have been presented in an authoritative voice; during the inquiry process, I came to grips with the prevailing impact that spiritual exercises, such as prayer and meditation, have had on my restorative journey towards wellness and my challenging venture approaching dissertation completion. Six years after being told that I may only have six months to live, I appeared in front of an examining committee and successfully defended my dissertation.

Researcher's focus on ten participants' stories

As part of the inductive analysis of the data, the foregoing reflective step enabled me to acknowledge some of my own standpoints about spirituality (Rockford, 2003). I was aware throughout the process that I was grounded in a Christian belief system, with Aboriginal and Buddhist influences. However, if I held these influences totally in suspension, I would become incapacitated and unable to proceed with the inquiry. While focusing on the process of data collection, I questioned how participants had negotiated their own meanings of spirituality, and how certain notions came to be considered their truths. Thus, rather than placing findings in a pre-constructed puzzle, I observed a fresh outline evolving, during the examination of data from three different sources, which were e-mail interviews, web-page discussions and some telephone follow-ups. This evolving outline helped me to categorize the findings into a religious, temporal, and life-enhancing context, which characterizes a triangulated qualitative approach to framing data (Rockford, 2003). A triangulated approach to inquiry encourages the application of three lenses when examining responses to the research questions (Mathison, 1988). It also leads to a deeper understanding of the questions with less bias.

As suggested by Bogdan and Bilken (2003), the new outline emerged from the bottom up "rather than from the top down. . . . [This] process of data analysis is like a funnel: things are open at the beginning (or top) and more directed and specific at the bottom" (p. 6). In this study, I started my data analysis from a macro perspective based on my literature review, which is like the open top of a funnel. From the literature I learned that there are multiple perspectives on "spirituality," which is an inchoate term still in the developmental stages of being clearly defined. Then, from a newly constructed micro-outline of the study, I searched for meanings in the data related to the spiritual experiences ten participants had and how they interpreted these experiences.

Like observing the narrow opening at the bottom of a funnel, I then examined data from a micro-perspective. For example, I noted that when two public school educators had attempted to dialog about spirituality within their workplaces, they were silenced or re-oriented to another topic by their peers. From a micro-perspective, this acknowledgement indicates that some educators had learned to negotiate a non-spiritual discourse to express certain experiences they perceived as being spiritual; it does not suggest, from a macro-viewpoint, that all educators share this same experience.

Comparable to the centre of a funnel, new themes were emerging and key concepts formerly mentioned were being identified. Bogdan and Bilken (2003) claimed this approach to data analysis is an example of qualitative researchers being "concerned with . . . participant perspectives" (p. 7). In this study, I acknowledged my interests in spirituality by stating them earlier in this chapter. This step within the research process helped me to keep the inquiry focused on ten participants' perspectives of spirituality.

Qualitative researchers have a choice about whether to "hand-analyze" data or to use a computer (Creswell, 2002). According to Creswell,

> hand-analysis of qualitative data means that the researchers read the data, mark it by hand, and divide it into parts. . . . A computer-analysis of qualitative data means the researchers use a qualitative computer program to facilitate the process of storing, analyzing and making sense of the data. These computer programs provide a data organizing, managing, and searching tool. (p. 261)

To examine data in this study, both hand-analysis and computer-analysis, using Atlas.ti microcomputer software were applied.

As part of the inductive process, both approaches to data analysis assisted in: 1. the coding process, which comprises segmenting and labelling text to form descriptions that evolve into themes in the data; 2. setting up codes to describe a segment of text; 3. finding "text segments," which are sentences or paragraphs related to a single code; and 4. collapsing codes into threads, which are similar text segments aggregated together to form a major idea in the data base (Creswell, 2002). In this study, the codes were collapsed into "ordinary" threads, "unexpected" threads, "hard-to-classify" threads and "major" and "minor" threads, which all had a thematic context. After the threads became developed to points of clarity, examples of narrative descriptions and visual displays related to dominant threads in the data were selected and recorded.

Young (1999) suggested that the method selected for qualitative research, such as having a researcher-participant relationship is guided through the literature review. In this study, major text segments shaped the research design towards: applying a triangulated qualitative theoretical approach, selecting ten participants; using on-line interviews; and engaging in a participatory electronic discussion activity by a web-page. "Triangulation is the process of corroborating evidence from different individuals and different types of data or methods of data collection" (Creswell, 2002, p. 280). If the data collected from various means matched, then the researcher can feel more confident about the accuracy of the study findings (Gay & Airasian, 1992).

In this study, I examined ten different educators' perspectives on spiritual leadership, which were communicated by an on-line interview, web-page discussion, and follow-up telephone conversations. Exploring data from on-line interviews, web-page discussions and telephone conversations enabled me to apply three different approaches to data collection, which supports a triangulated theoretical approach. Applying a triangulated qualitative approach to data collection reflects an epistemological paradigm shift in educational research methods that encouraged researchers to apply one approach to data collection.

Epistemological Paradigm Shifts Noted in Research Methods

New ways of viewing cultural assumptions about the world has led to an epistemological paradigm shift in educational research methods. Consequently, there are tensions about what theoretical approaches to select for research about leadership in education (Toulmin, 1997). Those researchers who endorse Platonism believe strongly in a scientific model, which assumes the only authentic knowledge is "universal, general and timeless" (Toulmin, 1996, p. 206). However, Aristotelean traditionalists believe that various kinds of inquiry seek out different kinds of knowledge with a variety of methods that suit the subject matter, as Aristotle treated "the multiplicity of intellectual disciplines in a democratic ... way" (p. 207). Thus, action research could be considered an intellectual descendent from the Aristotelean method of inquiry that aims to affect educators' beliefs and actions.

Action inquiry research approach

As a process consisting mainly of "sequences of interactions" (Ellis & Bochner, 2000, p.743), action research can challenge the hegemony of an established knowledge and power system (Salas & Tillmann, 1998) and focus on introducing new strategies for educational leadership (Gay & Airasian, 1992). Such strategies may encourage leaders to share personal narratives about spiritual experiences with one's peers.

An action inquiry approach to research focuses more on discovering the practical effects of a study than developing new theoretical rigor (Gay & Airasian, 1992). "Its purpose is to improve school practices and at the same time to improve those who try to improve the practices: to combine the research processes, habits of thinking, ability to work harmoniously with others and professional spirit" (Best & Kahn, 2003, p. 20). In action research, as applied to leadership studies, the knowledge generated has been referred to as "practical wisdom" (Toulmin, 1997).

Exchanging personal narratives is one means of connecting action research and connecting participants with the researcher (Connelly & Clandinin, 1990). Sharing stories is also a primary step in breaking down stereotypes and connecting theory with humanity. As noted by Vanier (1998),

> stories seem to awaken new energies of love; they tell us great truths in simple, personal terms and make us long for light. ... When we tell stories, we touch hearts. If we talk about theories or speak about ideas, the mind may assimilate them but the heart remains untouched. (p. 90)

To awaken hearts and increase understanding, Jesus told parables, Hasidic Jews and Sufi teachers told tales and Hindus introduced stories.

"Storytelling can provide an opportunity for one to imaginatively engage in dissonant situations thereby increasing one's capacity to see the world through more than one window" (Shakotko & Walker, 1999, p. 207). In this study, I attempted to understand participants' truths from multiple theoretical standpoints, which is an approach commonly used in action research. Schratz and Walker (1998) point out that action research encourages reflection about life experience and story-telling, which are keys to learning. "Being able to speak to ourselves and others about what we experience provides a means of editing and rewriting scripts of everyday life, which enables the building of a mental reference system . . . and allows us to build the narratives that give meaning and interest to our lives" (p. 197). Sharing stories is an important means of constructing knowledge and creating teachable moments (Mishler, 1986).

Action research enables participants and researchers to engage in a storytelling process that generates new insights and new knowledge, and creates opportunities for participants to improve their own lives and the lives of their students (Mishler, 1986). For example, in this study participants were encouraged to question what assumptions they took for granted about educational leadership and the effects of them muting discourses about spirituality within the school environment. Pyrch (1998a) views action research as a form of co-operative inquiry with a commitment and ability to collapse the division between objectivity and subjectivity.

Reason (1998) suggested action research "can be seen as a spiritual imperative" (p. 149) that objects to the Western world-view, as "based on a fundamental epistemological error that humans are separate from each other and the natural world" (p. 157). This form of co-operative inquiry is a means to obtain more accurate and more ethical data, because the research is based on people's experiences and "engaged with people rather than doing research on people" (p. 149). Therefore, participants were not treated like subjects. Action research is a way of interacting with other individuals who share common concerns and interests; the goal is to make more sense of life, construct new and creative ways of viewing life and "above all to heal the alienation, the split that characterizes modern experience" (Reason, 1998, p. 162). Action research is a holistic approach to inquiry.

Although the researcher is actively engaged with the study participants, each person's approach is individualistic (Marshall, 2001). Applying Mill's (2003) approach to inquiry as a guide, the process in this study consisted of the following four steps: 1. identifying spirituality in leadership as the focus; 2. collecting data; 3. analysing and interpreting the data by identifying themes; and 4. developing an action plan. Action research studies provide educators with data that can be used formatively to affect positively an educator's professional disposition. The action plan that was developed in this study was a schemata suggesting ways educators could cultivate spirit within leadership in their workplaces.

As a constructive mode of action research, appreciative inquiry illuminates factors that serve to nourish the human spirit and furnish new alternatives for social action (Ludema, Cooperrider & Barrett, 2001); asking positive questions during this inquiry about spirituality could have ignited transformative dialog and action within human systems, as suggested by Ludema, Cooperrider and Barrett. For example, study participants may have been motivated to dialog about and practise spiritual leadership within their workplaces while being actively engaged in cooperative relationships during the data-collection process.

Action inquiry as an ideal for studying spirituality

Rather than select an activity related to spirituality that is measurable or interpretable by a researcher, a person may choose to walk or sing as an expression of their spirituality (Mathews & Clark, 1998). Because only the walker or singer truly knows their intent, an outsider could not be certain whether or not this activity could be viewed as spiritual or non-spiritual. Taking this perspective into consideration, if a researcher attempted to analyse or dissect another's perceptions of spirituality through a quantitative approach, misunderstandings could occur (Ulich,1945). "Spirit may erupt at any moment and from any genuine act of creativity" (Fox, 1995, p. 123). Furthermore, telling a divine story that one has been "graced to breathe" (p. 121) could be an epiphany resulting in a true sense of connection with the divine. As stated by O'Murchu (1997), "meaning is embedded in story, not in facts" (p. 199). The challenge of attempting to measure or to explain an epiphany may have discouraged many researchers from studying spirituality. Matthews and Clark (1998) state,

> researchers have measured subjects' religious involvement or religiosity, rather than spirituality in almost all the faith-factor studies. . . . For example, from a researcher's point of view, looking at the frequency of church attendance among patients is a simple, valid, and easily measurable variable that can be used to compare patients' religiosity. There is no such variable to define or identify people who are spiritual but not religious. (p. 185)

Therefore, research approaches such as inquiry action research help deepen an understanding of the spiritual aspect of human existence. Reason & Bradbury (2001) claim action research "places human persons and communities as part of their world-both human and more-than-human" (p. 7). On the other hand, Loder (1998) states that "human spirit is the uninvited guest in every study. . . . It is relational, transformational, self transcending; it is the dynamism that drives human development forward" (p. xiii). As a result, asking researchers to bracket their beliefs and knowledge, could be like requesting them to ignore their spirit if the process involves personal reflection (Loder, 1998).

While encouraging further dialog amongst participants and attempting to bring a sense of spirit into the process of triangulation, I tried bracketing my own beliefs about spirituality. However, as noted by Loder, trying to bracket beliefs is comparable to attempting to ignore a part of my essence, my own spirituality. At times, I felt spiritless when trying to be objective during the analysis process. Thus, I refrained from efforts to bracket my own beliefs and alternatively acknowledged and applied them to the analysis. Qualitative research encourages a subjective approach to research which suggests taking the researchers beliefs into consideration during analysis. When in the commencing stages of analysing the data, I dialoged with participants by e-mail and telephone in attempts to confirm or challenge my interpretations of the data.

Feminist research approach

Like action research, which engages participants in cooperative relationships, feminist research supports a triangulated perspective of research. Through the use of interviews, feminist researchers such as Smith (1979) recognized the value of examining the world from one's standpoint, in one's everyday life. Feminist researchers were known to challenge the traditional objective/subjective split in some research methods and move "the field of qualitative research toward greater concern with the relationships between researchers and their subjects" (Bogdan & Bilken, 2003, p. 19). They believed a focus on subjectivity defies prevalent sociological methods, which may have oppressed women in their research methods (Maynard, 1990). They also reject the assumption that theory is superior to experience, and that researchers should be separated from participants for the sake of objectivity (Lazar, 1998). According to Smith (1990), "the only way of knowing a socially constructed world is to know it from within" (p. 22). Similarly, Maynard (1990) discussed applying "the story-telling approach" (p. 275) as a research method that enables individuals to present accounts of their own lives, "in their own terms and in their own chronology" (p. 275).

The work of many action researchers has been inspired by feminist theories, epistemologies, and methodologies (Maguire, 2001). "The power of the feminist lens is its ability to focus on the gaps and blank spaces of male-dominant culture, knowledge, and behaviour" (Gosetti & Rusch, 1995, p. 14). By applying a feminist lens, one can see how gender characteristics associated with leadership have been constructed from the assumptions and beliefs of the dominant male culture. Feminists' concerns about traditional research methods led to the adoption of the "participatory model," which aims "to produce non-hierarchal, non-manipulative research relationships" (p. 34). The interviewer establishes a comfortable interview environment and connects with the interviewees, by giving them voice.

Before Smith (1979) proposed conducting research from a feminist standpoint, Schutz (1970a) argued from a phenomenological perspective that one's experience of the everyday world includes both a natural and a cultural view according to an individual's perspective at the time. Feminism is not merely a "perspective (way of seeing) or an epistemology (way of knowing)" (Stanley, 1990, p. 14); like phenomenology, "it is also an ontology, or way of being in the world" (p. 14). Since qualitative research methods, such as participatory action, enable participants to have some say in the process, they can more completely articulate their life experiences. Thus, participants can construct versions of themselves within a triangulated relationship "represented by the interviewer, interviewee, and audience" (Gosetti & Rusch, 1995, p. 45).

Spirituality is the phenomenon being studied in this phenomenological inquiry. The purpose of phenomenological research is to "describe one or more individuals' experiences of a phenomenon [through a] data-collection method of in-depth interviews with up to 10 people" (Johnson & Christensen, 2000, p. 314). During the interview process, an individual's inner world or consciousness and world of immediate experiences, referred to as their "life-world" are explored. "From a philosophical perspective . . . wonder is the central methodological feature of phenomenological inquiry" (van Manen, 2002, p. 5). In addition to commencing in wonder, phenomenological methodology must induce wonder. "Wonder is that moment of being when one is overcome by awe or perplexity – such as when something familiar has turned profoundly unfamiliar . . . when our gaze has been drawn by the gaze of something that stares back at us" (p. 5). This wonder could happen as a result of having a peak spiritual experience.

Phenomenologists assume that some commonality in human experience exists, and by interviewing participants, they aim to understand characteristic viewpoints. Called an "essence," this commonality of experience is "often more abstract than literal descriptions of particular experiences" (Johnson & Christensen, 2000, p. 317). For example, while analysing data, I noted elements of caring, compassion and wonder expressed in stories shared by participants. As noted by van Manen (2002), during interviews "words may infect the reader with a sudden realization of the unsuspected enigmatic nature of ordinary reality" (p. 4). Thus, dialoguing about spirituality on the web-page may have infused participants with a sense of spirit.

A phenomenological approach to data analysis involved listing significant statements, determining their meanings and identifying the essence of the phenomenon being studied. I made note of my standpoints about spirituality and leadership before engaging in data analysis, and acknowledged them during the analytical process. Before commencing my data analysis, I implied my standpoint about spirituality by examining some personal experiences connected with spirituality.

In phenomenological research, the interview is used to explore and gather experiential accounts that could help develop a broader understanding of human phenomena, such as leadership (van Manen, 1990). Additionally, the interview is used as a method of developing a conversational relationship with the interviewee about the meaning of an experience. "Researchers in the phenomenological mode attempt to understand the meaning of events and interactions to ordinary people in particular situations" (Bogdan & Bilken, 2003, p. 23).

In this study, a phenomenological method provided snapshots of the ways individuals in the study perceived leadership and spirituality and how they acted on it. Phenomenological research provides explanatory associations between the micro activity and broader cultural, political and economic processes (Foley, 1999). Ballou (1995) stated that,

> phenomenology and non-rational modes offer promising access to knowledge of spirituality. . . . Its strength is the placing of reality in experience and the mode of knowing in the perception of experience. Basing knowledge claims on actual lived experience is an effective way of generating knowledge because it requires careful attention to the actual experience rather than connections between parallel methodologies imposing structure on that experience. (p. 12)

Ballou's (1995) viewpoint that sharing lived experiences offers "access to knowledge of spirituality" supports Hawley's (1995) position on gaining more insight about spirituality.

Hawley (1995) suggested that when individuals attempt to express their spirituality with words, "descriptions hang around in their minds, not quite making it to their hearts" (1995, p. vii). Experiencing spirit is the only way an individual can understand it, which affirms its subjectivity. "Relating metaphorical incidents (stories) is a more . . . experiential way of conveying spirit. From stories, we each get what we need at the moment" (p. vii). A phenomenological approach to research gives participants the opportunity to share stories and involves examining delineations through different lenses (Psathas, 1973). Phenomenology seeks "not to explain the world, but to describe as closely as possible the way the world makes itself evident to awareness, . . . to give voice to its enigmatic and very-shifting patterns" (Abram,

1996, p. 35). Therefore, because a person's perceptions about leadership and spirituality are understood according to which lens is applied, utilizing different perspectives to the examination of participants' experiences was important (Gosetti & Rusch, 1995).

In a phenomenological inquiry, a study of the phenomenon of understanding stems from a coevolving relationship with the researcher and the data obtained from interviews with participants. During the process of analysis, I attempted to explore the data from an indexical and reflexive perspective; therefore the meaning of participants' articulation of the phenomenon being studied leaned on the context of spirituality that they suggested; and the context of their articulation about the phenomenon being studied depended on the meaning they attributed to spirituality. "Phenomenologists believe that multiple ways of interpreting experiences are available to each of us through interacting with others, and that it is the meaning of our experiences that constitutes reality" (Bogdan & Bilken, 2003, p. 23). One person's reality, however, may not reflect the way another person interprets truth. As the researcher, I attempted to communicate the truths of ten participants' spiritual experiences. While spirituality is inherently personal in nature, it is also constructed with attention to social referents. Therefore, people's efforts to understand spirituality are valuable, despite the shortcomings in their efforts to understand the phenomenon.

Schutz (1973) suggested conventional research methods have limitations when studying a social concept from an individual's perspective. Some traditional approaches support the natural science paradigm that the social world comprises an objective world separate from the interpretive actions of individuals. However, phenomenologists argue that the objective reality of society, organizations, and communities is subjectively experienced by men and women (Schutz, 1973). Therefore, these researchers pay close attention to how a person perceives his or her reality (Freeman, 1980).

Since phenomenological methodology involves exploring phenomena as they are understood in their immediacy by the study participant (Wallace & Wolf, 1995), this methodology should be considered when studying qualitative aspects of leadership. Because this study was conducted on-line, participants were free to share their spiritual experiences during their own preferred times, rather than having a scheduled interview. Therefore, the immediacy of their experiences may have been communicated on-line, in response to the questions or in a discussion on the web-page. Such an immediacy of experience would be difficult to measure quantitatively.

Triangulated Paradigms Applied to Research Methodology

The theoretical framework for this study is a combination of phenomenological, feminist, and action research paradigms, and is applied to give voice to participants and to the researcher. Thus, as stated earlier, this inquiry design is an application of a triangulated research approach, which encourages the application of three lenses when examining responses to a research question (Mathison, 1988). However, this triangulated approach to research did not result in an equilateral triangle. The phenomenological and feminist tools for data collection using an interview proved more effective than an action inquiry approach on-line.

Phenomenological inquiry assisted in the discernment of "representational knowledge," which is gained from study participants "re-describing or re-presenting the object of knowing, as this re-presents itself over and over again for interpretation" (Park, 2001, p. 83). In this study, the object of knowing is described by participants as "spirituality." Park (2001) suggested that feminist inquiry supported ascertaining "relational knowledge" which has potential for bringing people together in empathy and "making it possible for them to know one another as human beings [and to] strengthen community" (p. 83). When participating in the web-page discussions, study participants connected with one another as an on-line small community' and later they requested an opportunity to meet one another for coffee. In association with relational knowledge, Park noted that "as feminist scholars have taught us, we make these connections not just with our heads but with our hearts as well" (p. 85).

Lastly, action inquiry helped me to explore "reflective knowledge" that is oriented to action. "This kind of knowledge requires the mobilization of rationality that includes knowledge of moral values relevant in everyday living" (Park, 2001, p. 86). During the research process, I worked towards examining unexamined truths about religion, spirituality and morals and I conducted my own critical analysis accordingly. This introduced fresh ways for me to understand and articulate spirituality and its relationship to morals. Also, from the data, I developed two schemata that suggested ways to cultivate spirituality within self, and to cultivate spirit within leadership practices within the workplace.

As noted in preceding heart graphs, the heart is an organizing framework for showing triangulated relationships. Heart graph no. 3 is a conception of the application of three research theories to this study which constitutes a triangulated approach to data collection and analysis. The theoretical framework could be associated with the knowledge domains introduced in heart no. 2. The flow lines show that although all three theories were applied throughout the research process, feminist and phenomenological approaches to inquiry (interviews) were applied to the major stages of data collection. Action research involved a web-page discussion, which provided less data than the interviews.

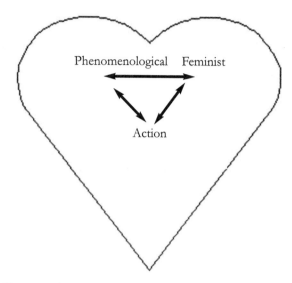

Heart graph no. 3: Triangulated theoretical framework

Using more than one lens is a strategy that reduces bias (Mathison, 1988). Furthermore, applying three theoretical paradigms, which all suggest using interviews for data collection, overcomes some weaknesses of utilizing only one theoretical argument. Similar to Mathison's stand on applying three lenses to the examination of a research question, Young (1999) proposed applying a procedure, called "multi-focal research" that uses more than one theoretical frame. "The process involves viewing from one lens and reconsidering the phenomena from another; using more than one frame will increase the trustworthiness of the findings" (p. 679). Using Chamber's term "eclectic pluralism," Pyrch (1998b) also discussed the application of more than one lens and points out that different action research approaches can constitute a "family." This research approach encourages a kinship enabling researchers and participants to share "from the heart as well as the head" (p. 653). Action research gives researchers the chance to walk their talk, be spiritual, create community, "love, feel close to people, and to participate within the safety of a system" (p. 660) while discussing aspects of educational leadership. This theoretical framework was applied in this study about educational leadership.

Participants Selected

The key concepts and triangulated methodology that evolved from the literature review influenced a decision to select ten public school educational administrators (Young, 1999). A gender balance was important in the group of participants so that male and female perspectives were represented equitably. Five women and five men who had worked or were working in leadership positions in the field of public education and who had openly articulated a spiritual approach to leadership comprised the selected grop group of participants. Participants were selected on the basis of their experience of the phenomenon being studied (Anderson, 1993). Thus, they were credible and considered to have authority in the area under investigation.

All Alberta participants had attended University of Calgary Faculty of Education graduate seminars that addressed spirituality within leadership. When I was a guest lecturer in these seminars and mentioned my research, they offered to participate. I did not know these participants prior to meeting them in the seminars. Ontario participants had voiced an interest about spirituality within leadership after they heard about my inquiry and later they volunteered to participate in the research. I was familiar with some of these participants' work within the field of education but she did not know them personally.

To ensure that I more fully understood the latitude of the participants' experiences, the group of participants was kept small, as advised by Omery (1983) and Johnson and Christensen (2000). Having ten individuals participate was sufficient to create a healthy dialog within the group. "Purposive" selecting of a group (Wilson, 1985) was applied to the participant selection process for this study. "In purposive sampling, the researcher selects a particular group or groups based on certain criteria" (p. 219) and uses their own judgment to decide who would be ideal participants. As Morris (1997) suggested, an available group of participants who met the criteria and were willing to participate in the study were sought and interviewed separately.

I invited a "convenient" group of leaders, who were working or had worked in the field of public education in Alberta or Ontario who ranged in age from 35 to 65, and who were interested in spirituality within educational leadership. This age range helped to reflect the paradigm shifts that have taken place in leadership practices over the past three decades, and added richness to the data. In accordance with the University of Calgary ethical policies, participants were informed by e-mail that they had the right to withdraw from the study at any time, but were advised that whatever they had contributed prior to their withdrawal would be considered data. The ethics review committee accepted the research proposal that stated consent would be communicated by e-mail.

Data Collection Process For This Inquiry

Applying a triangulated approach to the study enabled the research project to be grounded in the contextual reality of the modern computer technology of the schools, within which the educational administrators in the study are working or have worked. Additionally, the design acknowledged "multiple realities" (Goddard & Foster, 1999) represented by the individual unique experiences of each participant. Being able to connect with participants and encourage their connection with one another in shared experiences may have been what Wadsworth (2001) was suggesting as a way of "breathing life into each other" (p. 426) and what van Manen (2002) indicated was a means of stirring up wonder among participants.

After acknowledging my standpoint about spirituality, as advised by Smith (1992), I introduced the questions, initiated on-line dialog, and became a connector in the feedback network. During the web-page discussions, I assumed an active role of facilitating dialog amongst participants, which according to Ludema, Cooperrider and Barrett (2001) permits an inquiry that could nurture their spirits. They claimed this process "can unleash a positive revolution of conversation and change in organizations . . . creating new voices and new discoveries and expanding circles of dialog to provide a community of support for innovative action" (p. 189). Similarly, Loder (1998) stated that in such a position, a researcher "must in itself be spirit" (p. xiii). Throughout this research process, the researcher I aimed to reflect spiritual values by treating participants with dignity and respect while I was a "facilitator of inquiry," assisting them to arrive at their own "truths" as related to the study (Wadsworth, 2001, p. 420).

The task of facilitating involved a "collective undertaking" shaped by the participants' feedback (Wadsworth, 2001). Thus, to keep the process going, the researcher "kept watch" to ensure interaction was taking place. This process involved "clarifying, offering, watching for the response and being guided by it" (p. 421). As an "energy worker," the facilitator of an inquiry works with the energies of the participants by responding and driving the inquiry forward to prevent participants' loss of purpose and direction.

In reference to Cowan's (1998) list-server e-mail discussion group, Wadsworth (2001) stated that a facilitator's role is "sending out probes which reflect back the person's current position and possible direction" (p. 426). Heron and Reason (2001) explained "the primary procedure is to use inquiry cycles, moving several times between reflection and action" (p. 179). Marshall (2001) referred to this process as paying attention "to the inner arcs, seeking to notice myself perceiving, making meaning, framing issues . . . assumptions, repetitions, patterns, themes, dilemmas, key phrases which are charged with energy" (p. 433). This multi-dimensional framing enabled me to connect data that reflected intellectual, practical, intuitive, sensory and "imaginal knowings (p. 433)." The data was collected through dialog with the study participants.

With the intent of creating dialog amongst participants, data collected for this study was mainly conducted by electronic mail. As noted by Anderson and Kanuka (2003), to date the internet is commonly being used as a tool for data collection, analysis and dissemination of the findings. "Currently, the internet has replaced all other research networks . . .with . . . 10-20 million people using it just for E-mail" (Dillenbourg & Schneider, 1995, p. 1). Robertson and Webber (2000) note the list-server's usefulness as a leadership development tool.

After studying the cross-cultural and cross-role dialog that occurred within web-page discussions, such as the Change Agency, Robertson and Webber (2000) noted the capacity of email to exceed boundaries commonly imposed by cultures and institutions (Robertson & Webber, 2000).The list-serve "provided participants with an asynchronous forum for discussion where responses could be made at times that suited the respondent" (p. 319). Goddard and Foster (1999) point out that with e-mail, participants have the chance to think over their responses and edit them. Also they can retain a copy of their responses for verification. To conduct interviews by e-mail, Goddard and Foster suggest forwarding two questions at a time.

After the responses are received, the next pair of questions can be forwarded (Goddard & Foster, 1999). This step restricts the amount of knowledge the participants have with respect to additional questions (Goddard & Foster, 1999), which reflects a phenomenological hermeneutic interview approach that encourages participants to make sense of their own experiences (van Manen, 1990). A phenomenological interview approach to interviewing participants was ideal for this study. "Much of the research in . . . education focuses on processes that cannot be seen and measured with external and quantifiable tools" (Anderson & Kanuka, 2003), such as the mental processes of learning and spiritual experiences. The internet appears to be efficient and effective at collecting non-quantifiable data by on-line interviews and is capable of "reaching population samples that might otherwise be inaccessible" (Anderson & Kanuka, 2003, p. 28). In addition to providing a platform for anonymity, it can overcome cultural, disability and language barriers. However, collecting data on-line could also cause communication breakdowns.

Methods of Data Collection

The literature review for this study resulted in these key concepts that were expanded further during the data collection phase of this study: 1. muting discourses about spirituality within educational systems; 2. examining moral issues within educational values; and 3. shifting paradigms affecting educational leadership. At the outset, an on-line triangulated research design was shaped, framed and conceptualised, which was "compass work" guided by these key concepts (Bunning, 2000).

As explained in previous heart graphs, the heart image is an organizing framework demonstrating triangulation. Heart graph no. 4 is a conceptualisation of a triangulation of the three key concepts derived from the literature: muted discourses about spirituality within educational systems, moral issues within educational values, and shifted paradigms within educational leadership. The flow lines show the inter-relationship between the three key concepts. Moral issues and muted discourses about spirituality have a synergistic relationship which is influenced by shifted paradigms within educational leadership.

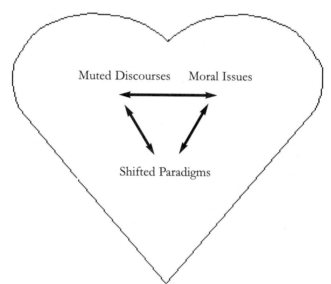

Heart graph no. 4: Triangulated key concepts derived from literature

Rationale for the selection of questions for participants

The literature indicates an inter-connective relationship between the key concepts, in relationship to spiritual leadership is evident. Among his four classifications, Wilber (1996) introduced an interior and exterior collective context that promote the development of spirituality. In different cultures, spiritual leaders have taught about awakening "divine states of mind" (Vanier, 1998, p.127) that shape a person's moral conduct; consequences of muting discourses about spirituality can be spiritual amnesia and moral confusion (Griffin, 1998; Myss, 2002). Ryan (1999) associated the degeneration of spirituality culturally with individual moral scepticism, and he connected moral erosion with a separation of spirituality from educational values.

Connected with the key concept "examining moral issues within educational values," Wheatcroft (2003) and Hunter (2000) suggested spiritual development results in moral conduct and moral conduct leads to further spiritual development. Education becomes nearly incomprehensible when disconnected from its fundamental moral purpose. "The literature on educational administration increasingly is giving attention to the importance of spiritual or ethical/moral dimensions" (Thom, 1993, p. 109). The key concept "shifted paradigms within educational systems" identified in the literature review suggests that some educators increasingly acknowledge inter-relationships between spirituality and moral values and they question whether or not spirituality is morally laden (Vaill, 1995; Walker, 2002). As noted earlier, many educators recognize their innate need to reconnect to their mind to heart and spirit, and become more socially active in mentoring moral values (Simington, 2003). As part of a global paradigm shift, they are moving away from heart and mind dualisms within their leadership practices.

The key concepts guided the development of the two core questions and four sub-questions. Additionally, appreciative inquiry was applied to the context of the questions. As one approach to action inquiry, "appreciative inquiry asks two basic unconditional positive questions (Ludema, Cooperrider and Barrett, 2001, p. 193). To guide the development of my research questions, I reviewed the "Appreciative Interview Protocol" (p. 193) questions applied to Ludema, Cooperrider and Barrett's action research inquiry. Their research questions, such as " 2. what do you value most about yourself, your work and your organization?" [and] "4. what are the unique aspects of your culture that most positively affect the spirit, vitality and effectiveness or your organization and its work?" appear to be leading. However, appreciative inquiry questions "set the stage for what we later find and discover. The concept of the unconditional positive question assumes that whatever topic we choose to study, we can study it unconditionally, and in so doing, significantly influence the destiny of our organizations" (p. 189).

As suggested by Ludema, Cooperrider and Barrett (2001), I used leading sub-questions with the aim of focusing attention towards affirming matters within the participants' personal and professional lives:

1. having peak experiences
2. acknowledging spiritual values and moral beliefs that influence effective leadership practices
3. recognizing changes that have added spirit and enthusiasm to their leadership and

4. noting effective leadership practices worth recommending to other leaders.

Within my working definition of spirituality, I state that the terms "enthusiasm" "excitement" and "spirit" are interconnected with the term "spirituality;" this enabled me to apply these terms within the second set of questions. As noted earlier, the literature review demonstrates there is a synergistic relationship between moral beliefs and spiritual values. Paradigm shifts toward practising spiritual leadership within educational systems are "a form of moral action" (Thom, 1993, p. 102) that encourage administrators to be "leaders with a conscience, without apologizing (p. 110). In connection with the key concept "muting discourses about spirituality within educational systems," some leaders practising spiritual leadership are being given opportunities to move beyond muted discourses about spirituality within educational systems (Thom, 1993).

Prior to data collection, I used an action research appreciative inquiry approach to developing my research questions. Drawing from the first key concept, 1. muting discourses about spirituality within educational systems and the second key concept, 2. examining moral issues within educational values, I developed and forwarded the first core question and two sub-research questions to participants:

First core question

How are the spiritual experiences of educational leaders understood and articulated by educators?

Sub-question related to first core question and first key concept

1. Think of a time when you felt the most excited, most engaged and most alive. What was it about this peak experience that you would define as being spiritual?

Sub-question related to the first core question and second key concept

2. What are some of the spiritual values and moral beliefs that influence the effectiveness of your leadership practices?

To answer the above research questions, data were collected on-line by giving participants questions by e-mail. The feminist and phenomenological approach to the interview involved an interpersonal interaction in which participants were encouraged, by the questions, to share details of their experiences with the researcher, as suggested by Valle and Halling (1989). During an on-line interview with the researcher, participants were asked to reflect upon a specific instance, situation, person or event and then to explore the experience. This on-line interview served as a means to establish a relationship with each participant about what the experiences meant them. Throughout the process, the interview was guided by appreciative questions guided by key concepts located within the literature.

For each question, participants were requested to give a one-page (250 word) response within a month. After participants had answered the first set of questions, I pasted their responses on a web-page and encouraged them to anonymously engage in an on-line discussion for two weeks. To keep the research process active and check out how participants were handling their commitment to the study, I contacted all participants by telephone. After a month, the process for administering and answering the first set of questions was repeated for the second set of sub-questions associated with the third key concept "shifting paradigms affecting educational leadership," and the second core question. Also, the discussion page was also left open for further discussions.

Related to the third key concept, 3. shifting paradigms affecting educational leadership, I developed and forwarded the second core question and sub-research questions three and four to participants:

Second Core question

In what way would this articulation best contribute to the development of effective leadership?

Two sub-questions related to the second core question and third key concept

3. What are some changes in leadership practices that have added enthusiasm and spirit to your leadership?

4. What effective leadership practices would you recommend to other educational leaders?

The second core question was not forwarded to participants. Responses to this question were extracted by me as a secondary level of analysis wherever this question was answered within follow-up web-page discussions and by the responses to the sub-questions. As with the first set of questions, participants were interviewed on-line by the researcher before answers to their questions three and four were posted on the web-page for fellow participants to review and respond. When three weeks had passed, I contacted all participants as a follow-up. Participants were given the opportunity to answer questions on-line within the next week, or by a telephone interview with the researcher.

During the delay, two participants had gone on holidays for two weeks and two were ill. Therefore, I allowed two more weeks to respond to the research questions. All ten participants responded within that time frame. One week after the questions had been answered and posted on the web page, I noted that only four participants were active in the web-page discussion. Therefore,

I contacted all ten participants by telephone to either thank them for participating in the web-page discussion or to question them about their inactivity in the discussion. I was informed that the inactive participants were facing leadership challenges and paper-work demands at work. After keeping the web-page open for one month, I informed all participants that the data collection had been completed and the web-page would be closed. I thanked them for their rich contributions to the study.

Summary of how data were collected and stored

Data were collected during a six month period from on-line e-mail interviews, along with web-page and telephone discussions with participants. Because the research involved human subjects, I obtained ethics clearance before commencing my study. After ten participants were recruited, and had signed a consent form, the on-line interviews were initiated by direct e-mail with the researcher. Although e-mail interviews and web-page discussions were the two main sources of data collection, the research design process evolved to include some telephone communication, where I took on the role of facilitator, as suggested by Wadsworth (2001). Being a facilitator involved keeping the dialog going among the participants and with the researcher. Therefore, I conformed to the needs of the participants, which included discussing the questions by telephone.

Because the questions were given just prior to the Christmas season, there was a delay in receiving responses. Furthermore, a virus was discovered on a disc containing data from the individual e-mails. Therefore, I contacted all the participants by telephone, to keep the research process active and investigate the accuracy of the answers to the first questions, posted on the disc. Although the first core question was presented to the participants to help explain the study, participants chose to answer this question in addition to the sub-question one and two. However, the second core question was extracted by me for a secondary means of analysis.

I checked the web page daily to see who was and was not participating. If an absence of involvement from a certain participant was evident, I contacted them by telephone, along with the active participants, to keep the process going. Participants gave me permission to post their comments, which were made during a telephone conversations. Also, one participant chose to respond to the others' answers by privately e-mailing her comments to me. However, this participant gave me permission to post a summary of her comments on the web-page.

Because the foregoing circumstances delayed the research process, I informed participants about the delay, and encouraged them to participate on the discussion page. As suggested earlier by Wadsworth (2001), the researcher continued to drive the research process and send out probes, despite barriers. During the delay, I summarized responses to the first sub questions and e-mailed the summary to participants, before posting it on the web-page. At this time, I questioned whether or not participants were reacting negatively to my study or if they were encountering challenging issues at work that were a priority. When speaking to participants by telephone, I was informed that they were appreciating participating in the study because answering the research questions had encouraged them to take time out for reflecting upon positive occurrences happening within their workplaces. Two participants, however, stated they would have preferred addressing the topic of spirituality while being face-to-face with the researcher. If I were to repeat the research, I would include face-to-face interviews.

After all answers to the third and fourth sub-questions had been received, I posted participants' responses on the web-page. Then, I e-mailed each participant, encouraging them to participate in the web-page discussion. When communicating with participants by e-mail, I suggested that they e-mail an example of their favorite expression of spirituality, such as a photo, song, poem or affirmation. Within a month, I received these expressions from all participants. As another encouragement to keep the discussion active, I e-mailed a summary of the responses to sub-questions three and four. The discussion page was left open for a month, but was inactive after two weeks.

After all data were collected, the e-mail interviews, web-page discussions, and notes from telephone conversations were filed with pseudonyms on disc and transferred to an Atlas.ti computer program, which was used for part of the data-analysis. This stage of research involves examining the systems, rationale and interrelationships within the data base (Giorgi, 1975;Valle & Halling, 1989). After storing the files for five years, data will be destroyed to support the University of Calgary confidentiality requirements.

Data-analysis tools used

Reinforcement of research findings can consist of a triangulation process, where the researcher compares different kinds of data from alternative sources to see whether they support one another (Seale, 1998). As Seale explains, "data relating to the same phenomenon are compared but derived from different phases of fieldwork, different points in time, accounts of different participants, or using different methods of data collection" (p. 231). In this study, as suggested by Stringer (1993), data analysis involved the use of two core questions, the key questions that commenced the research inquiry. While applying these questions, I compared the key concepts found in the literature, with data obtained from on-line interviews and, web-page discussions and telephone follow-ups.

Applying "multiple lines of sight" (Berg, 2001, p. 4), which were the three lenses derived from 1. the literature review, 2. on-line interviews and 3. web-page discussions, to the examination of the data assisted me in the analysis; these three lenses provided perspectives other than mine, which made the data more credible when reinforcing the findings. As stated by Berg (2001), "by obtaining several lines of sight, researchers obtain a better, more substantive picture of reality" (p. 4) and a more complete means of verification. Comparable to the generic definition of the application of a heart as an organizing framework, noted in previous graphs, heart graph no. 5 is a triangulated heart shaped image that conceptualises three "lines of sight" applied to the study: the literature review, on-line interviews and a web-page discussion.

The flow lines show that the literature review and on-line interviews were the stronger tools applied to the inquiry and that each approach to inquiry was conducted separately.

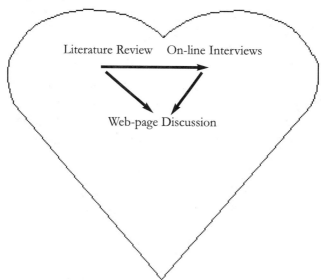

Heart graph no. 5: Triangulated "lines of sight" applied to data analysis

The commencing line of sight for this study, a literature review, demonstrated how others had perceived and researched the topic of interest. After formulating two core questions, along with four sub-questions from the literature, applying a phenomenological and feminist interpretation to the on-line data enabled me to broaden, strengthen and refine some concepts and themes found during the first step of the research. van Manen (1990) states that in phenomenological research, the interview assists researchers in grasping how they come to interpret their own and other's experiences as meaningful through the conceptual tools "indexicality" (meaning depends on context) and "reflexivity" (context is constitutive of the meaning of an action).

Seale (1998) suggested that in feminist inquiry, which is mainly dialectical and action driven, the interview serves as a means to establish an interactive relationship with participants about the meaning of their experiences. In phenomenological or feminist inquiry, the researcher is expected to be sensitive to what participants are attempting to communicate (Seale, 1998; van Manen, 1990). However, because this study did not give me the benefit of seeing participants' faces, hearing their actual tone or voice on-line, or seeing the environment for which they communicated, the interpretive process of the on-line data was challenging. Therefore, telephone follow-ups were beneficial additional interactive approaches to data collection, as part of action research inquiry.

Telephone interactions with participants evolved as a reaction to circumstances; this approach to data collection was not part of the original method proposed for the study. However, in common with feminist, phenomenological and action research inquiries, the metaphor of "giving voice" to participants was an objective that was met by telephone conversations, in addition to on-line communication. The application of an electronic tool for data collection and analysis in this study will be discussed further in subsequent chapters.

Considered as another triangulated line of sight, action research inquiry enabled participants to dialog with one another, through a web-page, and gave participants an opportunity to personalize their narratives while communicating (Mills, 2003). During collaborative inquiry, the researcher and participants engaged in a systemic inquiry as a cyberspace learning community (Mills, 2003). In this study, having access to a web-based action research resource provided participants and I with an extended sense of community, available from their homes, schools or office computers. As stated by Mills (2003), "regardless of the degree to which you participate in this activity with others, the ability to interact with other practitioners by the internet can provide a valuable support system, a way to become connected to others with similar goals and interests" (146). Also, on-line learning is perceived as a major element of action research.

Throughout the web-page discussions in this study, participants shared their spiritual experiences in leadership and provided feedback to one another's postings. After data collection was completed, some participants requested an opportunity to meet the other participants face-to-face. As suggested by Maguire (2001), the relational process established during action research can "facilitate silence breaking" (p. 63). Breaking the silence about spirituality within educational leadership was one goal of this study. Action research is also credited for providing participants with an opportunity to reflect on their own practices (Creswell, 2002). While responding to the interview questions and participating in the web-page discussion, the educators involved in this study were given opportunities to be reflective. As part of the process of cooperative inquiry, they were also given the opportunity to examine their own experiences and actions carefully in collaboration with others who shared similar concerns and interests (Heron & Reason, 2001).

The progression towards applying inquiry action research models to the study of educational leadership commenced with identifying a process for examining certain phenomena (Creswell, 2002). Methods applied to this type of study were adapted in response to the researcher/facilitator's objectives to better comprehend spirituality within educational leadership. The action research process of "looking, thinking and action" (p. Creswell, 2002, p. 610) was a reflective triangulated inquiry paradigm.

When communicating with ten educational leaders, the researcher/facilitator's role in this study involved attempting to apply five skills, introduced by Heron and Reason (2001):

1. being present, open, and empathetic;
2. doing some bracketing and reframing, which means refraining from imposing the researcher's beliefs on the participants;
3. being focused on the purpose of the study;
4. experiencing non-attachment and meta-intentionality, to ensure that the researcher was not investing her total identity and emotional security in the research;
5. having emotional competence, which is the "ability to identify and manage emotional states in various ways. (Heron & Reason, 2001, p. 184)

Heron & Reason (2001) stated that applying these skills "improves the quality of knowing" (p. 184) and ensures the data collection is done cooperatively with the participants. Although I attempted to apply these skills throughout the process, I did not experience non-attachment and meta-intentionality. Throughout the inquiry process, I felt like I was struggling to retain an identity, beyond being a researcher.

Summary of Chapter

The research design that framed the collection of data and analysis for this study is outlined in this chapter. The chapter commences with an introduction to the rationale for the design and methodology. After a presentation of some major epistemological paradigm shifts in educational research, which influenced the selection of a triangulated research design, the layout for the method was introduced. The subsequent literature demonstrated how feminist, phenomenological and action research ideology were suitable for this study. The selection of participants, methods of data collection, and collection and storage of data were later presented. This section included an outline of how I developed and forwarded each research question to participants and ways these questions were answered by study participants. The chapter ended with a summary of the data analysis tools applied to the study.

4
Results: Dialoging About Spirituality

The chapter has eleven sections, organized according to participant profiles, five e-mailed questions, threads in findings, and results from web-page discussions. The sub-questions were developed from two core questions: 1. how are the spiritual experiences of educational leaders understood and articulated? and 2. in what ways would articulating the spiritual experiences of educational leaders contribute to the development of effective leadership? To indicate contributions made by participants, examples of individual responses are provided in each section of the threaded key concepts, followed by a summary of the findings. Responses are recorded alphabetically, with the exception of the final follow-up group discussion. The chapter begins with profiles of each participant; all names are self-selected pseudonyms.

Profiles of Participants

The ten study participants ranged in ages 31 to 65. Four participants were ages 31-40; one was 41-50; four were 51-60, and one was 61-70. All had worked or were working in administrative positions in educational leadership in Ontario or Alberta Public School systems. Fifty percent of the participants were male and fifty percent, female; half of the respondents were from Alberta and half from Ontario. Participants' religious backgrounds were not taken into consideration during the participant selection process.

At the time of the study, Airjordan was age 51-60, with a Bachelor of Arts (BA), and Masters in Education (MEd), 18 years teaching experience and 16 years educational administrative experience. His religious background was Roman Catholic and his spiritual group affiliations were Marriage Encounters and other couple support groups. He worked as an Education Officer for the Ontario Ministry of Education on the coordination and implementation of Secondary School reform. When addressing spirituality within the study, he stated that spirituality meant "being more Christ-like."

Armary was age 61-70, with a BA and BSc, 10 years teaching experience, seven years Head of a Public School Guidance Department, and 23 years as school principal. After retirement from principalship, he continued his formal education in religious and spiritual studies. His religious affiliation was Roman Catholic and he was involved in the Catholic Charismatic Renewal movement. He also traveled across Canada to teach about spirituality in small communities and on native reserves. When addressing spirituality within the study, he stated humans are "spiritual by nature and not by any decision on their own."

Ayla was age 41-50, with a MEd, seven years teaching experience, and 15 years in educational administrative positions, including principal and public school supervisor. Her past religious affiliation was Roman Catholic, but at the time of the study, she considered herself a believer in spirituality with no particular religious affiliation. After leaving a principal position, she became an Ontario Public School Board office administrator. When addressing spirituality within the study, she stated spirituality is "not limited to any religion or cultural group of people because it is about universal respect for all human beings."

Beau was age 31-40, with a MEd, 14 years teaching experience, four years administrative experience with the Calgary Board of Education, two years Curriculum leader, two years Assistant Principal and two years in a public school principal's position. During the study, he was working as an Alberta public school principal. He was raised as a Mormon but left the Church of Jesus Christ of Latter-Day Saints to attend a United Church. When addressing spirituality within the study, he stated that spirituality is being "intricately connected to our own sense of self and having a deep understanding of our self and the world."

Habs was age 31-40, with a BEd, 12 years teaching experience and four years in an Alberta public school principal's position. During the study, he was employed as an Alberta public school principal. He was a member of the United Church, and considered parenting to be a spiritual role. When addressing spirituality within the study, he stated that "spirituality is lighting the souls of others when they feel their souls can not ignite any longer."

Luv was age 31-40, with a MEd, 17 years teaching experience and two years in a principal's position. During the study, she was employed as an Alberta public school principal. She did not claim to have any religious affiliation, but said she studied spirituality in courses and her readings and was informed about Christian beliefs within her childhood years. When addressing spirituality within the study, she stated that spirituality is taking "the synergistic approach to leadership . . . [which] enhances the spirit of . . . all members of the learning community."

Meiling was age 51-60, with a MEd, 23 years teaching and 17 years in an educational administrator's position. During the study, she was employed as an administrator and teacher within the Alberta public school system. She was of a Protestant denomination and attended the Christian Community Church. When addressing spirituality within the study, she stated "spirituality is tied up in considering the whole person and the relationship that educators have between class, curricula and themselves."

Newday was age 41-50, with a BEd, 11 years teaching experience and two years educational administrative experience. During the study, he was employed as an Alberta public school principal. He was a member of the Catholic community in the past, but later referred to himself as being Pentecostal, after having had a born-again experience within the Christian community. When addressing spirituality within the study, he stated "leadership that is spiritual should put others above self."

Sara was age 51-60, with a MEd, 32 years teaching experience and 23 years administrative experience, as a Public School principal. During the study, she was in the stages of preparing to retire from her position as an Ontario public school principal. In the past she attended a Presbyterian church, but referred to herself as a "secular humanist" who does not attend church. When addressing spirituality within the study, she stated that spirituality is to "show that she operates with . . . heart as well as . . . head."

Stider was age 51-60 with a MEd, 25 years teaching experience and 19 years administrative experience in a public school system. During the study, she was employed as an Alberta public school principal. Her past religious affiliation was Roman Catholic, but she referred to herself as a Christian. When addressing spirituality within the study, she stated "spirituality cannot be denied; . . . it is my silent partner."

First Core Research Question: How are the spiritual experiences of educational leaders understood and articulated by educators?

When answering this questions, six participants suggested that spiritual experiences are not clearly understood or articulated in words by educational leaders. The other four participants indicated that actions express one's spirituality better than words.

Not Clear by Words

Six examples of participant responses regarding communication about spirituality include:

Airjorden: I don't believe the spiritual experiences of educational leaders are understood very well and I believe they are seldom articulated. . . . My understanding of spirituality, from a more traditional sense, would be that it guides my behavior. That is, I would ask myself "what would Christ do in this situation or, how would he react to this person"? I don't articulate this to people; it would be too embarrassing. Plus they would think I was losing it or feel that it was quite inappropriate in a publicly funded system. Or, if I was speaking to a group of people, they might get offended or just walk out. In fact, I was at a seminar once when the person made reference to Christ and a number of people got up and left.

Ayla: Spirituality for me has become very broad and yet very narrow to define. Broad in the sense that it is not limited to any religion or cultural group of people whatsoever because it is about universal respect for all human beings. Narrow, because that's what it is for me: respect for the dignity of human beings and doing the right thing. Not an easy task, but certainly a good "lighthouse" for me to use as I make both personal and professional decisions every day.

Beau: While I can speak of my own spiritual experiences I believe that these are often very private and dependent upon the experiences one has had.

Luv: What I would call spiritual experiences, are very private and personal. They evolve from taking care of my own wellness. In that regard, they are not publicly articulated. However, it is my hope that they are understood by those with whom I work, in that I hope that others are attending to their own spirit and wellness. So, whether or not educational leaders' spiritual experiences are fully understood is not clear. I would suggest that because, in my case, it is such private work, it is not intimately understood by others and I do not articulate my spirituality in a conventional fashion.

Meiling: Spirituality is tied up in considering the whole person and the relationship that educator's have between class, curricula, and themselves.

Stider: When you are a school administrator in a public school, there seems to be no place for spirituality. One can talk about school climate, school culture, school spirit-building (rah rah) but not spirituality. Although there is some sense that conditions may be changing and that people may be more receptive to acknowledging the spiritual nature of being. I have heard references to principals whose religion is apparent in their operation of the school and these references have generally not been positive. Although religion and spirituality are not necessarily one and the same, without deliberate explanation, a spiritual person is quickly pigeon-holed into a religious framework which, in the modern world, is much maligned. So how are the spiritual experiences of educational leaders articulated? Very carefully. Spirituality cannot be denied. Yet, I am careful to keep conversations that refer to spirituality between those I trust and those who understand. Spirituality is my "silent partner." My relationship with my Creator is the source of my strength when

I need it and I believe that there our times when God works through me thereby making me feel humble yet worthy.

Articulate Primarily By Action

In response to the first core question, four participants stated that one's spirituality is expressed mainly by one's actions.

Armary: May I conclude that the awareness of one's spirituality will be first evident in the manner in which they relate to others. The articulation, then, of one's spirituality will be in action, not in words.

Habs: The spiritual experiences of leaders are articulated by walking the talk. Effective leaders show compassion and care for others. . . . Spirituality is lighting the soul of others when they feel that their soul can not ignite any longer. Spiritual leaders in essence walk the talk. To be a great spiritual leader you need to be a servant of others and your main purpose is to help them. In education, you see educators who do this with their students on a regular basis; their primary function is to serve their students and help their students achieve the stars.

Newday: The spiritual experiences of leaders are articulated through one's lifestyle. My spirituality is the very essence of who I am. Who I am should be communicated by my actions. The old adage, actions speak louder than words, is true as actions speak to what we believe. . . . values and priorities are demonstrated through what we do. Leadership that is spiritual should put others above self. Actions by leaders, who put others first, articulate that priorities should always be people. The best example of articulating this is for leaders to be willing to do the "lowly" jobs by setting an example that they are not above others. The principal should be willing to sweep the halls, teach classes or clean a toilet instead of imposing this on others. When people see this they learn to serve and are less apt to feel part of a hierarchy. It is crucial for leaders to be spiritual examples in their community. When leaders understand this crucial role they realize that the health of the community depends upon their modeling this to others. This articulates a flattened system where all individuals are equal, from the caretaker to the principal.

Sara: Spirituality is expressed through our words and actions. The consistency of how we deal with others and how we show our priorities through our words and actions is important in showing who we are and what we believe. As a principal, I need to show that I operate with my heart as well as my mind.

Beliefs and Life Experiences Affect Understanding of Spirituality

In response to the first core question, some participants' answers introduced more than one thread. In addition to the foregoing responses, four participants associated their beliefs, and four connected experiences with their understandings of spirituality. Armary, Beau, Meiling and Newday stated their beliefs affected how they understood spirituality.

Armary: I believe that we are "spiritual" by nature and not by any decision of our own. Our personal decision does determine how we respond to this built in desire to fulfill our "Holy Longing." As educational leaders, we address this reality primarily through our attitude to those whom we serve and with whom we work. There is an intrinsic value to everyone and this value is independent of what one knows, what one can do or who one knows. This includes both students and staff. . . . The "spiritual experience" of an individual may take on many forms. Enlightenment, conversion, inspiration, transcendence, covenant and communion are only a few terms which may express a deep personal experience. Whatever term is used, the outcome results in unconditional respect for the human condition.

Beau: In order for educational leaders to "have" spiritual experiences, I believe that we must be intricately connected to our own sense of self and have a deep understanding of ourselves in the world. For me, spirituality in leadership is connected to my sense of stewardship. . . . This becomes connected, then, to a need to serve others and to develop a consensual quest to help each other become our best. . . . Spiritual experiences of educational leaders are intricately connected to beliefs about how human beings interact, and a sense of moral integrity. . . . In the work of educational leadership, one must be careful to ensure that "above all, do no harm." . . . A spiritual experience, then, is to be able to see amazing potential rather than to harbor an understanding of downfall.

Meiling: One of the biggest challenges when looking at this question is what one is meaning by the term "spiritual experiences." Is the meaning, one of faith? . . . Religious involvement? . . . One that incorporates one deep psyche? . . . One's soul? Is it one that moves us to a point of being so engaged with the content of the subject that it becomes part of ones ultimate belief system?

Newday: My spiritual example was Jesus Christ who said that he who would wish to be the greatest among you should be the least. The lifestyle of a servant was His way to create a community of equals. Underscoring the reality that all of us are different but that our contributions are significant when applied to the ultimate goal before us. His goal was to build into His disciples the willingness not to compete but to cooperate. To have unity as the essential endeavor of building a healthy school community should be every leader's goal. This is best understood and articulated through a lifestyle of servanthood. Continuous and authentic selfless actions, that places the essential good of others before self, thereby creating a truly spiritual community.

Ayla, Beau, Luv and Sara provided examples of experiences that affected their awareness and understandings of spirituality.

Ayla :I have had spiritual experiences throughout my life. They have occurred through everyday interactions and observations of people, as a result of life crises such as family death and divorce, and in the tremendous challenges that I have faced as an educational leader. As these experiences force me to delve deeper into my own spirituality, it seems that it gets easier to define as I move forward. . . . I think that as I lived my life, what I had learned during the "Catholic" portion of my upbringing certainly influenced the way I thought and behaved (for fear of being punished by God!!), which obviously was the precursor to a greater question for me: the importance of choice and freedom as long as we respect the right of all other individuals and accept the consequences for our choices. I am not saying that I blame the Catholic society for causing the end of my marriage; this was just a catalyst into a very personal journey to define what my spirituality is about. . . . Religion does not have proprietary rights over someone's spirituality.

Beau: While we can possess any amount of leadership background and understanding of organizational behavior, it is through effective, dynamic relationships that an organization "comes to life." Educational leaders who "have" spiritual experiences dwell, perhaps, in a spiritual place in all aspects of their lives so that all the experiences are connected on that plane and are not identified by specific happenings.

Luv: When considering "spiritual experiences" I think of interior activities that aid in maintaining a balance in one's life. In the context of educational leadership, I believe spiritual experiences are the activities in which individuals engage to maintain and sustain themselves in what is very demanding, challenging, and potentially draining exterior work with others. . . . These demands are personal, important, intellectual, emotional and sometimes physical. To be able to attend to these demands with sensitivity, efficiency and compassion, I feel it is imperative, at least for me, to constantly work on my 'interiority' or spirituality. Without my own spiritual strength, I would not be able to meet the thousands of daily demands of the position of educational leadership in which I work. In a position of leadership, supporting staff and students in their educational endeavors is at the heart of what I do. However, as with any job dealing with people, it is not only professional obligations that have to be met. Real life, and personal matters are all a part of every person in my building. . . . In order to provide leadership in both arenas, I make time to replenish my supply of emotional support on a regular basis.

Sara: This morning I dealt with a number of incidents related to your study. These incidents show the need for compassion and understanding that school leaders must not only truly feel and show, but must be perceived as showing from those they deal with on a daily basis.

Summary of Responses to Research First Core Question

All participants answered this question. The following text summarizes responses to each of the four threads associated with the first core research question, "how are the spiritual experiences of educational leaders understood and articulated"? Seven participants' responses to this question supported more than two threads. The thread "not clear by words," which was endorsed by six participants, had the highest number of responses 6 (of 17). This finding indicates participants made a strong statement that spirituality is not clearly understood or articulated with words. For example, Ayla suggested spirituality was difficult to define; Airjordan stated that he seldom observed any references to spirituality made by educational leaders.

Supporting the notion that spirituality is not clearly understood or articulated with words, four participants indicated spirituality was expressed mainly by actions. Thus, four (of 17) responses were connected with the thread "articulated primarily by action." An equal proportion of responses four (of 17) were associated with participants' beliefs and four (of 17) with their life experiences that affected their standpoints about expressing spirituality.

Data demonstrate the threads are inter-connected in relationship to insights gained from the first core question. Each thread is part of a synergistic "multidimensional framework" (Abbott, 1984) representing how spirituality is awakened, signified and cultivated. Within this framework, the whole is greater than the sum of its parts, as noted by Wilber, (1996). Findings also demonstrate that spirituality within leadership reflects a post-modernist worldview, rather than a Cartesian reductionism perspective.

The core question was an introduction to the first set of questions given to participants at the commencement of the study. Sub-question one and two were part of this set of questions administered by e-mail.

Sub-question One: Think of a time when you have felt the most excited, most engaged and most alive. What was it about this peak experience that you would define as being spiritual?

In response to sub-question one, all ten participants shared peak experiences that made them feel excited, engaged and alive; then, they commented about how these experiences could be defined as being spiritual. Five participants defined "spiritual" in the context of professional experiences, and half connected the meaning of "spiritual" with personal experiences.

Professional and Personal Experiences

Airjordan, Armand, Habs, Luv and Newday acknowledged peak professional experiences they defined as being spiritual.

Airjordan: A time when I felt most excited, most engaged and most alive. I will relate them to education and think of an occasion or two when all of the descriptors above came into effect. One of my recollections goes back to when I was teaching a Physical Education class when I was teaching at a local high school.

Armary: Many years ago, as a swimming instructor, I had an adult class who were so full of "the fear of water" that it was impossible to teach them how to swim. I prayed! At the next class I told them to forget everything I taught them in the first class. I was not going to teach them how to swim. Rather, I would teach them how to teach their children how to swim. They all learned how to swim. This was a lesson I never forgot. It was not of my own knowledge that I discovered the solution. With that experience, I learned a lesson, which sustained me in my career as an educational leader.

Habs: For myself there are many experiences that I could say that I was alive. In regards to teaching, it is when I have helped a student(s) achieve something that they once thought was unreachable.

Luv: My most concrete example of a peak experience is an everyday activity that is always enlightening if not rewarding in some way. Every day I do bus supervision in the morning and after school. In the morning most learners are tired and not particularly keen on chatting, despite my cheery "good morning" and "How are you today?" However, at day's end, they are often bursting with energy and willing to "kibbitz" with me as they head to the buses for the journey home. At that time of day, many students are smiling, laughing, busily visiting with friends and making plans for the evening. They are so alive and full of energy that it is almost tangible. . . . Walking amongst the students as I do, casually chatting and jesting with them is magic.

Newday: The time I was most excited and engaged spiritually was when I was in a close community of friends and we worked together on a project for young people. It is the sense of community that engaged my spirit because we all had a common goal and direction. We accepted each other with all the baggage and did not let small obstacles divide us. Unity is a very spiritual concept because of the blessings that come to every member of the group. True unity drops one's guard and exposes the true self. It lifts the façade and makes one vulnerable. It speaks from the heart and does all in its power to build up and protect the other.

Ayla, Beau, Meiling, Sara and Stider defined spiritual in the context of personal experiences.

Ayla: The prospect of a new job was exciting but that was on the surface. I viewed the position as a serious one in which there could be significant influence on a large scale and I wanted to make sure that I could deliver in a responsible manner. . . . I took a very significant personal journey before I decided to apply for the position. . . . I was totally engaged, excited and alive as I tried to understand why it was that I was even thinking of the leadership position that I have now. . . . The journey towards seeking the right answer for me took me through tremendous personal questions and a review of where my life had been and where it was meant to be going.

Beau: The easy answer to this question, is when I realized that I was in love with someone. The difficult reality of the question, is when that relationship ended my peak experience in actuality was when I went through the process of rebuilding myself. Feeling the most excited, most engaged and most alive happens for me when I have been through a dark time. It is my blessing to be able to experience most dark times with an understanding that remaining positive, and seeking growth are things I can do.

Meiling: I think of two experiences. The first involved a class in my Master's program where I was a student. We as a class were grappling with the question of what are curricula? Through the study of articles given by the professor, and personal reading to set the stage . . . the class involved sharing our own beliefs as to what curricula was. I discovered that other educators were struggling with similar issues . . . and yet in my teaching career up to that point I had not been understood by many of my colleagues. The second involved a different class where I was given a lot of freedom to do my own personal study . . . rather than following a rigid prescribed curricula (This is not to say that required readings were not part of the study.) However, I was able to explore a path that I needed to deal with questions about education that I had for me.

Sarah: In general, the times when I feel most excited, engaged, and alive are the times when I've participated in something very successful. These feelings are directly related to the time and energy invested and are even more pronounced when they are preceded by very negative feelings such as anger, frustration, hopelessness, and even despair.

Stider: Peak experiences at work are as a result of feeling competent and from having handled a situation capably. However, my peak spiritual experiences have not been at school. These experiences have come after in reflection time when I think about the job and the people within whom I work.

Connection: Others, Community, World

In addition to defining "spiritual" in the context of professional and personal experiences, five participants, Armary, Beau, Habs, Luv and Meiling associated "spiritual" with having a sense of public connection with others, the community or the world.

Armary: Love generates love while hate generates fear. These beliefs are spiritual values addressed by most of the world's major religions.

Beau: I see myself as part of an eternal existence that requires growth in understanding of self and others. It is through relationships with others, and relationship with self, that we come to understand our potential, our connections with others, and our offerings.

Habs: I remember taking students on a sailing trip. We planned for months and worked very hard to achieve our goal of sailing on the west coast. The excitement in the students' eyes was well worth the hard work that we all put forth to go on the trip. What made this trip such a spiritual experience was to see the souls of the students enlightened and glowing. The heightened spirituality of the students enlightened my own spirituality. Helping others reach their goals helps all of us feel good about ourselves.

Luv: As a school we are doing work for local charities, the food bank and so on, and to see the effort and commitment of students to make these events a success is also what I would call a spiritual experience. This is positive, community oriented, selfless work and the students are taking it up with vigor.

Meiling: I was excited and very engaged . . . almost euphoric to know that there were others out there that were thinking "beyond the box" of what curricula meant. Perhaps because the discussion was getting at the heart of my belief system is one reason I was so engaged. I was able to read widely, and discovered that some of my struggles in being an educator where there were major philosophical differences in "what and how I was expected to teach" from my own experiences in what I knew intuitively would make students excited about learning. I had a framework to understand what I believed.

Connection: God, Self, Nature

The remaining five participants associated "spiritual" with experiences involving a connection with God, oneself or nature.

Airjordan: We were outside having a hockey class at a rink across from the school. I was just struck by the beauty all around me and how happy, youthful, energetic and playful the students were. The sun was sparkling over the snow and ice. The ice was crackling with the skate noise. This, to me, was the spiritual part. Particularly the students and their happy spirits and the beauty of nature and the feeling of connectedness I had with all that was going on around me. It most likely was being outside on such a beautiful day that was the catalyst. Everything seemed just right. I was sure at that point in time that there was a God out there somewhere orchestrating all this. I felt very alive at this time. Other experiences of this nature were similar. They usually involved people, and I usually felt a close relationship to them. Nature also seems to be a stimulus.

Ayla: I spent many hours over several weeks walking and walking, listening to music (but not really hearing it) reviewing my life, my relationship with my mother (who had been dead for over 10 years), my professional experiences, the "big" mistakes in my life and what I had learned from them. It was a journey where it seemed that every possible sense in me was acutely humming through this kaleidoscope so that I could reach the end and discover what the answer was from wherever. . . . There is a strong correlation for me between walks along the waterfront, watching the sunrise and the kind of work I do.

Newday: There is a scripture that states, "when we work together in unity, God commands the blessing." It is as if God allows His favour to rest on us as we encourage each other on. This principle works in any organization because a common focus creates momentum and inspires everyone to be diligent together. I can think of one example from the Bible that might be used as an example. When Jesus broke bread, and drank wine with His disciples, He was saying that He would always be part of them, in the deepest sense of unity. He would live on in their memories and in their lives for years to come. To this day, that time and those relationships live on in my memory. My heart has been touched by such intimacy.

Sara: To see something working well, to feel the energy and commitment of those involved, to see for a moment in time the perfection or the sense that everything is working in harmony, and to be a part of it, is such a good feeling that it must be cherished. These feelings are few and far in between which makes them more wonderful. Whether the feelings are the result of having a child attend school who has been consistently truant, or seeing a child happy and well-behaved who was previously angry and aggressive, or having a successful spirit assembly to culminate and award prizes for Reading Month, or seeing the Advisory Council working in harmony and with dedication, or seeing the staff get behind the implementation of a new program at the school, the feeling is always "This is the way it should be!" It's a sense of perfection, of things being in harmony, and a sense of being totally involved in the experience. In each case the experience involves others and their behavior and relationships. Each case is a success story.

Stider: The strongest association with spirituality is to sense that God has been at work through me. My life feels purposeful beyond my own needs to earn a living and fulfill my career obligations. This purpose is strongly felt when I know I have made a difference in someone's life and then I think about the importance of honouring each soul and the circumstances of each of our lives. This has come later in life for me. Sometimes through death one comes to understand the value of life and I have had many deaths in my family.

Summary of Responses To Research Sub-question One

All participants answered this question. The following text summarizes ten participants' responses to sub-question one, "think of a time when you have felt the most excited, most engaged and most alive; what was it about this peak experience that you would define as being spiritual?" This question generated a total of 20 threaded responses. Three (of 5) participants, who answered the question within the context of their professional experiences, articulated they felt a connection with others, the community and the world; this finding supports Tisdell's (2003) stand on the relationship between spirituality and community within the workplace.

Three (of 5) participants, who expressed how God, self, and nature had influenced their peak spiritual experiences answered sub-question one in the context of their personal spiritual experiences. This finding upholds Keen's (2004) belief that encounters with nature can awaken a person's spirituality. Findings demonstrate there are interconnections among four threads, related to sub-question one. Participants' spirituality was awakened by peak personal experiences within and outside of their workplaces; their shared experiences commonly signified "meaning-making moments" which were times of "significant learning" (Tisdell, 2003). Their responses reflect a "multi-voiced" (Lather, 1991) perspective of how spirituality is awakened; additionally, findings introduce transcendent and immanent domains of spirituality (Wilber, 1996), reflected within God, nature, and community. Connecting four threads may paint a more holistic picture of awakening spirituality, than having each thread expressed separately. Comparable to findings from the first core question, data from sub-question one demonstrate the whole is greater than the sum of the parts.

Like sub-question one, sub-question two was included in the first set of questions e-mailed to participants.

Sub-question Two: What are some spiritual values and moral beliefs that influence the effectiveness of your leadership practises?

In response to sub-question two, all ten participants associated their spiritual values and moral beliefs with viewing others as their equals.

Viewing Others as Equals

Airjordan: All people are people who are created in the image of God and therefore are deserving of care and respect and should be treated with dignity. I believe I became a more effective teacher when I really worked at trying to love those that were the most difficult to deal with. This also has influenced my leadership practices in that treating people I come into contact with dignity and respect is a basic building block for my continued interaction with them.

Armary: I believe that we are all equal because we are created in the "image of God." If we remove God from the equation then we are likely to believe that we are equal because of our inalienable rights (democracy). . . . I do not deny "rights" or "needs," but there is a value in the individual, which transcends both. Living the belief that equality comes from God has kept me sane in the demanding and sometimes competitive atmosphere of education.

Ayla: As a leader, I must show respect for all human beings and try to ensure that all people I meet feel like they have a valued place on earth. Therefore, I must acknowledge their value and encourage them to grow.

Beau: I highly value the worth of each individual person and try to "do no harm" in my relationships. I also believe that each person's journey is unique to them and that they bring specific gifts and talents to the work and to life and that it is our responsibility to help them discover those. In the forum of a school organization, the work is to help them find ways to contribute to the organization that are not in contradiction to their gifts and talents.

Habs: Another value that I am constantly working at, even with those that I have difficulty with, is to value each individual for who they are and not what I want them to be. In the text book, *Caring Enough to Lead,* the author talks about looking after your water buffalo. What he is saying is that leaders need to build relationships with their followers and truly look after them.

Luv: As a leader, I need to recognize that every child is capable of learning and growing and therefore I must see them as who they can become.

Meiling: I believe that every student has a right to learn and every teacher has a right to teach and when those aspects are being jeopardized (and they are) then there must be dialog to bring about understanding.

Newday: Showing his/her team that no-one is above the other, that everyone has are responsibility to serve and that the goals are best achieved when people willingly give of their time and talents to others. Serving is indeed the purest form of love because it is sacrificial. This was best demonstrated through the life of Christ who took on the role of a servant, loving the weak and was washing the feet of His disciples and ultimately giving all of Himself and all that He had to others.

Sara: I believe that all people are valuable within an organization and that everyone makes a specific and unique contribution to the overall effort. We are all of equal value although our roles differ. We should never look at our schools as a hierarchy but as a team, with everyone working together to achieve the goals of the organization.

Stider: I believe that God loves every individual and every individual in the eyes of God is worthy of love, so I should treat them accordingly. God loves even the lowest of the low. I am no greater or lesser than anybody else, so it's not my place to judge others. When we treat others like they are worthy of love, they feel worthy of being loved.

Practising Servant Leadership

Participants' answers to sub-question two indicate that in addition to treating others as equals, practising servant leadership is associated with spiritual values and moral beliefs. Six of the ten participants claimed servant leadership reflected their spiritual values and moral beliefs.

Ayla: I was put on earth to help make it a better place in whatever way that I can. Each one of us has a responsibility to move the world forward in some way. I believe there is a higher spiritual being that guides us to be moral and spiritual. We are role models, and this higher spiritual being holds us accountable for our actions. We are given challenges and our solidity is tested for a greater good.

Beau: I believe in teaching that we are to be good stewards of the gifts with which we have been blessed – as I see this work in some ways as a "calling" and a forum for stewardship.

Habs: What leaders need to remember, and many forget, is to lead with your heart and not just your head. Your heart will tell you what to do in regards to others and how to make them gain confidence to be successful. Leadership is like parenting. Parents want to see their children be successful and will do everything within their power to ensure that their children achieve their dreams and aspirations. . . . If you want others to follow you will need to look after them. By looking after your followers you will gain the trust which is essential to leading. Without trust, leaders will have no followers, and with no followers one cannot lead.

Meiling: One of my main ideas of leadership has always been to have a "servanthood" model and this has been especially true in the past two weeks . . . being available and welcoming to all. In this past two weeks with the onslaught of Bill 12, one of the main aspects of my leadership has been to listen, listen, listen and to let people talk. For some, this has meant they needed to come to my home and talk. Others have had to come and talk at all times of the day.

Newday: The beliefs that guide my practice are tied around the values of serving. Serving has much to do with leadership because it is a demonstration to others of humility and caring. It is the ultimate act of submission for a leader who holds power but does not abuse it. Servant leadership is a practice that really cares for others and demonstrates this through actions of compassion, giving and serving. It is the opposite of authoritarianism, that is often used in settings that demand performance and production. . . . Ultimately, serving creates the atmosphere where others can realize their own potential because there are no ladders to success when stepping on the back of your peer; there is equality striving together to the common ideal.

Sara: An organization is only as successful as the people in it. The ability to work together towards the goals of the organization determines how successful and organization is. I believe that our role is to ensure that today's children grow up to become educated, caring, responsible citizens. I believe that the more successful people feel the happier they are.

Having Personal Accountability and Positive Mentoring

Four participants connected personal accountability and three associated positive mentoring with their expressions of spiritual values and moral beliefs. Four examples of participant responses regarding personal accountability include:

Airjordan: I believe that what people value and how they feel about things are as important as their position in life or the level of education they have achieved. How people feel about things is important and as a leader I need to attend to them and listen attentively. People also need the opportunity to experience continued learning and personal growth. These are important and a leader needs to assist in providing opportunities for people to experience these. And a leader needs to be perceived as one who is also experiencing growth and continuing to learn. Lastly, I feel that my spirituality can help me be positive when things are difficult. As leaders it is important that we be leaders who provide hope, the hope that can spring from our spiritual beliefs.

Ayla: As leaders, it is our responsibility to awaken the spiritual values and moral beliefs in others, by our own actions and words. This means, we may be called to go into our souls and search deep for the right thing to do that will be the best for all. We are all born with the ability to tap into our souls and be spiritual beings, but this spirit needs to be ignited and lit up for people to recognize it. Leading with spirit is a highly developed skill that makes us aware of our moral obligation. . . . Being respectful, empathetic, fair and responsible are some of my moral values that when espoused, they help build character in others. Our actions need to be consistent with our words. We have to walk the talk. When we are in moral dilemmas, our higher spiritual being holds us accountable for our actions.

Meiling: Some spiritual values that I hold are how I view all students and staff, especially the difficult ones. When I feel an injustice is done to me or that I am not being heard, I have to stop and ask myself, how would Jesus respond? This has been so helpful at times, because I often find myself looking at them with a different eye. When I have staff complaining about students or coming with preconceived ideas, we have a discussion which may cause them to look at the child differently or I ask a question which may cause them to consider another way. I have Corinthians 13 on my office board that I read daily. This helps keep me centred. In terms of moral beliefs, I am a stickler for honesty and justice. This means that if I find that students' learning are being compromised by shortcuts taken by teachers or because of lack of funding due to changes in regulations of Alberta Education, then I will be a strong advocate for change.

Sara: I believe that we are all responsible and accountable for everything we say and do. Personal responsibility for our actions should guide how we interact with others and our expectations of them. We do not have rights without responsibilities. I believe leaders should always act with honesty and integrity. We should do what's right, not what others expect us to do or what is expedient. . . . We need to know who needs support and who needs encouragement. We need to understand human behavior and motivation in order to both lead and manage our organizations.

On the other hand, Habs, Luv and Newday viewed mentoring their spiritual beliefs and moral values as the ideal way to express them.

Habs: I believe some of the spiritual values and moral beliefs that influence my effectiveness as a leader are honesty. I need to be honest at all times with whoever I am communicating with. By being honest I will develop trust in others. As my father would say honesty is the best policy. Besides gaining trust, I will gain integrity from others by being honest with everyone. . . . In the book, *The Bonds that Free Us,* the authors talk in detail about relationships with others and if developed on a positive basis life will become complete. . . . What I try to do in my leadership role is to help others to be the best that they can become. Leadership is not about a position of power or control. Leadership is about helping others to reach for the stars. To be a great leader you need to be honest, open and sincere with everyone.

Luv: The spiritual values and moral beliefs that influence the effectiveness of my leadership practices are having honesty, integrity and respect at the head of what I do. I want to do what's best for the kids to practise fairness. My job as a leader is to help students gain self respect, and respect for others by demonstrating respect for myself and for them. Helping them to feel part of a community and giving them an opportunity to contribute to the community assists the students to learn values and morals. The clarity and consistency of the language I speak and my caring actions towards others, reflects my spiritual values and moral beliefs.

Newday In schools, where we are all working to better the lives of others a leader must lead by example.

Summary of Responses to Research Sub-question Two

All participants answered this question. The following text summarizes responses to research sub-question two, "What are some spiritual values and moral beliefs that influence the effectiveness of your leadership practises?" Each of the ten participants supported more than one thread, resulting in a total of 23 responses. Ten (of ten) participants discussed the thread, "viewing others as equals," and 6 (of 10) referred to "practising servant leadership," in association with spiritual values and moral beliefs. The other two threads included a total of 5 (of 10) responses; "having personal accountability," three responses and "having positive mentoring," two responses. Although the number of participants' responses supporting the different threads varied, each thread is equitable in the context of being a part of a whole set of attitudes, related to spiritual values and moral beliefs.

Viewing others as equals could result in practicing servant leadership, which would involve having personal accountability and positive mentoring within the workplace. Viewing others as equals supports Wilber's (1994) standpoint about natural hierarchy: although a "whole" is dependent upon parts, segments of a whole can exist independently; however, separately they will lack the effectiveness of functioning as part of a whole (p. 20). In educational systems, in which leaders treat others as equals and practise servant leadership, a natural hierarchy could be established. "A natural hierarchy is simply an order of increasing wholeness, such as: particles to atoms to cells to organisms" (Wilber, 1994, p. 28). As in previous findings, all threads associated with sub-question two are interconnected, synergistic, and part of a multi-dimensional framework, related to awakening, signifying and cultivating spirituality.

Results From Participant Involvement In Discussion About First Set of Questions

After participants answered three set number one questions, an on-line follow-up focussed discussion was initiated on a web-page, in response to comments given. All participants contributed to the discussion.; four (of ten) did one posting; three (of 10), two postings and three (of ten) three postings. Therefore, a total of 19 postings were made during the on-line discussion for this final component of phase one of data collection.

The number of postings made by each participant varied. Airjordan, Beau and Luv each contributed three (of 19) postings; Sara, Meiling and Stider, contributed two (of 19) and Newday, Habs, Armary and Ayla, contributed one (of 19). When articulating experiences related to spirituality, some participants found words insufficient to describe something they considered ineffable. Spirituality is still considered inchoate, without a clear language for its expression (Holmes, 2003). Therefore, each of the 19 postings is valued equally, and all participant contributions are perceived as important elements of the discussion, enabling the whole to be greater than the sum of its parts (Wilber, 1996).

Participant involvement fulfilled the study action research objective to move beyond muted discourses about spirituality. Postings demonstrated all participants were interacting and interconnecting during the discussion, which initiated a sense of community and may have assisted in the process of personal and professional spiritual development. The discussion was part of a triangulated research paradigm that may have encouraged the awakening, signifying and cultivating of spirituality within leadership amongst the 10 participants. Although the on-line discussion tended to be a series of monologs, some statements made by the participants were affirming to fellow participants. The participants' postings during the discussion were as follows:

Airjordan 1: There are many people in education known to have a strong spirituality, and in part at least, are looked to for leadership and are admired. I feel it depends a lot on how the individual personifies his/her spirituality. I really appreciated the many comments by participants who spoke about how their spirituality influenced their actions.

Airjordan 2: I particularly like Sarah's description of the two incidents she dealt with in the one day at school and the way in which she dealt with them. Her compassion and understanding were truly admirable! I see this as spirituality in action, a concept frequently referred to in the sharing by participants. This is most encouraging. I also liked the way Sarah summed her sharing up to: "how we show our priorities through our words and actions is important in showing who we are and what we believe. As a principal I need to show that I operate with my heart as well as my mind." Bravo. I felt that this is one of the keys to the role of spirituality in education. We need leaders who will operate with both their hearts and their minds. And it is imperative that we do so. We need the moral, the conscientious leadership.

Airjordan 3: In reaction to Luv specifically and to the other responses generally, I really appreciate the comments made by her in regards to identifying oneself as "religious" might be somewhat dangerous in that one could be "pidgeon-holed." I have noticed this as well and the fact that the person's ability to influence things was diminished. It also depends on the person however. It is my opinion that if people see your faith/religion as the way to salvation, they will be turned off. I feel that being closed-minded on this is not the way to create understanding or to promote the role of spirituality. Those who feel that their way is the only way would not be in a position to influence me.

Armary 4: I am very impressed with the statements of each participant but I guess I should not be surprised. During my career, I met many educators who lived their spirituality in love and respect for others and the situations of the lives they encountered. It is my observation and experience that there is a common sense of fulfillment when we are true to that inner voice of love for all and not an irresponsible emphasis on power and authority. I would like to meet all of you.

Ayla 1: The balance of professional commitments and family life leave little time for spending time on the computer. I know I need to further my technology skills but when I do have a little spare time, I need to do other things than "education" or educate myself!!! so I choose to paint, improve house, read and sew!!! Nothing that is educationally related, but is probably spiritually related.

Beau 1: Somehow, I have come to the conclusion that one can possess all the leadership theory in the world but without the ability to formulate relationships of trust and care and synchronicity we simply cannot be effective in our roles. Thinking about it, the leaders from whom I have learned the most and been the most willing to "follow"– have been the ones who have a deep sense of humanity, a belief that "above all, do no harm," and a desire to make me feel successful in what I am doing.

Beau 2: Today, in our staff meeting, I did something that I have never done before. Lately, I have been dealing with an enormous personal load in my life and some of the staff were aware of "tidbits" of what was going on. There was conversation amongst the staff about the load I carry, so I felt it necessary to share my story with the whole staff in order to alleviate unfound stories and also to comfort them with the understanding that I am okay. Unfortunately, but perhaps it was a good thing – I began to cry when telling my story. The staff began to tell me how much they appreciated my willingness to connect so personally with them. To say the least, I was concerned that they had seen me "break down" -- afraid that they would see this as a weakness I suppose . . . after all, my job is to keep them motivated, focussed and "on track." However, in the afternoon while I was in meetings of one kind and another the staff expressed to my secretary how close they were all feeling to each other and how our meeting had actually drawn us together closer as a team. Is this spirituality?

Beau 3: I find it interesting to attempt to choreograph what sometimes appear to be competing initiatives as groups of people come together. The skill in connecting all constituents in our dance of light and sound is delicate. Here again, it is important to teach meaning and context. For me, this comes through discourse. Our language tells us so much about who we are and what we believe. An example of this is in the challenge and conversations about what we celebrate as a community and what the celebration will look like. Our community was asked to reconsider what events like Halloween and Christmas look like in our school. The outcome was a shift in ownership from school staff to community members, including students, parents, and school staff. The resulting blast of fireworks was a beautiful display of an energized, involved group of diverse individuals who sought to have a common understanding of community. (This was a spiritual experience for me.) Fireworks are beautiful to me, as is an organization of human beings who are all unique and wonderful. I am highly energized by being in a place where individuals feel free to contribute in their own ways and where individuals are highly valued in the overall composition of light, sound and energy. As a leader, my work is to ignite ideas in others, not to make the organization live my ideas.

Habs 1: In regards to the topic of discussion, I think spirituality comes from the heart. The heart is what drives the soul and not the brain. What we need to do in schools is connect our souls together and we will find an inner peace along with effective teaching. This connection will build relationships, which are key to the success of teaching students. There needs to be time to connect our souls with each other and if schools made time for spirituality amongst staff and students they would find schools would be a better place for all. Spirituality carries no religious connection but only the connection of your soul and that of others. Our spirit is in us and if we can see the spirit of others then we will be able to see them for who they are.

Luv 1: Thank you to everyone for your insights and views in the discussion so far. Already I can see and feel that the reflections and discussions involved in this project are wonderfully meaningful professional development activities. Personally, I do not consider myself to be a religious person at all, but I certainly consider myself to be a spiritual being. That aligns with one of the previous questions of "what is spirituality?" I do believe that spirituality is very broad in its meaning and how it is manifested. In my perception it does not automatically mean something "religious." However, in my assumptions, as unschooled as they are, I would most likely understand religious activities to be inherently spiritual.

Luv 2: As clearly noted, in a public school setting, identifying oneself as "religious" might be somewhat dangerous in terms of being "pigeon-holed" or stereotyped by that designation. However, as we work on the ongoing development of ourselves and our changes in our schools, there is often discussion of the "spirit" of the learning community. There is perhaps, a greater willingness to discuss "spirit" without a religious context because of its generality versus perceived or real "confinedness" of specific religious designations. That said, I feel often that a "spiritual" curricular component would be of great worth to many in our learning community. The importance of the respectful treatment of self, others and the earth may not be specifically articulated in any one curricular area but it is integral to all that we do. Assisting students to understand that we are all a part of something greater than ourselves and that we need to strive to be our best in regard to ourselves, others and the earth is a huge task. This might also be called character education.

Luv 3 Working by myself and with others to achieve our potential in terms of respectfulness for ourselves, others and the earth is constant. As the baby-boomer generation is aging, we can see in popular culture that this is taking hold, as many people seek to improve themselves and contribute meaningfully to the world. Note the success of Oprah's magazine O that is dedicated to the re-generation and health of one's soul. The economic success of a plethora of writers who address the spiritual needs of today's consumers can be witnessed. The term "spirituality" is bandied about with much more comfort and frequency than previously. How this can more definitively be constructed in the schools is anyone's guess. Whether it would be possible or desirable is another question. By virtue of being a participant in this study, I recognize that my own work in this area needs to be constant. It is my belief that, as an educational leader, one person at a time I can assist people with spiritual development, whether I call it that or something else.

Meiling 1: I have been impressed with your thoughtful replies. Some common themes that resonate with me are the ideas that to show spirituality to co-workers is to be servant-like or Christ-like in attitudes towards students and colleagues. The thoughts of compassion for others and stopping to deal with the issues that encroach our planned day with joy and love are factors that I have been working through myself particularly these past two years. It is important for me at times to look beyond the immediate . . . spending time just talking to colleagues and students about what's going on for them . . . encouraging them and listening.

Meiling 2: Three years ago, I too thought that issues and ideas about spirituality was to be kept out of the workplace, that it was a private personal response. Although I used prayer in my workplace . . . praying for students in distressing events, and colleagues etc., it was done in private. This past year one of my colleagues in the department that I provide leadership to is facing death due to inoperable cancer. She has a deep faith and she was not afraid to show the importance of that faith and her spiritual beliefs to colleagues who were really struggling with her illness. What she did was smash open the doors to deep discussion. Although she is now on sick leave, there are many deep discussions with colleagues ongoing. In opening up the dialog, it has made for a deepening of relationships with one another. I have noticed that this year despite much turmoil within the school due to renovations, overcrowding, lack of space, no work room etc., that the staff have a closeness, a community of care and concern for one another and for students that I have not seen so clearly before.

Newday 1: I had a chance to quickly review answers to questions and I noted some commonalities in perspectives on spiritual leadership. As a leader, I aim to be used effectively for what God has equipped me to do spiritually. With whatever gifts I have been given, I want to use in a ministry to touch people's lives and use these gifts to the fullest. I agree with some of the other participants that our spirituality is innate and inherent. It is a part of who I am; it is what enables me to view others as my equals. I believe faith without works does not awaken one's spirituality; it keeps it asleep which may make it feel as if it is dead. One cannot separate morals from leadership; without having moral integrity, a person can't be a true leader. Servant leadership means putting others above oneself, not being arrogant, and leading by example; I aim to be a servant leader. In response to participants' comments about their spirituality being awakened by nature, things such as observing a sunrise . . . how much time does an administrator, who is also a parent have time to commune with nature? I feel my spirit being awakened when I'm with my family, praying with the kids and going to church with them. I feel my spirituality when there's lots of laughter and meaningful exchanges with family members, peers, and students. My spirituality is more evident to me when I take off my professional hat and allow myself to be childlike. My busy schedule at work and family obligations has made it difficult for me to find time to participate in the discussion.

Sara 1: I did read all the responses last week but really had no comment to make. I did a cursory reading of all of the responses but was unable to bring them back to the screen to read a second time for a more thoughtful reading. However, from my initial reading I felt many of the responses were focused on the religious component of spirituality. When I think of spirituality, I think of the heart connection to the mind, and associate it with care and compassion. That said, I feel often that a "spiritual" curricular component would be of great worth to many in our learning community. The importance of the respectful treatment of self, others and the earth may not be specifically articulated in any one curricular area but it is integral to all that we do. Assisting students to understand that we are all a part of something greater than ourselves and that we need to strive to be our best in regard to ourselves, others and the earth is a huge task. This might also be called character education.

Sara 2: In my role as an educational administrator, I often look at the misdemeanors of my students and conceptualize their behaviors in terms of themselves and the bigger picture. Very often they can only consider their actions in the small picture and they often need exposure to the bigger picture effects of such behaviors and attitudes. I view this as spiritual work. Work with students, parents, teachers and myself, frankly, to maintain perspective and to try to attain what is the best resolution for ALL parties involved in situations that are a challenge. To attempt to bring people to work together in a win-win situation instead of a win-lose scenario which is so often more instinctive than the win-win situation, is ongoing. To have compassion, care and understanding for all parties, as opposed to only the self (and that includes me), is something which I try to instill in those people with whom I interact. This is a draining and rewarding aspect of the job.

Stider 1: It is interesting to see the common threads between the participants. I struggled to answer these two questions because they are deeply personal. However, I am encouraged by those common threads we share. In many ways administration is very lonely. Lonely, with hundreds of people at our door and because we must be strong for others. Others expect it of us and more importantly, we expect it of ourselves. And where can we go to build our strength but in a faith in a spirituality that sustains us.

Stider 2: I have finally had time to sit at the computer and read the responses that have been added since last time. I have been searching for articles on spirituality and education. There is such a sweep of material on spirituality but it is still taboo to talk about it at school (out loud). I found a term I quite like called "spiritual intelligence." Just like emotional intelligence, spiritual intelligence has certain characteristics that are evident in a person. From what I have read and believe, these things are not necessarily learned in Church or Bible study or at the equivalent in any religion. They may be innate and developed by study, reflection and life experiences. A Christian might say that it is the life experiences that are provided us which bring us closer to God. This is my personal experience and that has made me a student of spirituality. What I want to do now is apply spiritual intelligence to my work without crossing the line of taboo. And, I think it can be done.

Second Core Question: In what ways would this articulation best contribute to the development of effective leadership?

The second core question which guided sub-questions three and four was not forwarded to participants by e-mail. The researcher extracted the responses to this question from data, generated web-page discussions and all sub-questions. Three examples from the web-page discussion are 1. Beau stated that when openly sharing a painful story in his workplace, which resulted in his coworkers expressing their appreciation for him trusting them, he had articulated spirituality and acted effectively as a leader; 2. Luv suggested that when bringing people together into win-win situations and expressing compassion, care and understanding towards them, she had articulated spirituality and reflected effective leadership; and 3. Habs indicated that when showing respect for others and taking time to connect and build relationships with staff and students, he had articulated spirituality and been an effective leader.

After discussing the answers to the first set of questions, participants were given a second set of two questions to answer individually by e-mail. The following question was the sub-question three from the second set of questions.

Sub-question Three: What are some changes in leadership practices that have added enthusiasm and spirit to your leadership?

In response to sub-question three, seven (of ten) participants stated that affirming themselves and others added enthusiasm and spirit to their leadership roles. When responding, participants communicated more than one thread.

Affirming Self and Others

Airjordan: Changes in my leadership practices that have added enthusiasm and spirit to my leadership primarily include a willingness to step out and take risks. Earlier in my career I would have held back, but as my confidence built I was willing to take on more of a leadership role and put myself out "on the line" more. Some of the factors that influenced me included affirmation from individuals around me as well as a feeling, more spiritual than anything, that I was doing this for the benefit of students and teachers. This was quite a new feeling for me.

Beau: Changes in leadership practice that have added enthusiasm and spirit to my leadership are varied. I am assuming that in this question, "leadership" refers to the enthusiasm and spirit that have been brought to the organization. My assumption is based on my belief that when I am within an organization that is enthusiastic and spirited, I am that way also. I have found that positive energy is more effective than negative energy when dealing with others. It is far more productive for me to work with someone from a perspective of what they can offer rather than from a perspective of what they are not offering to the organization. As an example, a teacher who is struggling with constructivist theory on our staff is more effectively motivated when I review the things she is doing well, and teach her some ideas that she might try to enhance her practice – than if I simply told her that her current practices are not satisfactory.

Luv: It is my belief that everyone in the learning community should have the opportunity to feel like a meaningful and purposeful member of that community. That means being respected, appreciated, and valued. To affirm and reaffirm the contributions and worth of all members of the learning community these are a few of my / our practices: 1. I place beautiful and peaceful landscape images in the staff washrooms for all to enjoy. 2. My principal and I regularly provide muffins and doughnuts to our staff to show our appreciation. 3. Twice each term, we provide an appreciation luncheon. Once each term, we hold a social for staff. With my staff and students I practice "random acts of kindness" just because. These can include cards, flowers, candy, smiles, a thank-you, photos, bookmarks, and inspirational postcards. 4. Consistent and constant use of language which models respect for others and self is something both I and my principal employ.

Meiling: I take time for myself in solitude to renew my spirit so that others can be renewed. This includes closing my door for a short period in the day to read and reflect. Also I have uplifting music that I put in my CD player while working on the computer. I spend some time daily with staff and students providing encouragement and a word of praise. I try to be available and build in time to really listen to what staff are saying. I have a confidant at work who will listen and give feedback on difficult issues at work. This is important to me because it provides a person who is a sounding board and who is extremely discreet. I have let go of the having to perform; rather I do what I can and find ways to prevent burnout for myself and others. I model and practice what I desire others to do.

Habs: Effective leaders help light the fire of others and keep the fire burning even when others believe the fire has no more wood to burn. Effective leaders are caring for their followers, like Gandhi did with his organization. Leaders realize that the only way anyone will have success is that they need to engage everyone within the group. The success of the group is only as effective as its weakest link. Leaders no longer are the boss, to speak of, but are someone to help direct others in the right direction. In his book, *Caring Enough to Lead,* the author states leaders need to be servants of their followers. This would not have been seen by leaders on a regular basis in the past but leaders need to remember the group is everything and a leader is not everything.

Newday: People are unique and have diverse opinions that they hold dear. I respect people when I accept this and let go of my agenda and let them live out theirs. Systems also have a personality that is part of the collective sum of its parts. My influence is just one piece of the whole. I must continue to let go of the school and trust God that He is looking after the big picture.

Stider: A practice is to take a little more time with things. Sometimes someone will come in and they are obviously stressed and I will use whatever strategies I have to calm them down. Someone I know well, I will encourage to take a deep breath or I will go get them a glass of water to drink. I overtly remind everyone to relax. If it is a student, I start to talk about other things before we get to the point in somewhat of a Detective Columbo style. It puts people at ease when they talk about other things first. The term often used is to get "grounded". . . . Leadership practices that I have added include improving my listening. I'm not sure how it happened but I believe my increased awareness of the spiritual nature of each living being has helped me to honor the person as an individual. Therefore, it is easier to be intrigued by what they are saying and I find myself almost "studying" them. I have seen results in that people look at me and there is an eye-to-eye connection that tells both of us we are really communicating. Of course, there are times this doesn't happen. Our school environments are so disruptive.

Applying Faith

Five participants stated that applying faith to their leadership added enthusiasm and spirit to their leadership. Examples of participant responses regarding this thread include the following:

Airjordan: I would ask what would Christ do in this situation and experience the feeling that "if what I was doing was good He would be with me." And I did a number of things that were very risky and quite altruistic. I have never shared this with anyone before this study. Another aspect is the motivation that comes from my spirituality is me asking what would Christ do in this situation? What is best for the persons involved? It is more a private motivation. What is best between me and my God? A part of that is to give the world the best I have. I will be fully "spent" in the end, but I feel that is the way I want to live my life.

Beau: I find that if I pray, and study my beliefs, and remain in tune with my own spirit, I am a far more enthusiastic, compassionate and effective leader. When I am out of balance myself, I note that my organization and the people therein become out of balance too. I see the practice of shared leadership and self nurturing, both of which add enthusiasm and spirit to the "leadership within."

Meiling: I have a Bible study group that meets twice monthly. This is a group of people who care for me and provide a safe place to share needs and give insight for me spiritually. They pray for me and for difficult issues at work. This keeps me grounded beyond the tyranny of the immediate.

Newday: I believe that the main change that has assisted me in leadership is to let go and to let God. As a young principal I struggled to influence and change people and systems. I have since realized that my efforts are arrogant and often counterproductive.

Stider: Sometimes, I have to ground myself. I do this with my faith. I give my problems to God when they become too big for me. I try to trust that I will be given the strength to do the right thing for others and for myself. In short, prayer helps. Another practice is to model happiness and a positive attitude. It really is a choice and if others see you as a leader practicing it especially when things get tough; then this attitude gains credibility. Believing in God should make a person happy, not just pretending to be happy but really happy.

In addition to the above responses to sub-question three, three leadership strategies were identified by nine participants, as contributors to the development of their professional spirituality: 1. shared leadership; 2. increased accountability; and 3. vision and mission Additionally, these strategies were improved as a result of participants' spiritual awakenings. Representative examples of these strategies follow. For a complete presentation of participant responses.

Sharing Leadership, Increasing Accountability, Having a Vision and Mission

Four participants stated that sharing leadership added enthusiasm and spirit to their leadership. Airjordan said he encouraged staff "to carry the water buckets," as part of collaborative leadership; Armary pointed out the value of using his peers as "the first line of resource within the system;" Beau claimed "sharing the responsibilities of leadership is important because as people take ownership of the work, they become happier about doing it," and Luv asserted that having a "belief in a flatter leadership model [and] inviting input from all stakeholders in the learning community" resulted in increased enthusiasm and spirit within her leadership role.

Three other participants claimed that an increase in their accountability as leaders added enthusiasm and spirit of their leadership roles. Ayla said educators "are becoming more and more accountable to . . . school councils . . . communities and to the province (eg. testing results)" since school systems have progressed toward "site-based management," and leaders have started focusing "on being instructional leaders as opposed to being managers." Habs noted that aside from being managers, educational "leaders provide inspiration and hope for others which in turn builds enthusiasm and spirit in others." In a similar vein to Ayla and Hab's insights about increased accountability, Sara pointed out that "principals have shifted from being academic school leaders to being building managers and systems leaders as well as multi-skilled workers. During labor disputes [they] have assumed the role of secretaries, custodians, teachers, Special Education assistants, Early Childhood Educators, lunch supervisors, etc."

Two participants associated having a clear vision and mission with their spiritual development within their leadership. Armary noted "if an organization has a specific philosophy and style which has clear articulation and training, then the organization will flourish better." Comparable to Armary's acknowledgement, Sara stated that "articulating the vision and direction for the school" brings enthusiasm and spirit into the school setting.

Summary of Responses to Research Sub-question Three

All participants answered this question. The following text summarizes participants' responses to research sub-question three: "What are some changes in leadership practices that have added enthusiasm and spirit to your leadership?" Participants introduced more than one thread in their responses. The majority of the total 21 responses was associated with the thread "affirming self and others" which received seven (of 21) responses. Creating fruitful interaction and a team feeling through affirming self and others is a process related to establishing a clear vision and cultivating spirituality within the workplace (Vaill, 1998). Four (of ten) participants addressed the thread "applying faith." They suggested faith meant having a belief and trust in a God of their understanding. Other participants may have associated faith with believing in the strengths of their co-workers and thus affirming them, based on this faith. Applying faith to leadership assists leaders to clarify their mission and open their hearts to divine guidance (Janis, 2000).

The remaining three threads had a lower number of responses to sub-question three: sharing leadership, four (of 21); increasing accountability three (of 21), and having a vision and mission, two (of 21) had lower numbers of responses to sub question three: "sharing leadership" four (of 21); "increasing accountability," three (of 21) and; "having a vision and mission, two (of 21)." Although the number of responses to each thread varied, all threads are associated with changes in leadership practices that have added enthusiasm and spirit to participants' leadership. Applying faith and affirming self and others in the workplace may result in shared leadership, increased accountability and having a clear vision and mission. Therefore, as noted previously, these threads are synergistic, and each thread contributes to a more holistic dynamic (Wilber, 1996) and a multidimensional framework (Abbott, 1984) representing cultivation of spirituality within leadership.

Sub-question Four: What effective leadership practices would you recommend to other educational leaders?

After answering the third sub-question within the second set of questions, participants progressed to sub-question four. Ten participants contributed more than one response to the fourth sub-question. Within the total responses, seven leadership practice types were identified by participants. Six participants suggested that "engaging in team work," and six stated that "believing in self and others" are necessary for effective leadership; four suggested mentoring, three, continuous learning, two, being true to self, two, connecting with others, and two, having clear goals. The following text outlines six examples of how team work results in effective leadership.

Engaging in Team Work

Airjordan: Effective leadership practices that I would recommend to other educational leaders are largely reflected in my answer to the first question, since these have added enthusiasm and spirit to my leadership. These include being highly collaborative and one who involves others in decision making. I feel these are the most important since we need to involve others and gain their support when so many of our tasks seem so complex and demand so much of us. We need to empower others to carry forward our work. We need to trust people and not be too controlling.

Armary: Within the Education environment there are a number of opportunities that can be used. First there must be regular meetings within the peer group of administrators i.e., superintendents, principals, vice-principals, consultants and department heads. These would be more or less frequent depending on need. Within regions or families of schools there may be occasions for gatherings of leaders based on mutual interest, mutual concern or mutual responsibility. Such issues as sequence of skills in a specific curriculum, resource materials and how they are introduced, special education, violence and school safety or orientation programs to schools as the pupils progress.

Ayla: We often talk about believing in the ability of others but how do we demonstrate that belief on a daily basis? It is critical that as leaders, we delegate and then let go and keep our hands off (unless things are really falling apart). One of the most rewarding experiences that we have as leaders is to see the result after we have allowed someone to take something to a successful conclusion. There is real truth in the more power you give away, the more powerful you are.

Habs: Get to know the people within your organization. They are your greatest asset and without them you have very little. By creating this team, you will be able to move mountains. Do not get caught up in the power game. Power is for managers, not leaders. Power has no role in leadership. Power is only good to control others and will have no positive effects if you wish to become effective leaders. Take care of others like they are your family. This will help create a bond that never separates you, especially in difficult situations. Be honest and fair. Gandhi spoke only the truth and leaders need to remember this principle. Only expect of others that which you are willing to do.

Meiling: I fully believe in team work and team mentoring of one another. I maintain that the most effective practice is one of servant leadership where others are put ahead of personal agenda, although there is a balance. For example, sometimes things in my job must take priority and then I just explain to my staff that for the next day that particular issue must take precedence. Most of the time though I am conscious and proactive in dialoguing with staff and listening to them . . . at times challenging them with questions or encouraging personal reflection of educational practices.

Sara: We need to work with others to get the job done – communicate, delegate, lead by example, provide support and assistance, work as a team, and ensure that everyone feels valued and appreciated as a contributing team member.

Believing In Self and Others

Five participants viewed believing in self and others as necessary qualities for effective leadership.

Airjordan: I feel the ability to take risks is also an effective leadership characteristic. Also, the support of others who are willing to take risks is an important attribute. People are much more willing to follow someone who supports them. Without followers there can be no leader. A leader needs to be able to articulate what the group or organization is all about.

Ayla : As a superintendent (and formerly as a principal), other people turn to you often expecting you to have the answer. It is very important to help the person find his/her own answers and solutions. This choice can be detrimental to the development of the skills and in the confidence in our school leaders. All leaders and teachers must be actively engaged in all dialog and decision making. This ensures growth and learning for all. . . . In order to persuade successfully, a leader must develop a strong intuitive sense so that s/he can capitalize on the strengths of those around him/her in order to make things happen. Persuading someone to do something we want them to do must be done with genuine belief in the other person's ability and absolute respect. Honesty and integrity are significant qualities in order to be successful at persuasion.

Habs: Believe in each other. If you believe in each other them you will be able to move in the right direction. Trust others and do not fear others. Trust others for what they have to offer and do not fear others who may not have the same plan as yourself.

Meiling: I have goals for me each year as well as attend at least two outside workshops per year. This keeps me fresh and renewed. This keeps my practices from getting old and stale. This generates new ideas.

Newday: I let go and let God. Leaders are facilitators, not dictators. It is wonderful to realize that one's leadership can be best demonstrated by listening, advocating and enabling others to be the best they can be. Realize that every school has latent potential and skills necessary to produce the desired community. A good leader is able to assist change by wise and patient service to others. Let go, be authentic and serve the school community.

Sara: I believe that personal power is very important in running an effective school. If staff like and respect the principal they are much more willing to work co-operatively with the principal. . . . My former Director of Education advised principals that in these times of fast paced change, school autonomy, and accountability, principals need to "kiss ass, kick ass, and read everything." We don't have time to let change evolve; we must lead the change by knowing the people we work with and what we expect from them. We need to know how to motivate people who work with us and we must be the leaders of the cause.

Mentoring and Continuous Learning

Seven of the total responses to sub-question four were associated with the threads: mentoring: four (of ten) participants, and continuous learning, three (of ten) participants. Habs stressed the importance of walking the talk: "leaders need to do what they say they will do. . . . A leader is one who knows the way, goes the way and shows the way." Similarly, Luv stated "leading by example is the most effective leadership practice in any organization." She added "this means being compassionate, respectful and committed to one's leadership position." Meiling thought modelling was the "most effective practice" in leadership and Sara said "treating each other with respect and courtesy and setting a good example for staff must not be undervalued in its power to effect meaningful change; the relationships in a school are key in how successful it is."

Of the three participants who viewed continuous learning as a factor influencing effective leadership, Airjordan stated, "that a leader needs to be perceived as a learner and one who supports learning in the organization." Luv argued, "lifelong learning is not just a catch phrase but an integral part of being an effective teacher-learner-leader. If we want our students and staff to commit themselves to teaching and learning, we must demonstrate that ourselves." Sara pointed out that educators are "totally responsible and accountable for everything and everyone in [their] buildings; therefore [they] need to have a knowledge base through reading, networking, experience, [and] working with others."

Being True To Self, Connecting With Others, Having Clear Goals

Two (of ten) participants commented about the value of being true to one's self in order to practise effective leadership. Stider said, "It is more important to be true to your beliefs even if you have to use "I" language." Being true to self involves sheltering one's "soul with experiences that build community, [such as] reading, meditating, singing, praying, going to church." Luv believed that having balance in one's life and "looking after oneself is an important precursor to being able to be an effective leader."

Two (of ten) participants argued that connecting with others helped them to be effective leaders. Luv stated "making the time to connect with individuals, not only when difficulties arise, is a worthwhile investment of one's time. This relates to parents, students and staff." Sara claimed effective leadership involves determining where people are at, what motivates them, and what the best way to get them on board with the program. Her claim suggests effective leadership is associated with manipulating staff, which may or may not be perceived as a spiritual approach to leadership.

Two other participants stated that having clear goals encourages effective leadership. Airjordan suggested that educators "need to be setting goals and constantly looking for how [they] can do things better." Ayla stated that effective leadership involves aligning "the heart and mind to work together towards a goal."

Summary of Responses to Research Sub Question Four

All participants answered this question. The following text summarizes ten participants' responses to sub question four: "What effective leadership practices would you recommend to other educational leaders"? Of the total 25 responses to this question, the highest number of responses were associated with the two threads, "engaging in teamwork" six (of 25) and "believing in self and others" six (of 25). Thus, responses affirm that effective leadership involves moving beyond one's ego (Chee, 2002) and recognizing the spark of the divine within oneself and others (Bohac Clark, 2002).

Four (of 25) responses were connected with the thread "mentoring others" and three, with "continuous learning." This insight is consonant with literature that suggests that to mentor spiritual leadership, a person needs to reflect personal growth, kindness towards peers and a healthy working environment, which assist educators to be in tune with their hearts (Palmer, 1998). The fewest responses were associated with the threads: "being true to self," two (of 25); "connecting with others," two (of 25) and "having clear goals," two (of 25). These responses support literature (Arieti & Wilson, 2003; Caroll & Tober, 1999; Curtis & Eldredge, 1997; Ocker, 1999) indicating that introducing a "heart-centred" approach to leadership will renew educational systems for the betterment of humanity.

Each thread represents a valid segment of a multidimensional framework (Bateson, 1994) related to signifying and cultivating spirit within leadership. Thus, in addition to the two threads with the highest number of responses, the other threads: mentoring others, continuing learning, being true to self, connecting with others and having clear goals are synergistic in signifying and cultivating spirit within the workplace. Thus, the interconnection of threads, related to sub-question four support Wilber's (1996) statement that the whole is greater than the sum of parts.

Results From Participants in Discussion About Second Set of Questions

After answering the second set of two questions, participants had the opportunity to dialog on-line with a web-page, where all their responses were posted. Four participants did postings for the second discussion. The following text is their postings on the web-page.

Stider There was once a boy who the teacher recommended for retention. I reviewed his file and as I had been quite involved in his case for the second time in my long career endorsed the recommendation. The parent trusted us and her son repeated grade six. I do not really think retention works past grade one but that is a personal bias. This boy once again had an unsuccessful school year as he was very unmotivated and now alienated from his friends who had moved on to the next grade. I had an opportunity to place this boy in a vocational program so once again I reviewed his file and recommended this placement. The parent agreed and since then, fortunately, this student has experienced success. The whole process had a profound effect on me that has made a "spiritual" difference. I realized the authority and trust that had been vested in me as a principal and how my decisions could have a profound impact on the individuals I work with. Although I had sincerely worked in the best interests of that student, I connected with an essence of his life and his spirit and what was right for him. I knew that important decisions are best made on a deep connection with the person it affects. Although this was not a "moment" in time, it was an epiphany of the true nature of our work. The spirit is a part of everything we do.

In Beau's two postings, which followed Stider's, he expressed his connection with other participants which gave him a sense of hope.

Beau 1: I have been reading our responses to questions three and four, and am interested and delighted to see the similar ways we have all responded – especially as we do not even know each other. This gives me hope for the work we do as leaders in education. Reading your responses makes me want to meet you in person! We could have a great conversation!

Beau 2: Here in Alberta, we are currently experiencing what will soon be horrific times in public education, and great challenges to educational leadership. It makes one really focus on "uplifting" the organization, but also makes it difficult to find the "right" time to challenge practice. Does anybody have any suggestions?

Airjordan responded to Beau's postings.

Airjordan I agree that there are many similarities. The most common appears to be the importance of personal growth and the development of coping mechanisms. The importance of listening, of being collaborative and of having an optimistic attitude appear central. The organizational structure one works in was also mentioned as an important component. The one difference appears to be in how principals view their role; are they managers or curriculum leaders within the school?

In his posting, Armary relates to the other participants' abilities to practise spiritual leadership by following their inner calling to help others transform.

Armary As I was reading the material presented by you, I was reflecting on the significance of the work each of you are doing and could capture the profound effect you are having on education and the equally profound effect your work is having on you. The Education profession has obviously been impacted by the philosophies and learning theories of the society in which we live. Much of what drives the theories of today are the secular philosophies of humanist psychologists. Each of us has within us the ability, skill and talent to become "self actualized" so long as we learn the proper attitudes to drive us on to this state of "self fulfillment." What I see in the respondents who have answered the questions in this exercise is another understanding of "self" and of the students whom we serve. That is the call to "transformation" and not just "fulfillment." As spiritual beings there is another dimension beyond what is recognised by secular humanism . . . the spiritual. This explains for me the joy you each seem to find in helping others on their journey. It also addresses the humility we experience knowing that even though we know we have made a contribution the affect on the student and those with which we work is always greater than the contribution we have made. We are instruments in a process which transcends us. I have always liked the quote of George Bernard Shaw, "I am not a teacher, but a fellow traveller who points the way ahead. Ahead of me as well as you."

Fewer than half, four (of ten) participants, contributed to the above discussion in response to the second set of questions. Stider made one posting, Beau two, Airjordan one and Armary one.

Researcher Follow-up by Telephone to Second Set of Questions

As a consequence of a lack of participation in the follow-up web-page discussion, I telephoned all ten participants, but only took notes on the dialog with the six inactive participants. The four active participants were thanked for their contributions. A common response to being questioned about not participating in the on-line discussion was that they were too busy at work or dealing with the politics, related to Bill 12 to engage in an on-line discussion. Four inactive participants in the web-page discussion were from Alberta and the other two lived in Ontario. The following text is taken from the researcher's notes.

Ayla: I'm too busy to go on line and participate. I am tied up with the politics behind a school closure. In response to the questions, spirituality to me is mainly a sense of presence.

Luv: In response to Bill 12, the staff is downtrodden and tired. They are trying to make their voices be heard. The dreary long winter is also bringing the staff's spirits down. I have been too busy and tired to go on line.

Newday Since Bill 12, the staff morale is low. It is killing the school spirit. Staff feel betrayed by government. People at work are frustrated and the atmosphere does not feel positive. This has been tiring me out.

Sara: I haven't had time to participate in the discussion. It is report-card time. But here are my thoughts about the research questions: we need to differentiate between religion and spirituality. Right now, in the name of religion, there are many wars going on. Also, in the school system, we need to take some course content out and leave time for interaction and connection. We have an "overloaded" system leaving both students and teachers frustrated. Consequently, there is a ripple effect of this frustration in the community. Educators are expected to be "all things to all people." This is what kills spirituality within schools.

Habs: I haven't been on-line because I don't have a computer at home and I am on a sabbatical. Also, I am getting ready to take my kids to Disney World.

Meiling: The work load has been heavy and staff morale has been down, since Bill 12 was implemented.

Spirituality: Unconventional Means of Articulation

During the data collection related to the study, all participants suggested that spirituality is an experience that exceeds conventional ways of expression. This finding supports literature (eg. Vaill, 1998; Walsch, 1995) that indicates only using a linguistic definition to express spirituality may sound artificial or preachy and therefore be misunderstood. For the sake of this study, participants forwarded unconventional expressions of spirituality by e-mail: poems, photographs, song lyrics and affirmations, which they claimed had a spiritual influence on them. For examples of participants' unconventional means of articulation, check the following text.

Airjordan: Attached is a picture of my first granddaughter . . . and her mother. The admiring look on her mother's face says it all. When I get a little tired or discouraged I can just click on this picture and things are looking hopeful again. A baby is truly a little miracle, and gives my faith a boost.

Armary: When I reflect on spirituality, I think of a pregnant woman; it is life within life; one is pregnant with God . . . with spirit. The amazing spiritual leader Jesus came to earth through a pregnant woman. Spirituality is the coming together of our divine and human nature. We are on a spiritual journey to be transformed and divinised into God-like beings. We are spiritual beings having a human experience.

Ayla: It is a song by Whitney Houston: "The Greatest of All" It's a song that is very special to me. . . . It speaks volumes about being a person and about kids . . . and our responsibility to them. The opening is, I believe the children are our future; teach them well and let them lead the way; show them all the beauty they possess inside. Give them a sense of pride to make it easier. . . .

Beau: As Einstein stated, "great spirits encounter violent opposition from mediocre minds." This is one of my favorite quotes I think about when I am being challenged about taking a spiritual approach to leadership.

Habs: On my refrigerator, I have this quote as my spiritual reminder. It states, "you don't get to choose how you're going to die or when; you can only decide how you're going to live." This quote reminds me to live in the moment and be thankful for what I have now, as I can't know what will happen in the future.

Luv: This John Donne poem makes me think of the importance of connection with others and team work: "No man is an island, entire of itself; every man is a piece of the continent, a part of the main. If a clod be washed away by the sea, Europe is the less, As well, as if a promontory were, As well as if a manor of thy friend Or thine own, were. Any man's death diminished me, Because I am involved in mankind, And therefore, never send to know for whom the fell tolls: It tolls for thee."

Meiling: Certain songs get me in touch with my spirituality. Some of my music that I listen to is a CD called *Miracles*. One of my all time favorite songs is "As the Deer." The song goes "As the deer pants for living water, So my soul longeth after you. You alone are my heart's desire and I long to worship you. You alone are my strength, my shield. To you alone may my spirit yield. You alone are my strong high tower and I long to worship you."

Newday: Let go and let God is my daily affirmation.

Sara: The northern lights remind me of my spirituality. As stated on a purchased card, designed by Marion Storm, the artist who sketched this painting of the Northern Lights "I live in a reality bounded by the limitations of time and space. There is however, a magical peace in all of us where we become as children enveloped in the fantasy of stars. Where the stars are the limitations is the place I have found myself and have usually transferred those same feelings."

Stider: This photo of mine gets me in touch with my spirituality whenever I look at the forest and the mountains in it. It makes me think that great or small, God loves us all. In one breath of nature, spirituality can ground and inspire us.

Summary of Chapter

In Chapter four, the study findings were presented. Organized by profiles of participants, responses to the research questions, and two follow-up webpage discussions, the chapter was divided into 11 sections. To indicate contributions made by ten participants who answered the questions, examples of individual responses were provided for each section.

The ten participants ranged in ages 31 to 65 and all had worked or were working in administrative positions in educational leadership in Ontario or Alberta school systems. When answering the first core question "How are the spiritual experiences of educational leaders understood and articulated?" six participants suggested spiritual experiences are not clearly understood or articulated in words and four indicated actions express one's spirituality better than words. Three (of 5) participants who answered sub-question one in the context of professional spiritual experiences, articulated that they felt a connection with others, the community and the world; three (of 5) who responded to the same question in the context of personal spiritual experiences, stated that God, self and nature had influenced their peak experiences.

In response to sub-question two, all participants agreed that viewing others as equals was their strongest moral belief. In the follow-up web-page discussion from the first set of questions, the ten participants contributed. Their involvement fulfilled the study action research objective to move beyond muted discourses about spirituality. From the first set of questions and the web-page discussion, the researcher extracted responses that addressed the second core question "in what ways would articulating the spiritual experiences of educational leaders contribute to the development of effective leadership?" For example, during the web-page discussion, one participant stated treating others respectfully contributes to effective leadership.

In response to the third sub-question, seven participants indicated that "affirming self and others" is a change in their leadership practices that added enthusiasm and spirit to their leadership. In response to the fourth sub-question, six participants associated "engaging in team work," and six connected "believing in self and others" with effective leadership practices.

Fewer than half of the participants contributed to the second on-line webpage follow-up discussion. As a consequence of a lack of participation, the researcher telephoned the six inactive participants and took notes. Participants stated that being busy with accountability issues within their workplaces influenced their inactivity.

After introducing participants' reasons for being inactive on the final webpage discussion, the chapter ends with participants' introductions of an unconventional means of articulation of spirituality that added enthusiasm and spirit to their leadership.

5
Discussion: Connecting Key Concepts, Threads and Themes

Within this fifth chapter, findings are discussed and woven into a synergism composed of key concepts, threads, and themes. The overarching key concepts found within the literature established a foundation for this synergism: 1. muting discourses about spirituality within educational systems, 2. examining moral issues within educational values, and 3. shifting paradigms affecting educational leadership. An analysis of common threads found within the data precedes the three emergent themes: the thematic sections are as follows: 1. awakening spirituality within self, 2. signifying spirituality within the workplace, and 3. cultivating spirit within leadership practices. A schemata for cultivating spirit within leadership practices at work is provided as a conceptual framework, identifying how participants have cultivated spirit in their workplaces after their innate spirituality was awakened and signified. A concluding summary is provided.

Examining Participants' Spiritual Experiences Through a Triangulated Lens

Applying a triangulated methodology to this study was an effective research approach to elicit professional and personal spiritual experiences of ten educational leaders. The method was congruent within feminist, phenomenological and action research paradigms that helped guide the research. Examining spirituality from the participants' own standpoints in their everyday lives, as suggested by Smith (1992), a feminist, and Schutz (1970a), a phenomenologist, helped to heighten awareness of how the innate, noetical and relational influences on participants' views of spirituality, related to people, values and systems. As noted in Chapter Four, participants adopted standpoints that a person's spirituality is innate, inherent and natural. For example, Armary and Newday adopted the standpoint that spirituality is innate; Airjordan and Luv each took a noetical stand that people's spiritual development is associated with continuous learning; and Meiling and Habs embraced the relational standpoint that building relationships and being positive mentors fosters spiritual leadership. Thus, spirituality has internal and external components.

The findings indicate how ten educational leaders perceived their own experiences of spirituality within the context of their moral interactions with others, and leadership practices within their employment systems. Personal realities, discussed in on-line interviews, manifested how they had conceptually awakened, signified, and cultivated spirituality within themselves and at their workplaces. Phenomenology aims to describe the ways the world presents its truths through an individual's awareness (Abram, 1996). Thus, whatever was important to the specific topic addressed in the research questions was subjectively viewed by participants as being "motivationally relevant" (Schutz, 1973). This viewpoint indicates the leaders' perceptions of spirituality were directed by relevancies they had interpreted as being part of their reality (Sergiovanni, 1996).

While some participants spoke about how communing with nature awakened their spirituality, others claimed they cultivated their spirituality throughout their lives, with prayer, meditation and continuous learning. Their acknowledgements suggest their notions of spirituality are constructed from past interactions and kept active by current ongoing interaction. This standpoint coincides with theoretical paradigms (e.g., Mead, 1982; Schutz, 1970a; Smith, 1979) associated with phenomenological and feminist perspectives of research, as discussed in Chapter Three. During the interviews, participants' understandings of how particular experiences had awakened, signified and cultivated their spirituality introduced fields of consciousness that affected their viewpoints about leadership. For example, Ayla's response to sub-question one suggests that the prospect of getting a new job affected her field of consciousness and standpoint about spirituality within leadership. As noted in Chapter Four, she claimed this professional experience resulted in her feeling "totally engaged, excited and alive." On the other hand, Beau's field of consciousness and standpoint related to how spirituality was influenced by a personal experience of falling in love and then facing the dark time of a severed relationship.

Participants answered questions by directly responding by e-mail to the researcher; they had not reviewed one another's responses prior to making their own contributions. This interview approach is a phenomenological/feminist method of research (Schutz, 1979; Smith, 1992) which can raise participants' awareness of the topic being studied, as suggested by Maguire (2001). For example, during the research process, Airjordan, Ayla, Armary and Sara became aware that they needed to operate with their hearts as well as minds to be an effective leaders.

Their shared experiences support literature (Ludema, Cooperrider & Barrett, 2001) which indicates appreciative inquiry, within action research, encourages conversations of possibility. Asking positive questions promotes transformative dialog, giving participants a sense of hope and optimism about their futures. During this inquiry process, they had opportunities to rethink former ideologies that had shaped reality, and to formulate fresh perspectives about truth. For example, Armary pointed out the value of being true to the inner voice of love, rather than power and authority; Beau stated that without having the ability to formulate relationships of trust and care, leaders cannot be effective; Airjordan claimed he had not shared specific spiritual experiences before this study; Ayla indicated the research questions forced her to go deep and reflect. Findings such as these indicate a feminist/phenomenological-/action approach to inquiry was suitable for this study of leadership and spirituality.

The language participants applied to articulating their spiritual experiences, such as Armary's mention of "enlightenment, conversion," and Hab's description, "lighting the soul," demonstrated their means of attempting to make sense of their spiritual worlds. When addressing how they cultivated spiritual leadership, they appeared to be presenting "recipes," as described by Schutz (1973) earlier, to understand and validate their own and others' spiritual life experiences. For example, one ingredient of spiritual leadership that all participants agreed as an essential component of spiritual leadership in workplaces was "treating everyone as equals." This value meant showing dignity and respect towards co-workers. As well, teamwork and affirming self and others were viewed as basic ingredients of spiritual leadership. These components of leadership also signify a humanistic and compassionate approach to leadership or a means to keep the profit margin topmost. Therefore, teamwork and affirming others cannot be exclusively perceived as components of spiritual leadership.

Furthermore, as an inquiry action approach to research, in the follow-up web-page discussions, participants had opportunities to review one another's responses and dialog with other educators involved in the study. This on-line opportunity to share spiritual experiences may have enabled participants to contemplate their "beyond humanness" and experience different ways of being together as a community (Reason & Bradbury, 2001). For example, one participant praised a fellow participant for her compassion and understanding in the workplace and another educator thanked all fellow participants for sharing their insights about spirituality. Participants had opportunities to connect with other educational leaders and learn about their perspectives on spiritual leadership, which could be perceived as a means to engage in cooperative relationships. Presenting an opportunity for participants to dialog fulfilled part of the study mandate, which was to move educators beyond muted discourses about spirituality into sharing their experiences in ways that may have cultivated further spiritual development within their leadership practices. Conversely, the choice of internet may have discouraged expressions of spirituality, as was suggested in the follow-up web-page discussion in response to the second set of questions.

During the follow-up web-page discussions, participants moved beyond silencing their discourses about spirituality within a professional role when they dialoged on-line about their personal experiences and responded to one another's postings. This approach to data collection enabled these educators to share their spiritual experiences at their preferred times, without having scheduled meetings. As noted by Pyrch (1998b), such an approach to inquiry action research enables participants to create a kinship wherein they feel comfortable sharing experiences both from their hearts and their minds. An immediacy in communication appears to create a sense of nearness amongst participants (van Manen, 2002).

As noted by Hawley (1995), relating stories of spiritual experiences is the one way individuals can understand them. In the web-page discussions, Beau shared an experience of crying in the presence of co-workers; Meiling revealed she was working on her personal growth by setting aside meditative times to pray within the school setting. Additionally, three Ontario participants voiced a strong interest in breaking their anonymity and having the opportunity to meet fellow research participants face-to-face, to share more spiritual experiences; these three people met with me and each other for coffee, after the data collection was complete. They reviewed some findings and agreed to continue dialoguing with one another about spirituality, by e-mail. In addition, three Alberta participants met me for coffee, after the study concluded and discussed the inquiry process.

In the discussion following the first set of questions, all participants contributed postings; furthermore, they commenced a web-page interaction that resulted in multiple postings by seven of the ten participants. Their postings addressed the first set of questions and the second core question. Participants' responses suggested that awakening spirituality involved being in close community with others, experiencing continuous learning, and being competent when handling a situation; whereas, signifying their spirituality was related to assisting others to actively reach for the stars; and cultivating their spirituality involved taking care of their own health; and, spending time in prayer or meditation.

Although fewer than half of the participants four (of tem) participated in the web-page discussion following the second set of questions, their contributions supported the validity of applying an appreciative inquiry action methodology to the study. Stider commenced the on-line dialog with a heartfelt story about a process to assist a student, which resulted in an epiphany experience that made a spiritual difference in her leadership practices. Beau responded to her posting by stating her story gave him hope for professional development as leaders in education. Airjordan stated that personal growth and development of coping mechanisms can be gained by dialog with peers; and Armary stated that reading others' postings led him to reflect on the significant role of an educator. The discussion enabled some participants to tell stories and reflect about their life experiences, which may have generated new insights about their leadership roles (Mishler, 1986; Schratz & Walker, 1998).

Reasons for Attrition

Participants claimed busyness in their workplaces was the major reason they did not continue engaging more in on-line dialog during phase two of data collection. Three participants from Alberta, Luv, Newday and Meiling, cited Bill 12, the Alberta Government "Education Services Settlement Act," as a major barrier to participation in the on-line discussion. During the researcher's telephone follow-ups, they made reference to the Alberta Teacher's Association President's statement that "this Bill is an assault on the civil liberties of teachers and has created a chill in classrooms and staff rooms and a climate of fear and uncertainty in the province of Alberta." They claimed the effects of Bill 12 were causing the workplace to become "dispirited" and full of fear. Despite her anonymity in the study, one participant asked not to be quoted by the researcher, for fear of being discovered, imprisoned or fined. This participant did not participate in the on-line discussion. Three other participants said they felt reluctant to dialog about spirituality, since the new Bill was initiated. They indicated their freedom of speech had been reduced by the new piece of legislation and suggested the "spirit of teaching" had been crushed in their schools since its initiation.

One Alberta participant, Habs, did not address Bill 12; on sabbatical, he felt distant from the issue. In addition to acknowledging the effects of Bill 12, Luv also attributed her lack of on-line participation to seasonal conditions lowering her spirit. The remaining two Ontario participants, who did not engage in on-line dialog, said they were preoccupied by the politics of a school closure and preparing report cards. These observations suggest participants experienced increased professional accountability pressures, which deterred them from further participation in the study. Therefore, this finding is contrary to data that suggested having more accountability within the educational system was related to cultivating spirituality within the workplace. It is possible that at another time in the year, retention in the final component of a research study might be higher.

Analysing Key Concepts Guiding Research Questions

Responses to the first core research question "How are the spiritual experiences of educational leaders understood and articulated by educators?" presented in the first set of questions, were connected with the key concept, "muting discourses about spirituality within educational systems." Findings indicate that life experiences and beliefs are determinants affecting how spirituality is signified, which supports Tisdell's (2003) findings. Also, the threads "not clear by words" and "articulate primarily by action" reflect Albright and Ashbrook's (2001); L'Engles' (1997) and Walsch's (1995) perspectives about some challenges faced when attempting to verbally articulate spirituality. Four participants' responses indicated spirituality is signified primarily by actions. Associated with the same key concept, sub-question one resulted in the common threads, "professional experiences," "personal experiences," "connection: others, community, world," and connection: "God, self, nature." These threads demonstrated that participants' spirituality had been awakened by professional and personal experiences that involved connections with their internal and external worlds. Findings reinforce literature (e.g., Fox, 1995; Glazer, 1999; Palmer, 1999a; Pearsal, 1998) that addresses the relationship of spirituality to re-awakening the sacred spark within the self and connecting with the experience of having heart.

The main threads associated with participants' responses to sub-question two were guided by the key concept "moral issues within educational leadership." The threads: 1. viewing others as equals, 2. practising servant leadership 3. having personal accountability, and 4. having positive mentoring exemplify ways that spirituality can be awakened within self, signified within the workplace, and cultivated within leadership practices. These findings support the literature (e.g., Dallaire, 2001; D. Jones, 1995; Vaill, 1998) that indicate spiritual conditions, such as viewing others as equals, relate to leaders' capacities to be moral agents by re-thinking and re-examining basic values within themselves and their workplaces.

Participants' postings on the web-page discussion addressed the second core question guiding the second set of questions: "In what way would this articulation best contribute to the development of effective leadership?" It appeared their articulation of spirituality assisted them in acknowledging their own and each other's ways of awakening, signifying and cultivating spirituality, personally and professionally. Their postings suggested that cultivating spirituality within their workplaces enabled them to be more effective leaders.

Answers to sub-question three, shaped by the key concept "shifting paradigms affecting educational leadership," had five connecting threads within the responses, 1. affirming self and others; 2. applying faith; 3. sharing leadership; 4. increasing accountability, and 5. having a vision and mission. These threads suggest how spirituality can be awakened within self, signified within the workplace and cultivated within leadership practices. Responses to sub-question four, within the same key concept, had seven threads representing participants' responses. They include, 1. engaging in team work; 2. believing in self and others; 3. mentoring others; 4. continuing learning; 5. being true to self; 6. connecting with others, and 7. having clear goals. These threads are associated with ways spirit may be cultivated within the workplace. Emergent themes from the data were woven from "threads" associated with the process of awakening, signifying and cultivating spirituality, personally and professionally.

Emergent Themes From Data Base

Phenomenological themes are "structures of experience" (van Manen, 1990); part of analysing data is identifying these structures of experiences. Analysis of data in this study resulted in three emergent themes: 1. awakening spirituality within self; 2. signifying spirituality within the workplace, and 3. cultivating spirit within leadership practices at work. These three prominent "structures of experience" noted in the data were cited as themes connecting threads introduced by participants' responses reported in Chapter Four. As explained in association with previous heart graphs, a heart-shaped image may be used to conceptualise triangulated relationships. When adapted in the context of spiritual experiences, heart graph no. 6 symbolizes a synergistic triangulated relationship between the following emergent themes: awakening spirituality within self, signifying spirituality within the workplace and cultivating spirituality within leadership practices. After awakening spirituality within self, a leader can signify spirituality within the workplace and cultivate spirituality within leadership practices. The flow lines on the graph indicate spirituality needs to be awakened before a person can signify of cultivate spirituality. However, signifying, cultivating and re-awakening spirituality is an on-going cycle.

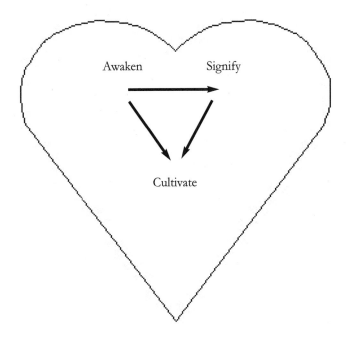

Heart graph No. 6: Triangulated emergent themes from data analysis

Awakening Spirituality Within Self

Data uphold Park's (2001) standpoint that representational knowledge involves participants re-describing or re-presenting the object of knowing, which were their peak spiritual experiences. Also, the antecedent event of having a peak experience could lead to the probable consequences of signifying and cultivating spirituality within the workplace. Experiences associated with "awakening spirituality within self" varied amongst all ten participants, who presented them within the context of peak spiritual experiences. Airjordan associated his spiritual awakening with becoming more Christlike, positive and creative; he was spiritually awakened when he allowed his Christian consciousness to guide his behavior. For example, if confronted with a tough decision or judgment call, he would question what Christ would do in the same situation. Airjordan also described a beautiful outdoor nature scene that awakened him to the divine presence of God and a feeling of connection with his students.

Armary used the terms: "enlightenment," "conversion," "inspiration," "transcendence," "covenant" and "communion" to describe a spiritual awakening. He believed that to be spiritually awakened, people need to be true to an inner voice of love for all, rather than live with an emphasis on external power and authority. As a swimming instructor, it was difficult to teach his students how to swim until he started empowering them to learn. When he stopped being authoritative, his students more deeply internalized their learning, which awakened him to a fresh way of teaching.

Ayla was awakened spiritually as a result of life crises, such as a family death and divorce. These experiences forced her to question her religious upbringing and to delve deeper into her own spiritual core. Additionally, she experienced another spiritual awakening when she went on a significant personal journey before applying for a new job. The journey was a review of where her life had been and where it was meant to go and involved asking reflective questions.

Beau stated that falling in love with someone and later having the relationship severed were both peak spiritual experiences. During those times of being spiritually awakened, he became more intricately connected with self, gained a sense of moral integrity and saw amazing potential in self and others.

Habs claimed that helping students achieve something they once thought was unreachable gave him a peak spiritual experience. Additionally, he referred to having his spirituality heightened while communing with nature on a sailing trip with students and observing their enlightenment.

Luv's peak spiritual experiences were associated with interactions with her students during bus supervision in the mornings. Walking amongst a joyful group and chatting and joking with them was magical and spiritual for her. Additionally, working on her own "interiority" to maintain balance within her life, enabled her to become spiritually attuned.

Meiling addressed peak experiences, related to continuous learning, which she viewed as spiritually uplifting. Gaining new knowledge and studying with others enabled her to feel connected with peers and inspired her to explore alternative paths in education. She felt "very engaged, almost euphoric" when acknowledging oneness between herself and others while engaging in a learning process.

Newday's spiritual awakening was associated with a heart-felt experience of being in close community with friends and with students. It was a sense of having common goals and unity that engaged his spirit; the unity he felt assisted him to lift his facades and be vulnerable. Thus, it enabled him to be in touch with his heart.

Sara associated her successful ventures with peak spiritual experiences. After investing time and energy into something, which moved her beyond feeling anger, frustration, hopelessness and despair, she became spiritually uplifted. Feeling the energy and commitment of others involved and noting the perfection of everything working in harmony triggered spiritual awakenings for her.

Stider identified a sense that God had been at work in her, as being a peak spiritual experience. This sacredness was sensed when she became aware she had made a difference in someone's life. She also associated the death of a family member to experiencing a spiritual awakening.

Throughout the interview period and following the on-line dialog, participants appeared to reflect a belief that their spirituality was not a choice, a dynamic which was reported in the literature (Griffin, 1998; Purpel, 1989; Rolheiser, 1999; Simington, 2003). Three participants suggested that everyone is spiritual by nature and not by any decision of their own. These findings support literature indicating all humans have an innate spirituality that can be awakened (e.g., Fox, 1995; Janis, 2000; Palmer, 1998; Pearce, 2002; Urantia Foundation 1999).

In the study, ten participants described different ways they had become sensitised to having had spiritual awakenings. Here are six examples: 1. acknowledging a sacred presence in self, others and nature (Bohac Clark, 2002; Fox, 1995; Glazer, 1999); 2. being a part of a community (Curtis & Eldredge, 1997; Janis, 2000; Ulich, 1945); 3. being in love and expressing love (Fox, 1991; MacDonald, 2000; Simington, 2003); 4. operating with heart and mind (Janis, 2000, Simington, 2003; Vaill, 1998); 5. connecting with self and others (Chee, 2002; Tisdell, 2003); and 6. maintaining balance and harmony in one's life (Fox, 1991;Vaill, 1998). As well, three participant suggested a person who has been spiritually awakened will have "moral integrity," which guides them to act with honesty, justice and respect towards others (Urantia Foundation, 1999). These findings support literature (Holmes, 2003; Rolheiser, 1999) that indicates spirituality does not have a standard definition or developed language; data also suggest that spirituality and morals have a synergistic relationship (Dallaire, 2001; Thom, 1993). Although spirituality is inherent, it is also latent until it awakens to sacred truths. Once a person's spirituality has been awakened their moral leadership and values could be effected.

Literature (e.g., Rolheiser, 1999; Simington, 2002) and data suggest that spirituality is predetermined by the essence of being human. However, studies about spirituality can serve to enlighten the field of educational administration by encouraging educators to dialog about spirituality and by proposing fresh holistic leadership models. Outlining alternative leadership models that reflect an effective approach to leadership gives educators an opportunity to alter and enhance their approaches to leadership.

When referring to peak experiences, participants addressed "spirituality" in the contexts of their innate, noetical and relational worlds. Therefore, their peak experiences involved reflective (innate), learning (noetical), and social (relational) practices that had a spiritually uplifting effect.

Participants addressed how innate peak experiences involved connections with God, nature and self, their noetical encounters, with continuous learning, and their relational insights with connections with others, communities and the world. These data upholds other research (Fox, 1995; Yob, 1994) that suggest continuous learning and a strong sense of connection with self and others are major elements of one's spirituality. Findings also support Tisdell's (2003) study, which reported that educators' shared experiences often reflected hope, healing, or affirmation during "meaning-making" moments that were times of "significant learning." Participants' peak experiences were perceived as meaning-making moments resulting in them gaining new insights about spirituality.

Closely examining participants' accounts of spirituality, looking for common patterns and questioning how their notions of spirituality were awakened is using a phenomenological/feminist approach to analysis (Schutz, 1973). It helps identify major influences on the awakening of spirituality within these leaders. Experiencing an innate sense of knowing God, falling in love, having a life crisis, helping students excel, and communing with nature were all ways in which participants' senses of spirituality were awakened. These experiences prefaced their signifying spirituality within the workplace. Further, participants' views of spirituality were influenced by family interactions, other people's persuasions, along with personal educational backgrounds and religious beliefs; these influences also affected their approaches to signifying spirituality within their workplaces (Tisdell, 2003). However, as noted by Myss (2001), a true spiritual awakening manifests itself as an urge to be of service to others, an action that the data in this study supports.

Exploring my peak experiences during inquiry

For me, peak innate, noetical, and relational spiritual experiences occurred during my literature review, data collection and analysis process when – 1. I was discerning multiple perspectives of spirituality from the literature and participants' responses to the questions, 2. facilitating and observing the follow-up web-page discussion, and 3. witnessing the literature and data evolving from key concepts initially, to threads and then to emergent themes. I sensed that – 1. I became more in tune with my Creator, 2. I acknowledged that my heart and mind were functioning synergistically, and 3. I was engaged in healthier, more nurturing relationships. My research journey demonstrated that the triangulated methodology selected for this study about spirituality emerged into a holistic mind-and-heart centred paradigm for spiritual inquiry. The inquiry process enabled me to become more spiritually attuned, balanced, and accountable, and enabled me to move beyond muted discourses about spirituality within my personal leadership practices.

Signifying Spirituality Within the Workplace

Data support Park's (2001) perspective on relational knowledge; this type of knowing plays a major role in strengthening community and gaining personal insights. During the interviews and web-page discussions, participants suggested spirituality could be signified by connecting with others through affirmative actions, which supports Park's (2001) standpoint that "relational knowledge grows out of active communal life" (p. 86). In congruence with other literature (L'Engle, 1997;Ulrich, 1945;Vaill, 1998), six (of ten) participants addressed challenges they faced when attempting to articulate "spirituality" exclusively verbally while in the workplace.

One participant stated spirituality is mainly signified by actions and gestures. Another participant suggested that before using the term "spirituality," a person needs to clearly define what spirituality means by asking if it is a religion, or a belief in a higher being or something divine. Other participants indicated that spirituality is too broad and narrow to define in words; spiritual experiences are private; there is no place for spirituality when one is a school administrator. Although spirituality cannot be denied, conversations about spirituality should be kept among those one trusts. Spirituality is a silent influence often mistaken for religion. Another participant stated that she can assist people with spiritual development, whether she calls it that or something else. These findings support literature which suggest "spiritual dissonance" and "muted discourses about spirituality" are issues faced by educational leaders within public school systems (Dallaire, 2001; Griffin, 1988; Guzie, 1995).

Data also suggest spirituality can be tacit and thus, may be expressed in actions, rather than words. In the study four (of 10) participants did not support literature (Fox, 1995; Hawley, 1995; Stewart, 2000; Yob, 1994) that indicated "muted discourses about spirituality" is a structural barrier that discourages leaders from expressing spiritual leadership within the workplace. These four participants indicated a preference for actions when a leader is expressing spiritual leadership. Thus, they suggested muted discourses about spirituality in educational workplaces do not prevent leaders from expressing spirituality by their actions. They argued educators can actively signify spirituality by "walking the talk" and "operating with heart" as well as mind, in the manner they relate to others. For example, a true spiritual awakening manifests itself as an urge to treat others as equals (Myss, 2001).

Treating others as equals by showing them dignity and respect was the major means of signifying spirituality within the workplace that was agreed upon by all the participants. They indicated treating others respectfully as equals was their way of expressing spiritual values and moral beliefs within their workplaces. This stance meant demonstrating that no person is superior to another as a human being; it involved functioning as an interactive team, thus, challenging rigid hierarchical systems that judge a person's value on the position they hold within their workplaces.

Six participants stressed that practising servant leadership signified their spirituality within the workplace. Beau discussed the importance of demonstrating he was a steward of his spiritual gifts by following his sacred calling to serve others within the workplace; Habs stated that servant leadership meant leading with heart and taking care of followers' needs; Meiling suggested that listening was an important element of serving; Newday said serving is about creating an atmosphere where others can realize their own potential and is about demonstrating care through compassionate acts of giving and serving; Sara indicated servant leadership involves the ability to teach children to become caring responsible citizens.

Four participants suggested that signifying spirituality involved being personally accountable. Airjordan said that a spiritual leader needs to reflect personal growth, be positive, and provide hope to others; Ayla stated that it is her responsibility to awaken spiritual values and moral beliefs in others by acting respectful, empathetic, fair and responsible; Meiling pointed out the importance of being a strong advocate for positive changes by standing up for her moral beliefs; Sara asserted that leaders should always act with honesty and integrity.

Three participants indicated that signifying spirituality in the workplace meant acting morally and reflecting spirituality within their treatment of others. Habs insisted that he needed to be honest, open and sincere, to build trust in his students and peers; leadership is about helping others to reach for the stars. Similarly, Luv stated that demonstrating self-respect and respect for others with caring actions signifies spirituality in the workplace; and Newday argued that leaders must lead by example.

The findings support literature (e.g., L'Engle, 1997; Albright & Ashbrook, 2001) which suggest spirituality is signified more by actions than words. Palmer (1998) states that communicating spirituality is actively expressing kindness towards others, and Spink (1997) argues that expressing love with one's actions reflects spirituality in an ineffable way. As Vaill (1998) notes, non-verbal vocabularies are limitless sources of spiritual insight that can help cultivate spirituality within leadership practices.

All participants were contacted by e-mail or telephone during the data collection process; when communicating with the researcher, they indicated that spirituality is often an experience that exceeds words, which supports the literature (Janis, 2000; L'Engle, 1997;Vaill, 1998). Therefore, for the purpose of this study, they forwarded by e-mail: poems, photographs, song lyrics and written affirmations, which they claimed had had a spiritual influence on their leadership practices. These examples of spiritual expressions may be viewed as triggers that can help awaken, signify and cultivate one's spirituality.

Cultivating Spirituality Within Leadership Practices at Work

Cultivating spirituality within leadership practices is comparable to Park's (2001) standpoint about gaining reflective knowledge. He states that "human knowledge must not merely understand the world but also change it; it must be normative and oriented to action as well as descriptive or explanatory" (p. 86). Further, other literature indicates cultivating spirituality within leadership is preceded by 1. awakening one's innate spirit, (Newburg, D'Aquili & Rause, 2001; Wilber, 1996) with noetical (Vaill, 1998; Wilber, 1996) and relational peak experiences (Dallaire, 2001; Janis, 2000), and 2. signifying spirituality by facilitating a communal workplace (Park, 2001; Pearsal 1998; Vaill, 1998). Dallaire, Park, Vaill, and Wilber introduced leadership models that advocate ways of cultivating spirituality personally and professionally.

Data supporting the foregoing literature indicate that ten participants' spiritual leadership abilities were being cultivated in most aspects of their lives. The educators were constructing their own spiritual identities within their leadership profiles, according to their beliefs and interactions with others in the everyday world. This activism coincides with Schutz's (1970) belief that people construct their own worlds and Mead's (1982) view that the self is a person's perception of his/her individual and social identity. As children, participants had internalized certain moral values, attitudes and skills, related to their spirituality, which, as adults they cultivated from interactions with others, life experiences, and their education (Tisdell, 2003). This stance supports several theoretical standpoints (Anderson, 1993; Freeman, 1980; Schutz, 1973) about ways in which leadership can be cultivated.

Further, data suggest that cultivation of spirituality within leadership practices is a process that involves awakening the innate spirit, encouraging ongoing learning and connecting with others. Participants' peak life experiences were described as part of their spiritual awakening processes that resulted in signifying and developing spiritual leadership abilities. Half of the participants noted their religious beliefs or spiritual practices had awakened and influenced the evolution of their spirituality. For example, three participants claimed Jesus was their primary mentor for spiritual leadership. Their perspective supports (Solomon, 2002; Myss, 2001; Ulich, 1945) views that religious leaders may be spiritual mentors in aspects of educational leading.

Schemata of cultivation of spirituality within self

From the data, a schemata of cultivation of spirituality within self was developed from ten participants' shared personal spiritual experiences. The eight components of this schemata include 1. take care of health, 2. be childlike, 3. take time to reflect and meditate, 4. commune with nature, 5. take walks, 6. listen to uplifting music, 7. read positive books, and 8. have close community with friends. These components support the literature that suggests if leaders live more balanced personal lives, they will be more effective leaders within their workplaces (Chopra, 2000; Frankl, 1963; Drouin, 1997; Dyer, 2001; Fox, 1995). The components of the schemata were constructed from participants' responses to sub-question one, "think of a time when you have felt the most excited, most engaged and most alive. What was it was it about this peak experience that you would define as being spiritual?" For example, Airjordan and Stider associated awakening and cultivating spirituality with communing with nature; Meiling and Ayla suggested upbeat music helped them to tune into their spirituality, and Newday and Armary indicated that allowing themselves to be childlike cultivated their spirituality. The other four participants associated cultivating spirituality within self with the other

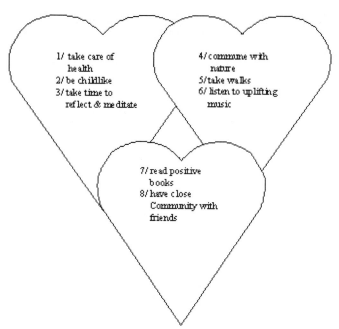

Heart graph no. 7: Cultivation of spirituality within self

components listed in heart graph no.7. Heart graph no. 7 is a metaphoric diagram symbolizing a heart-centred model for cultivating spirit within self. The graph also complements the triangulated research design applied to this study.

Schemata of cultivation of spirit within the workplace

From the findings, a schemata of cultivation of spirit within the workplace was developed from ten participants' shared spiritual experiences as leaders. The eight components of this schemata include 1. affirming self and others, 2. applying faith, 3. sharing leadership, 4. being accountable, 5. having a clear vision and mission, 6. being true to self, 7. being a positive mentor, and 8. being a continuous learner. These components support literature (Cully, 1984; Palmer, 1998; Sweet, 1997; Vaill, 1998; Yob, 1994) that indicates that leadership models include a heart-centred approach would place the needs of educators and students ahead of the materialistic concerns of a consumer nation. The components were constructed from participants' responses to sub-questions three: What are some changes in leadership practices that have added enthusiasm and spirit to your leadership, and sub-question four: what effective leadership practices would you recommend to other educational leaders?

In response to sub-question three, seven participants stated that "affirming self and others" added spirit to their leadership. Airjordan stated after being affirmed, he felt more confident about taking risks; Beau pointed out the importance of staying positive during challenging times; Luv said that to affirm the worth of her staff, she practises random acts of kindness, such as giving out inspirational cards, flowers, smiles and thank-you notes. She also provides muffins and doughnuts for staff. Meiling and Stider provided the gift of attentive listening; Habs and Newday affirmed themselves and others by practising servant leadership.

Five participants indicated that "applying faith to their leadership practices" added enthusiasm and spirit to their work. When he is feeling challenged, Airjordan questions what Christ would do in the same situation; Meilling, Newday and Stider said they lean on meditative and prayerful activity to help get them through difficult times at work. For example Newday applies the third step of Alcoholic Anonymous, "Let Go and Let God."

Four participants suggested that "sharing leadership" added enthusiasm and spirit to their leadership. Airjordan referred to applying a collaborative effort; Armary suggested giving front-line status to staff; Beau discussed sharing leadership his responsibilities; Luv supported endorsing a synergistic flatter leadership model, inviting input from all stakeholders in the learning community.

Three participants indicated that "increasing their accountability" added enthusiasm and spirit to their leadership. Ayla used the example of becoming more accountable in the community and province, while progressing towards site-based management; Habs stated that his role has moved beyond manager towards a role of providing inspiration and hope for others; Sara noted that she had become a multi-skilled leader, assuming various roles to help articulate vision and direction for her school.

Two participants associated "having a clear vision and mission" with bringing enthusiasm and spirit into their workplaces. Armary and Sara stated when organizations have a clear philosophy and articulate the school's mission, enthusiasm and spirit can flourish in the workplace.

In response to sub-question four, participants noted that being true to self, being a positive mentor, and being a continuous learner were effective leadership practices they would recommend to other leaders. Stider stated "being true to self" involves sheltering one's soul with experiences, such as reading, meditating, singing and praying. Similarly, Luv indicated having balance in one's life and taking good care of oneself is an important precursor to being an effective leader.

To "be a positive mentor" four participants indicated a leader must walk the talk by doing what they say they will do. For Luv this meant "leading by example;" and, for Sara it was treating others with respect to set a good example.

According to three participants, "continuous learning" is a factor influencing effective leadership. For example, Luv emphasized that "lifelong learning is not just a catch phrase but an integral part of being an effective teacher-learner-leader." Sara indicated that to be accountable, leaders need to retain a knowledge base through reading, networking, life experience and connecting with others.

In association with "shared leadership," six participants recommended working as a team. For example, Airjordan stressed the importance of empowering others to share his leadership role rather than being a controller; and Ayla stated that "the more power you give away, the more powerful you are." Additionally, in association with "affirming self and others," five participants suggested "believing in self and others" should be incorporated into one's leadership practices. Airjordan indicated a belief in self and others means taking risks and letting others do the same; according to Sara this belief involves knowing how to motivate staff. Also, affiliated with "affirming self and others" and "shared leadership," two participants suggested that connecting with others helped them be more effective leaders. Luv stated making time to connect with people is a worthwhile time investment and Sara said connecting with others involves sharing her leadership role. Associated with "having a clear vision and mission," participants indicated "having clear goals" encourages effective leadership. Airjordan stated that leaders need to set goals related to the school's vision and mission; Ayla argued effective leadership involves "aligning the heart and mind to work together towards a goal."

Different than the preceding six heart graphs and similar to heart graph no. 7, heart graph no. 8 portrays a conceptual framework for cultivation of spirit within the workplace. Applying heart-shaped images helps conceptualize a leadership model that aligns heart with mind. Half of the participants associated their experiences of cultivating spirit within the workplace with functioning with their minds and their hearts. For example, Sara stated that

Heart graph No. 8: Cultivation of spirit within the educational workplace

having a heart connection to her mind leads her to be more caring and compassionate towards herself and others. Heart graph no. 8 represents a heart-centred approach to cultivating spirit within the educational workplace. There is no significance in the order that the ways to cultivate spirit appear within the hearts.

The foregoing schemata (Heart graph No. no. 8) indicates that leadership models should contain elements of contemplation and action that assist educators to become more spiritually attuned to their hearts while at work, which supports literature (Dallaire, 2001; Noddings, 1992; Thom, 1993; Vaill, 1998).

The schemata also suggests that educators need to bring a spiritual condition into their workplaces by having a clear vision (Vaill, 1998). Like Wilber's (1996) model, this schemata places the cultivation of spirituality within the contexts of the interior, exterior, cultural and collective social. This schemata represents participants' indications that effective leadership practices involve applying mind and heart intelligence to decision making, which also supports the literature (Curtis & Eldredge, 1997; Newburg, D'Aquili & Rause, 2001; Pearce, 2002).

The emergent themes awakening spirituality within self, signifying spirituality within the workplace, and cultivating spirituality within leadership practices at work relate to the evolution of spirituality within leadership practices. These themes support Tisdell's (2003) and Bateson's (1994) beliefs that spiritual development is a continual process that involves both progression and regression. The themes demonstrate that personal and professional spiritual development can rotate between the three emergen themes. For example, when Armary was cultivating spirituality within his workplace by applying faith and affirming his students, he had a peak spiritual experience, which resulted in a desire to further signify spirituality.

Participants' shared experiences reported in the schemata also reflect Tisdell's (2003) assumptions about relationships between education and spirituality. The findings associated with 1. "applying faith" imply, although religion and spirituality are not the same, that they can be inter-related for some people; 2. "sharing leadership" honors the wholeness and interconnection of all things; 3. "having a clear vision and mission" demonstrates meaning-making within the workplace; 4. "affirming self and others" reflects that spirituality is always present; 5. "being true to self" indicates spiritual development involves moving toward a more authentic self; and 6. "being a continuous learner" indicates one aspect of spirituality is about how people construct knowledge, and integrate spiritual experiences, which often happen by surprise (Tisdell, 2003).

The findings address the two core research questions: 1. How are the spiritual experiences of educational leaders understood and articulated by educators, and 2. In what ways would this articulation best contribute to the development of effective leadership? Examining how ten educational leaders in Alberta and Ontario perceive their spiritual experiences facilitated the individual voice of these participants, which creates a better understanding of the process of awakening, signifying and cultivating spirituality personally and professionally within leadership. This articulation of spirituality could contribute to the development of more effective leadership practices, with the construction of models that cultivate spirit within workplaces. Further studies might indicate whether this schemata is universal, that is if other data are similar.

Summary

This study is an exploration and analysis of how ten educational leaders perceive their spiritual experiences. Applying a triangulated methodology involved exploring spiritual development phenomena as they were understood by participants. An analysis of the data generated a greater understanding of how a person's spirituality is awakened, signified and cultivated personally and professionally. The findings both supported and challenged previous research conducted on spirituality within educational leadership. Although the group studied was limited to ten participants, the study provides an indication of how more educators could benefit from incorporating a program for cultivating spirit within leadership and possibly affect the organizational system itself.

The key concepts from the literature set the foundation for a synergism: 1. muting discourses about spirituality within educational systems 2. exploring moral issues within educational values, and 3. shifting paradigms affecting educational leadership. These key concepts led to discoveries of threads within the data. After the threads were woven into synergistic patterns, they evolved into emergent themes and phases of spiritual leadership development. The phases of spiritual development include 1. awakening spirituality within self, 2. signifying spirituality within the workplace, and 3. cultivating spirituality within leadership practices. A schemata of cultivation of spirituality within self, and a schemata of cultivation of spirit within the workplace were outcomes of these phases. Both schemata framed ways that participants have cultivated spirituality within self and spirit within leadership, after their innate spirituality had been awakened. In sum, the findings were woven into a synergism composed of key concepts, threads and themes. The overarching key concepts set a foundation for the questions; the data collected from the questions evolved from threads into emergent themes. Then, the emergent themes were enfolded into two heart-centred schemata depicting the cultivation of spirituality within self and cultivation of spirit within workplaces.

6
Implications and Conclusions: Expressing Spirituality

Within this study, ten research participants indicated that establishing discourses about spirituality in educational leadership could assist them to examine their work through a new lens. In this chapter, the issues that inspired this research are revisited; a summary of the findings and limitations is presented and implications of the study and implications for professional education and policy development are discussed. The conclusion section is a discussion about cultivating spirit within leadership practices.

Revisiting the Scope of the Study

The study is an exploration of the spiritual dimension of educational leadership as it pertains to ten educators who have held leadership positions centred within the public education system. The two core questions and four subquestions were addressed in the overarching theoretical framework proposed in Chapter Three and through a qualitative analysis of the educator interviews, which was reported on in Chapter Four. Qualitative analysis of the data provided by participants responses by e-mail interview and follow-up on-line discussion and by telephone communication provided insights into these leaders' spiritual experiences. Findings are reported in Chapter Five. The culmination of these findings is proposed in two schemata: 1. Cultivation of spirituality within self, and 2. Cultivation of spirit within leadership practices.

Findings suggest that cognitive awakenings and spiritual awakenings are linked to meaningful ways educators attempt to apply these epistemological perspectives when reflecting on their leadership practices. For example, within phenomenological, feminist and action inquiry, there is "the spirit of . . . participation" (Park, 2001, p. 84), which ascertains relational and reflective knowledge that can strengthen community. The way educators perceive spirituality and their conscious awareness of this phenomenon reflects their understanding of how to apply spiritual values and moral beliefs to leadership practices. Their various ways of knowing indicate spirituality evolves according to people's pre-dispositions, peak life experiences, current circumstances and environments, as noted in the literature (e.g., Fox, 1991; Glazer, 1999; Palmer, 1999a; Vaill, 1998) and findings. For example one participant, Armary, stated that spirituality is a "holy longing" awakened by conversion experiences; Luv referred to her "interiority" as her spirituality, which requires that she take care of self to promote wellness in others.

Newday suggested that although spirituality is inherent, when it is not actively expressed with good works, a person's spirituality remains latent. Other participants indicated that awakening, signifying and cultivating their spirituality was influenced by family, society, religion, education, peers and their own free will, which supports the literature (Begley & Leonard, 1999; Creighton, 1999; Graham, 1990; Vaill, 1998.)

Participants' peak spiritual experiences ranged from communing with nature and connecting with others, to facing a major life crisis. After being enlightened by spiritual experiences, three participants claimed they adopted Christ-like attitudes and became more compassionate and caring towards others. Two others, Sara and Airjordan, suggested that putting spirituality into action cultivated spirit within their leadership practices. To demonstrate spirituality in action, another participant, Luv, brought muffins and doughnuts to her workplace and hosted appreciation luncheons for staff. Although she suggested this was a spiritual act, others may have judged her nurturing gestures differently.

Habs stated that walking the talk can light the souls of fellow employees and mentor spiritual leadership in his workplace. Ayla claimed that her leadership mission was to awaken spiritual values within others, and Airjordan stated that he aims to provide hope to fellow employees. These findings support the literature (e.g., Bohac-Clark, 2002; Chee, 2000; Donaldson, 2000 & Emes, 2000; Fox, 1991; Simington, 2003) which indicates that spirituality is one's true essence that rises above ego and becomes a circular process, driving one to function from both head and heart in a caring compassionate fashion.

Summarizing Findings

The first schemata, illustrated in heart graph no. 7, constructed from the findings, suggests educators need to cultivate spirituality within themselves before attempting to cultivate spirit within their work places. The second schemata, illustrated in heart graph no. 8, demonstrates that effective leadership models should include contemplative, verbal, and active spiritual conditions; this perspective complements a triangulated conceptual framework for putting spirit into action within workplaces. Data indicates that to cultivate spirit within their workplaces, leaders need to establish a vision and a credo, which incorporates being true to self, affirming self and others, and sharing leadership. By applying a vision and credo to infuse spirituality into leadership practises, educators could institutionalize a process for creating and re-creating the schemata that is illustrated in heart graph no. 7.

Giving five male and five female participants an opportunity to dialog openly about their spirituality may also have given them freedom to use the term "spirituality." Findings suggested there is a relationship between morals and spirituality and for some participants there was connections between religion and spirituality. Participants' responses further indicated that some educators are willing to move beyond muted discourses about spirituality.

Data supports the trend that paradigm shifts are taking place within educational leadership practices during the new millennium. However, one participant noted in this era, there is still no place for spirituality within educational administration. Paradigm shifts are comparable to what Palmer (1999a) calls a "movement mentality," leading to alterations in leadership practices despite "institutional resistance" (p. 10). A small group of ten educators within the study reflected some of the paradigm shifts within leadership paradigms that have been underway during the past few decades.

Noting Limitations of the Study

I had considered face-to-face interviews, but anticipated that with the sensitivity of the topic "spirituality" and popularity of e-mail, participants might be more comfortable communicating by e-mail and web-page discussions. Because many educators may be reluctant to talk about spirituality, I was fortunate to find ten participants who were willing to do so. However, face-to-face interviews or observational research in the workplace may have provided me with more insight into the ineffable elements of spirituality, such as the passion a person may be attempting to communicate through non-verbal expressions, when articulating a spiritual awakening or the demonstration of spirituality through actions.

On-line, a researcher cannot see the sparkle in participants' eyes, hear the joy in their tone of voice, observe their body movements, or have a sense of their spirituality. Likewise, participants may not be able to feel a relational connection with the researcher, with whom they cannot have eye contact with, or see an appreciative smile. Therefore, on-line data collection may have been too depersonalized for the study of spirituality. Also, it was likely the participants' responses were edited and re-written rather than spontaneous expressions of what they were feeling at the time. Additionally, political circumstances, including a teachers' strike and the initiation of Bill 12 were unexpected barriers to communication with participants which affected response rates.

I had envisioned an equilateral triangle when initiating a triangulated design for the research methodology. However, the active inquiry, in the second web-page discussion, was below expectations, and technical problems, such as receiving an on-line virus from a participant's transmission, were not anticipated. I did not anticipate that all participants would have Christian roots; after having heard them speak in seminars and at conferences, it was assumed their religious roots also included Aboriginal, Buddhist and Jewish traditions. However, having a particular religious belief was not one of the criteria set for participants. Also, participants may not have made a connection between spirituality and morals if I would not have provided a leading question.

Understanding and Articulating Spiritual Experiences

Findings indicate that outside of their religious contexts, participants' spirituality was silenced, not yet having developed into a clear discourse with other people in any aspect of life (Holmes, 2003). Discourses about spirituality were often muted within the workplace to reduce misunderstandings from peers and students. However, four participants believed actions speak louder than words when expressing spirituality. Additionally, in their examples of non-traditional means of articulating spirituality, five other participants suggested spiritual expressions can extend beyond language and alternatively can be communicated through music, photographs or nature, which supports the literature (Bohac-Clark, 2002; Goding, 1995; Vaill, 1998). Assuming that spirituality in educational leadership has existed for a long time, the value of this inquiry is the attempt to articulate spirituality to make the topic more mainstream.

Articulating Spirituality Contributes to Developing Effective Leadership

Findings helped provide greater insight into how spiritual experiences shared among educational leaders can have implications for their personal and professional development. It provides a profile of them being affirmed and validated through dialog with one another. Airjordan stated he had never shared this experience with anyone before this study, and Ayla claimed the questions forced her to reflect deeper than usual. If the dialog is caring, a sense of respect could be assumed by participants. Thus, a safe space is created in which intimate thoughts could be expressed. During the study, I treated participants with respect and demonstrated compassion and caring when they shared heart-felt experiences. For example, when one participant revealed that his mother had just been diagnosed with cancer, I took time to listen and empathize.

Throughout the research process, participants addressed a need for self-care and care of others, especially through affirmations. They suggested that treating others as equals was a universal way to act ethically and morally within their workplaces. This perspective supports literature in Chapters One and Chapter Two that indicates educational leaders can awaken or re-awakening the sacred spark within themselves and their peers by kind and caring acts (Graham, 1990; Noddings, 1992; Richmon & Allison, 2000; Vaill, 1998).

Participants also stressed the value of continuous learning as a means to cultivate spirituality within the workplace. As Sergiovanni (1996) claims, "if our aim is to help students become lifelong learners by cultivating the spirit of inquiry and the capacity for inquiry, then we must provide the same conditions for teachers" (p. 52). In sum, what was evident throughout the data base is the desire for more interaction about spirituality among educational leaders.

Implications for Future Research

This study raises questions that are potential areas for further research within the field of education. For example, how would results from a similar type of study be the same or different if a larger group of educators working in leadership positions was used or it the study was replicated in a faith-based system? How would the findings turn out if participants had non-Christian roots and were from different corners of the world. Further research needs to be conducted with a larger group of educators in leadership positions, to see how new data would extend results of this study.

More research aimed at further discovering the conditions under which spiritual leadership is developed and nurtured would be especially beneficial to educators who can influence leadership development in the school systems. Conducting similar research to this study but with other methods of data collection to obtain educational leaders' perceptions of spirit within leadership, would extend the scholarly dynamic and add value to the spiritual component of leadership. Research in this area could also reach beyond the field of education to leadership within other organizations.

Findings of this study, which are from the perspective of the educational leader, have the potential to influence further data collection on other leaders' perceptions of leadership. As noted earlier by Sullivan and Decker (1992), researchers should focus on the actions of leaders, rather than on their personality traits, when attempting to clarify the profile of a good leader. These findings, which suggest how spirituality within leadership may be awakened, signified, and cultivated personally and professionally, could inspire researchers to do further research on the behavior patterns, actions and non-verbal expressions associated with spiritual leadership within the workplace.

Data also suggest that cultivating spirituality within leadership may influence moral behavior within the work place

This study provides more clarity about how ten educators perceived spirituality within leadership and is an addition to the literature about spirituality within the workplace. Participants discussed eight major elements of cultivating spirit within leadership: 1. affirming self and others; 2. sharing leadership; 3. applying faith; 4. being accountable; 5. being true to self; 6. applying faith; 7. being a positive mentor; and 8. being a continuous learner. These perceptions reflect common perspectives of spiritual leadership models presented in other studies (Dallaire, 2001; Fox, 1995; Thom, 1993; Tisdell, 2003; Vaill, 1998) in which the data base was comprised of business, organizational and religious leaders.

Studies related to spiritual leadership, such as this one, could encourage researchers to conduct additional research from an educator's perspective and leaders working in other fields. A need for more research on spirituality within leadership is evident. Further research conducted on this element of leadership could reduce the neglect and misunderstood notions of spirituality found in traditional literature and ground the quest for understanding more about this aspect of life (Moffett, 1994; Fox, 1995; Goding, 1995; Thom, 1993). According to Heifetz (1994), the concept of leadership is still in a developmental process that is ongoing. Thus, to increase an understanding of what spirituality in leadership means to educators, more research needs to be conducted about the spiritual component of leadership. This study resulted in me gaining insight about how a select group of educational leaders in Alberta and Ontario perceive spiritual leadership.

Study Implications for Education, Practice and Policy Development

Considering that effective leadership is necessary for organizations, politics, the arts, schools and all the other institutions that determine the way we live, work, and relax (Bedeian, 1993), studies, such as this one about leadership, are significant. Working as a team, treating everyone as equals and "walking the talk" are three elements of spiritual leadership shared by participants. From an educational perspective, implications include applying the findings to understand better how to facilitate awakening, signifying and cultivating spirit within the educational workplace. Articulating the evolution of spirituality may assist educators to construct fresh leadership training programs that would apply the study's findings with other data that demonstrate similar results. For example, if persuaded spirituality is valuable within leadership, educators may consider establishing spiritual leadership programs within some schools. Additionally, combined with similar research, this study may help school boards move beyond muted discourses about spirituality and offer trustees instructional leadership programs about spirituality, to promote growth in student learning as well as enhance professional development.

Conducting research, such as this study, is a step towards encouraging the development of more spiritual and humanistic leadership models adept at dealing with diverse young and impressionable children. As noted earlier by Maxcy (1991), humanistic leaders foster team work, a group process to policy making, and a child-centred approach to education. Throughout the interviews, participants suggested that functioning from mind and heart and treating others as equals are attributes associated with applying spirituality to leadership. This research and other studies addressing spiritual leadership could assist educators to recognize that a spiritual approach to leadership is an asset that can introduce synergy into workplaces, and assist in cultivating a more humane productive world.

Findings associated with the emergent theme "cultivating spirit within leadership practices at work," combined with other types of data on leadership, could assist educators to establish clear mission statements within their workplaces. As Porat (1985) asserted, one who pursues a leadership position needs to be willing to grow, to be open-minded, and interested in new educational models. This type of research, along with similar studies, could help provide direction about how to awaken, signify and cultivate spirituality personally and professionally.

After comparing the findings with other data from similar studies, educators may acknowledge ways that they can cultivate spirit within their leadership and management practices. As a result, they could provide training programs on leadership that would help challenge the traditional power and control hierarchical models currently prominent in many workplaces. Furthermore, as an implication, this area of research offers great value for the importance of spirituality within leadership when engaging in a political decision-making process for policy development. Likewise, data suggest there is a need for policies that promote a synergistic, strong team approach to leadership within organizations. Incorporating a synergistic team approach to leadership practices may help educators to cultivate and signify spirituality within their policy-making procedures.

Personal and Professional Implications for the Researcher

The components of the first schemata (Heart Graph no. 7) reflect a variety of means that I have cultivated spirituality within my own life. Taking care of my health, being childlike (but not childish), taking time to reflect and meditate, communing with nature, taking walks, listening to uplifting music, reading positive books and having close community with friends are ways that I have nurtured my spirituality throughout the research process. Without first cultivating spirituality within myself, I would find it challenging to cultivate spirit within a workplace. Because spirituality is both an immanent and a transcendent dynamic, it requires internal and external cultivation to evolve.

I will continue working towards fulfilling my sacred mission to help awaken the latent spirit within whomever the Creator puts into my life. To fulfil this mandate professionally, I will implement heart-centred models into my leadership practices. My credo will be inspired by spiritual conditions for cultivating spirit noted in the research findings: affirm self and others; apply faith; share leadership; be accountable; have a clear vision/ mission; be true to self; be a positive mentor; and be a continuous learner.

Applying elements of schemata one and two to my personal and professional life is honoring Park's (2001) suggestion to broaden epistemological horizons within inquiries by discerning relational, representational and reflective knowledge. I gained relational knowledge by functioning with mind and heart when connecting with other graduate students and building community with them on the university campus. Functioning with "mind-and-heart [refers to] both cerebral and emotive functions" (Park, 2001, p. 85). To obtain representational knowledge, I presented sections of my research study at local, national and international conferences that involved "re-describing the object of knowing" (Park, 2001, p. 83), which was spirituality. Reflective knowledge came from actively conducting an inquiry about spirituality and then defending it. "Action is an integral part of reflective knowledge" (p. 86). As indicated by Park, acquiring these dimensions of knowledge during the research process has assisted me to gain connection, competence and confidence. These gains will help to give me moral courage when I attempt to move beyond muted discourses about spirituality within educational systems.

Summary of Conclusions

Study findings helped generate a better understanding of how spiritual elements of leadership are perceived by leaders within the public education system and demonstrated ways educators can work towards being paradigm-shift pioneers by cultivating spirit within their workplaces and by applying more heart-centred approaches to leadership practices. Outcomes of the research are an encouragement of more open dialog about spirituality within public educational systems and a contribution to the development of cultivation of spirit within leadership practice models. Additionally, answering the research questions provided an original contribution to knowledge that encourages more open communication about the spiritual elements of leadership amongst educators and leaders in other walks of life thus assisting them to move beyond muted discourses about spirituality.

This study involves an investigation about how ten educational leaders interpreted their spiritual experiences. Participants indicated that dialoguing about spirituality within educational leadership assists them to view their work through a fresh lens. An analysis of data generated a greater understanding of how a person's spirituality may be awakened, signified and cultivated personally and professionally. As noted earlier, findings suggest that workplaces could benefit from incorporating programs that cultivate spirit within leadership practices. For example, Ayla, Airjordan and Habs stated that if educational leaders mentored spirituality within their leadership practices, they could nurture moral values within students, ignite their souls and cultivate hope for a better future.

Discussing spirituality within educational leadership environments could transform more school systems from what Begley & Leonard (1999) have described as a state of "anomie and mediocrity," into places that help re-awaken students to a greater understanding of the spiritual nature of being human (Fox, 1995; Glazer 1999). However, leaders need to cultivate spirituality within themselves before attempting to better articulate and cultivate spirit within their workplaces. They require a sense of their own spiritual well being to support the emerging paradigm shift that explores how a spiritual place and voice within the academic world might be cultivated.

176 *Cultivating Spirituality in Leadership*

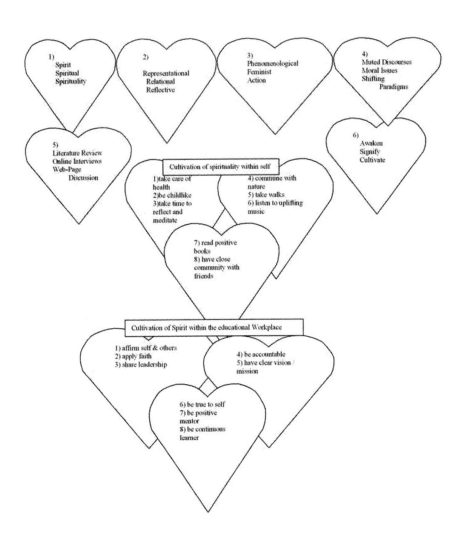

All Hearts

References

Abercrombie, N., Hill, S., & Turner, B. (1984). *Dictionary of sociology.* London, UK: Penguin Group.

Abbott, E. (1984). Flatland: *A romance of many dimensions.* New York, NY: Penguin Books.

Albright, C. & Ashbrook, J. (2001). *Where God lives in the human brain.* Naperville, IL: Sourcebooks, Inc.

Alexander, A. (1997). *The Antigonish movement: Moses Coady and adult education today.* Toronto, ON: Thompson Educational Publishing.

Al-Krenawi, A. & Graham, J. (2000). Islamic theology and prayer. *International Social Work 43,* (3), 289-304.

Abram, D. (1996). *The Spell of the sensuous.* New York: Random House.

Anderson, M. (1993). *Thinking about women: Sociological perspectives on sex and gender.* New York: McMillan.

Anderson, T. & Kanuka, H. (2003). *E-Research: Methods, strategies, and issues.* Boston, MA: Pearson Education.

Arends, C. (2000). *Living the questions: Making sense of the mess and mystery of life.* Eugene, OR: Harvest House.

Arieti, J. & Wilson, P. (2003). *The scientific & the divine: Conflict and reconciliation.* Lanham, ML: Rowman & Littlefield.

Armstrong, H. (2004, August). *Report on thesis: Personal and professional spiritual development.* University of Calgary.

Armstrong, P. & Armstrong, H. (1994). *The double ghetto: Canadian women & their segregated work.* Toronto, ON: McClelland & Steward.

Atlas.ti. (2000). [On-line] Retrieved November 21, 2002 from htpp://www.atlasti.de/atlasneu.htm

B. (anonymous last name), Mel (1991). *New Wine: The spiritual roots of the twelve step miracle.* Centre City, MN: Hazelden.

Baden-Powell, J. (1945). *Aids to scoutmastership.* Ottawa, ON: Scouts Canada.

Ballou, M. (1995). Women and spirit: Two nonfits in psychology. In J. Oshshor & E. Cole (Eds.), *Women's spirituality, women's lives* (pp. 9-19). New York: Harrington Park Press.

Banks, R. (2000). Moving from faith to faithfulness. In R. Banks and K. Powell (Eds.), *Faith in leadership: How leaders live out their faith in their work and why it matters* (pp. 1-20). San Francisco, CA: Jossey-Bass.

Barton, A. (1987). The teaching methods of three famous teachers: Lao Tzu of Ch'u Zeno of Elea and Jesus of Nazareth. *The Journal of Educational Administration and Foundations, 2* (1), 4-19.

Bates, R. (1993). On knowing: Cultural and critical approaches to educational administration. *Educational Administration Quarterly, 21*(3), 171-176.

Bateson, M. (1994. *Peripheral visions: Learning along the way*. New York : HarperCollins.

Bausch, W. (1984). *Storytelling, imagination and faith*. New Jersey, CO: Twenty-third Publications.

Beck, C. (1986). Education for spirituality. *Interchange: A Quarterly Review of Education, 17*(2), 15-20.

Beck, C. (1993). *Learning to live the good life: Values in adulthood*. Toronto, ON: OISE press.

Bedian, A. (1993). *Management* (3rd ed.). Forthworth, TX: Dryden Press.

Begley, T., & Leonard, P. (1999). *The values of educational administration*. London, UK: Falmer Press.

Bender, P. (2001). *Leadership from within*. Don Mills, ON: Stoddard.

Berg, B. (2001). *Qualitative research methods for the social sciences*. Needham Heights, MA: Allyn & Bacon.

Best, J., & Kahn, J. (2003). *Research in education*. (9th ed.). Boston, MA: Allyn and Bacon.

Bierle, D. (1992). *Surprised by faith: A scientist shares his personal, life-changing discoveries about God, the Bible, and personal fulfilment*. Lynnwood, WA: Emerald Books.

Blackmore J. (1999). *Troubling women*. Buckingham, UK: Open University Press.

Block, P. (1993). *Stewardship: Choosing service over self interest:* San Francisco, CA: Barrett-Koehler.

Bogdan, R., & Bilken S. (2003). *Qualitative research for education: An introduction to theories and methods*. Boston, MA: Allyn & Bacon.

Bohac Clark, V. (2002, June). In Search of school spirit: The cloud of unknowing in public education. *International Electric Journal For Leadership in Learning, 6* (10). Retrieved July 10, 2002 from http://www.ucalgary.ca/~iejll

Bohac Clark, V. (2002, July). *In search of school spirit: is there room for spirituality in public education?* Paper presented at the July Leadership Institute, Calgary, AB.

Bosetti, L. (1995). Teaching as heartwork. In D. Jones (Ed.). *The spirit of teaching excellence*. (pp. 31-47).Calgary, AB: Detselig.

Bunning, C. (2000). *Achieving success in post graduate action research programs*. Retrieved August 10, 2002, from http://www.mcb.co.uk/services/conferen/nov95-/ifal/paper2.htm

Burke, J. (2000). *Educational research: Qualitative and qualitative approaches*. Neigham Heights, MA: Allyn & Bacon.

Carroll, L., Tober, J. (1999). *The Indigo children: The new kids have arrived*. Carlsbag, CA: Hay House.

Change Agency (2000-1). Calgary: University of Calgary, AB. Retrieved July 2000 to August 2001, from Change-L@majordomo.ucalgary.ca, and acs.ucalgary.ca~cll/-CAN/frameset.htm

Chee, K. (2002, July). *The heart of leadership: Spirituality in educational leadership.* Paper presented at the Linking Research to Educational Practice II Symposium, Calgary, AB.

Chopra, D. (1994). *The seven spiritual laws of success.* San Rafael, CA: Amber-Allen.

Chopra, D. (2000). *How to know God: The soul's journey into the mystery of the mysteries.* New York: Harmony Books.

Chow, K., Ng, O., & Henderson, J. (1999). *Imagining boundaries: Changing Confucian doctrines, texts, and hermeneutics.* New York: State University of New York Press.

Christians, C. (2000). Ethics and politics in qualitative research. In N. Denzin and Y. Lincoln. (Eds.) *Handbook of qualitative research* (pp. 25-30). Thousand Oaks, CA: Sage. Publications.

Coelho, P. (1998). *The alchemist.* New York: HarperCollins.

Coles, R. (1990). *The spiritual life of children.* Boston, MA: Houghton Miffin Company.

Collingwood, R. (1940). *An Essay on metaphysics.* Oxford, UK: Oxford University Press.

Connelly, F.M., & Clandinin, D. J. (1990). Stories of experience and narrative enquiry. *Educational Researcher, June-July,* 2-15.

Cowan, D. (1998). ACTLIST E-mail listserver discussion group

Creighton, T. (1999). Spirituality and the principalship: Leadership for the new millennium. *International Electronic Journal For Leadership in Learning 3*(11). ISSN 1206-9620. Retrieved July 7, 2000, from www.acs.ucalgary.ca~iejll

Creswell, J. (2002). *Educational research: Planning, conducting and evaluating quantitative and qualitative research.* Upper Daddle River, NJ: Pearson Education.

Cruz, E. (2003). *Education as transformation newsletter.* Retrieved October 2, 2003, from www.educationastransformation.org.

Cully, I., & Cully, K. (Eds.) (1971). *Harper's encyclopedia of religious education.* San Francisco. CA: Harper and Row.

Cully, I. (1984). *Education for spiritual growth.* San Francisco, CA: Harper and Row.

Curtis, B., Eldredge, J. (1997). *The sacred romance: Drawing closer to the heart of God.* Nashville TN: Thomas Nelson Publishers.

Deal, T., & Peterson, K., (1999). *Shaping school culture: The heart of leadership.* San Francisco, CA: Jossey-Bass.

Dallaire, M. (2001). *Contemplation in liberation: A method for spiritual education in schools.* Lewiston, NY: Edwin Mellon Press.

DeBoice, D. (2003). *Backgrounder: Religion and public education: Public Consultation: Calgary Board of Education.* Retrieved June 28, 2003, from http://www.cbe.ab.ca./new/religion.asp

Dillenbourg, P., & Schneider, D. (1995, Feb.). *Collaborative learning and the internet. TECFA unit of educational technology.* Switzerland: University of Psychology. Retrieved March, 10, 1999, from http:/tecfa.unige.ch/tecfa/research/CMC-/colla/iccai95 1.html

Doetzel, N. (2003). Morals, religion, and spirituality in the leading of education. In D.

Thom(Ed.), *Disciplined educational leadership into the future.* London, UK: Ming- AJ Institute.

Donaldson, E. L. (1996). Imaging women's spirituality. *Comparative education review, May 40*(2) 194-204.

Donaldson, E. L. (1997). Images of the Goddess: Spiritual aspects of the women's life cycle. *Canadian Woman Studies 17*(1), 36- 39.

Donaldson, E. L. (1998). Three markers on the waves of the women's movement. *Interchange, 29*(2), 237-240.

Donaldson, E. L., & Emes, C. G. (2000). The challenge for women academics: Reaching a critical mass in research, teaching and service. *The Canadian Journal of Higher Education, 30*(3), 33-56.

Dossey, L. (1999). *Beyond mind-body to a new era of healing: Reinventing medicine.* New York: HarperCollins.

Drouin, H. & Rivard, D. (1997). *No stone unturned: Building compassion, community and spirituality in the workplace.* Toronto, ON: Family Service Ontario Publishing.

Duke, D. (1999). Envisioning the good organization: Steps toward a philosophy of organization. In P. Begley (Ed.) *Values and educational leadership* (pp. 9-24). New York, NY: New York University Press.

Dupuis, A. (1966). *Philosophy of education in historical perspective.* Chicago, IL: Rand McNally.

Dyer, W. (2001). *Ten secrets for success and inner peace.* Carlsbad, CA: Hay House.

Ellis, C., & Bochner, A. (2000). Autoethnography, personal narrative reflexivity. In N. Denzin & Y. Lincoln (Eds.), *Handbook of qualitative research* (pp. 733-61). New York: Sage.

Emmerich, K. (2000). Mentoring the next generation of faithful leaders. In R. Banks & K. Powell (Eds.), *Faith in leadership: How leaders live out their faith in their work and why it matters* (pp.109-20). San Francisco, CA: Jossey-Bass Inc.

Evers, C. & Lakomski, G. (1991). Educational leadership. *Knowing educational administration, 22*(2), 131-140.

Fairclough, N. (1992). *Discourse and social change.* Cambridge, ON: Polity Press.

Fenstermacher, G. (1990). Some more considerations on teaching as a profession. In J. Goodland, R. Soder, & K. Sirontnik (Eds.), *The moral dimensions of teaching.* (pp. 131-51). San Francisco, CA: Jossey-Bass.

Fisher, M. (1999). *Living religions* (4th ed.), Upper Saddle River, NJ: Prentice-Hall Inc.

ley, G. (1999). *Learning in social action: A contribution to understanding informal education.* New York: St. Martin's Press.

Fox. M. (1991). *Creation Spirituality: Liberating gifts for the peoples of the earth.* San Francisco, CA: Harper Collins.

Fox, M. (1995). *The reinvention of work.* San Francisco, CA: Harper Collins Publishing.

Fox, M. (1998). *A spiritual renewal of education.* Tikkum, 13(6), 49-50.

Foxworth, M. (1998). *Putting spirituality in public schools.* Tikkum, 13(6), 51-54.

Frankl, V. (1963). *Man's search for meaning: An introduction to logotherapy*. New York: Simon & Schuster.

Freeman, R. (1980). Phenomenological sociology and ethomethology. In J. D. Douglas (Ed.), *Introduction to the sociologies of everyday life,* (pp. 113-154). Boston, MA: Allyn & Bacon.

Friesen, J. (1999). Christian schools in a pluralistic society: A reply. *Interchange, 3*(2), 235-240.

Fullan, M. (1991). *The new meaning of educational change*. New York: Teachers College Press.

Fullan, M. (1998, April). Leadership for the 21st century: Breaking the bonds of dependency. *Educational leadership*, 6-10.

Gadamer, H. (1994). *Heidegger's ways*. Albany, NY: New York State University Press.

Gardner, H. (1999). *Intelligence reframed*. New York, NY: Basic Books.

Gay, L., & Airasian, P. (1992). *Educational research: Competencies for analysis and applications*. Upper Saddle River, NJ: Pearson Education.

Gilligan, C. (1993). *In a different voice: Psychological theory and women's development*. Cambridge, MA: Harvard University Press.

Giorgi, A. (1975). An application of phenomenological method in psychology. In A. Giorgi, C. Fiosher, & E. Murray (Eds.), *Duquesne studies in phenomenological psychology, 2,* (pp. 72-103). Pittsburgh, PA: Duquesne University Press.

Glazer, S. (1999). *The heart of learning*. New York: Tarcher/Putnam.

Goddard, T., & Foster, R. (1999, January). *Experiences of neophyte teachers: A critical assessment*. Paper presented at the International Congress for School Effectiveness and Improvement, San Antonio, TX.

Goding, B. (1995). Excellence has no seams. In D. Jones (Ed.), *The spirit of teaching excellence,* (pp.113-125).Calgary, AB: Detselig Enterprises.

Goodman, J. & Lesnick, H. (2001). *The moral stake in education: contested premises and practices*. New York: Longman.

Gosetti, P., & Rusch, E. (1995). Re-examining educational leadership: Challenging Assumptions. In D. Dunlop & P. Schmuck (Eds.), (pp.21-5), *Women leading education*. New York, NY: State University Press.

Graham, R. (1990). *God's dominion: A skeptic's quest*. Toronto, ON: McClelland & Stewart.

Greenfield, T. (1991). Reforming and re-valuing educational administration: Whence and why cometh the phoenix? *Educational Management and Administration, 19*(4), 200-217.

Greenleaf, R. (1991). *The servant as a leader*. Indianapolis, IL: The Robert K. Greenleaf Center.

Griffin, D. R. (1988). *Spirituality and society: Postmodern visions*. New York: New York State University Press.

Grimbol, W. (2000). *The complete idiots guide to spirituality for teens*. Indianapolis, IN: Alpha Books.

Grob, L. (1984). Leadership, the Socratic model. In B. Kellerman (Ed.) *Leadership multi disciplinary perspectives,* (pp. 17-25). Jersey City, NJ: Prentice Hall.

Groen, J., & Jacob, J. (2004, June). *Spiritual transformation in a secular context: A qualitative research study of transformational learning in a higher education setting.* Paper presented at the Humanities and Social Sciences, Canadian Society for Studies in Higher Education Congress, Winnipeg, MB.

Guba, E. & Lincoln, Y. (1981). *Effective evaluation.* San Francisco, CA: Jossey Bass.

Guzie, T. (1995). Change. In D. Jones, (Ed.) *The spirit of teaching excellence* (pp. 179-193). Calgary, AB: Detselig.

Guzie, T. (1999). Response to Doret de Ruyter. *Interchange, 30*(2), 241-245.

Guzie, T. (2000, February 17). *Spirituality in the 21st century.* Paper presented at Calgary Teacher's Convention, University of Calgary.

Handy, C. (1989). *The age of unreason.* London, UK: Arrow Books.

Hawley, J. (1995). *Reawakening the spirit in work.* New York: Barrett-Koehler Publishers.

Heifetz, R. (1994). *Leadership without answers.* London, UK: Belknap Press.

Helgesen, S. (1990). *The female advantage: Women's ways of leadership.* New York: Doubleday.

Helliwell, T. (1999). *Take your soul to work: Transform your life and work.* Vancouver, BC: Random House.

Henry, Bishop F. (2000, Oct. 24). *Education as a moral activity.* Paper presented at a Centre For Leadership Learning Seminar at the University of Calgary.

Henslin, J., & Nelson, A. (1996). *Down to earth approach to sociology.* Scarborough, ON: Allyn & Bacon.

Heron, J., & Reason, P. (2001). The practice of co-operative inquiry: Research 'with' rather than 'on' people. In P. Reason & H. Bradbury (Eds.), *Handbook of action research* (pp. 179-187).Thousand Oaks, CA: Sage.

Hesse, H. (1998). *The journey to the east.* (38th ed.). New York: Farrar, Straus & Giroux.

Hesse, M. (1980). *Revolution and reconstruction in philosophy of science.* Bloomington. IN: Indiana University Press.

Hill, M. & Ragland, J. (1995). *Women as educational leaders: Opening windows, pushing ceilings.* Thousand Oaks, CA: Kirwan Press, Inc.

Hochschild, A. (1983). *The managed heart: Commercialisation of human feeling.* San Francisco, CA: University of California.

Hodgkinson, C. (1991). *Educational leadership.* Albany, NY: SUNY Press.

Hodgkinson, C. (1999). The triumph of the will: An exploration of certain fundamental problematic in administrative philosophy. In Begley, & T. Leonard, P. (Eds.), *The values of educational administration* (pp. 6-21). New York: Falmer Press.

Hollaar, L. (2000, May 25). *Educational leadership is community building: A postmodern and independent school perspective.* Paper presented at the Canadian Association of Educational Leadership, Federation for the Humanities and Social Sciences Congress in Edmonton at the University of Alberta.

Holmes, P. (2003, Mar.). *Some of the problems studying spirituality: Facing its challenges, landscaping its domain.* University of Bristol, Graduate School of Education, unpublished research paper.

Hoyle, J. (2002). *Leadership and the force of love.* Thousand Oaks, CA: Corwin Press.

Hunter, W. (2000). Spirituality in the service of a larger moral education: *Religious Education, 88*(4), 595-605.

Jampolsky, G. (1983). *Teach only love.* New York: Bantam Books.

Janis, S. (2000). *Spirituality for dummies.* Foster City, CA: IDG Books Worldwide.

Johnson, B.,& Christensen, L. (2000). *Educational research: Quantitative and qualitative approaches.* South Alabama, AL: Pearsonallyn & Bacon.

Jones, D. (1995). *The spirit of teaching excellence.* Calgary, AB: Detselig.

Jones, L. (1995). *Jesus CEO: Using ancient wisdom for visionary leadership.* New York: Library of Congress.

Kass, J. (2003, December). Building confidence in life and self through spirituality. *Spirituality and health:The soul/body connection, 5,* 58-61.

Keen, S. (2004, June) What is power. *Spirituality and health: the soul/body connection, 7,* 30-35.

Keeney, B. (1996). *Everyday soul: Awakening the spirit in daily life.* New York: Riverhead Books.

Kersten, H. (1999). *Jesus lived in India: His unknown life before and after the crucifixion.* Boston, MA: Element Books.

Kessler, R. (1998). Nourishing students in secular schools. *Educational leadership,56* (4), 49-52.

Kiely, R. (1996). *The good heart: A Buddhist perspective on the teachings of Jesus: His Holiness the Dalai Lama.* Sommerville, MA: Wisdom Publications.

Kinjerski, V., & Skrypnek, B. (2003). Measuring spirit at work: Work in progress. In G. Biberman and A. Alkhafaji (Eds.) *Business research yearbook: Global business perspectives journal10,* 1015-1019.

Knitter, P. (2001, November 26). *Multifaith dialogue: More urgent than ever.* Paper presented at the University of Calgary Religious studies Swanson lecture series on Christian Spirituality, Varsity Acres Presbyterian Church in Calgary, AB.

Kuhn, T. (1970). *The structure of scientific revolutions.* Chicago, IL: University of Chicago Press.

L'Engle, M. (1997). *The genesis trilogy.* Colorado Springs, CO: Shaw Waterbrook Press.

Lambert, L. (2003, November 20). Eyes on leadership. Paper presented at the University of Calgary Centre for Leadership in Learning seminar, at the University of Calgary, AB.

Lashway, L. (1996, June). Ethical leadership. *Eric digest 107.* Retrieved May 1, 2002, from http://www.ed.gov/databases/ERIC Digest/ed397463.html, 1-4

Lather, P. (1991). *Getting smart: Feminist research and pedagogy within the postmodern.* New York, NY: Routledge.

Lazar, D. (1998). Selected issues in the philosophy of social science. In C. Seale (Ed.), *Researching society and culture.* (pp. 7-22). London, UK: Sage.

Lerner, M. (2000). *Spirit matters.* Charlottesville, VA: Hampton Roads.

Leithwood, K., Begley P. & Cousins, B. (1992). *Developing expert leadership for future schools.* London, UK: Burgess Science Press.

Leithwood, K., & Steinbach, R. (1995). *Expert problem solving: Evidence from school and district leaders.* New York: University of New York Press.

Leithwood, K., & Duke, D. (1998). Mapping the conceptual terrain of leadership: A critical point of departure for cross-cultural studies. *Leading Schools in a Global Era: A Cultural Perspective, 73*(2), 31-50.

Leithwood, K. (1999). An organizational perspective on values for leaders of future schools. In P.Begley (Ed.), *Values and educational leadership* (pp. 25-46). New York: University of New York Press.

Lockman Foundation (1977). *Holy Bible: New international version.* USA: Lockman Foundation.

Loder, J. (1998). *The logic of the spirit: Human development in theological perspective.* San Francisco CA, Jossey-Bass.

Lowe, G., & Krahn, H. (1993). *Work in Canada: Readings in the sociology of work and industry.* Scarborough, ON: Nelson Canada.

Lyons, L., & Chipperfield, J. (2000). De-constructing the interview: A critique of the participatory model. *Feminist qualitative research 28*(1&2), 23-46.

Ludema, J., Cooperrider, D., & Barrett, F. (2001). Appreciative Inquiry: The power of the unconditional positive question In P. Reason & H. Bradbury (Eds.), *Handbook of action research* (pp. 189-199). Thousand Oaks, CA: Sage.

Lusted, D. (1986). Why pedagogy. *Screen 27*(5), 2-14.

MacDonald, H. (2000). *A man who made a difference.*Victoria, BC: Trafford.

Maguire, P. (2001). Uneven ground: feminisms and action research. In N. Denzin and Y. Lincoln (Eds.).*Handbook of qualitative research* (pp. 60-69). Thousand Oaks, CA: Sage.

Manzer, R. (1994). *Canadian public educational policy on schools and in historical, political perspective ideas.* Toronto, ON: University of Toronto Press.

Marshall, J. (2001). Self-reflective inquiry practices. In P. Reason & H. Bradbury (Eds.), *Handbook of action research* (pp. 433-439). Thousand Oaks, CA: Sage.

Martin, J. (1985). *Reclaiming a conversation: The ideal of the educated women.* New Haven, CT: Yale University Press.

Mathews, D., & Clark, C. (1998). *The faith factor: Proof of the healing power of prayer.* New York, NY.

Mathison, S. (1988, March). Why triangulate?. *Educational Researcher, 17* (2), 13-17.

Maxcy, S. (1991). *Educational leadership: A critical pragmatic perspective.* New York: Greenwood Publishing.

Maxcy, S. (2002, July 8). *The moment of simplicity and the emerging E-earningculture:* Paper presented at the Linking Research to Educational Practice II Symposium, July 5-17, University of Calgary.

Mayer, R. (2000). What is the place of science in educational research? *Educational Researcher, 20*(1), 38-39.

Maynard, R. (1989, March). The new executive father. *Globe and Mail Report on Business Magazine, 44*(49), 51.

Maynard, M. (1990). The re-shaping of sociology? Trends in the study of gender. *Sociology, 24* (2), 269-290.

McKinnon, M. (2004). TPCP *Implementation secondary principals.* Unpublished masters thesis, University of Calgary, AB.

Mead, G. (1982). *The individual and the social self.* Chicago, IL: University of Chicago Press.

Mills, G. (2003). *Action research: A guide for the teacher/researcher.* Upper Saddle River, NJ: Pearson Education, Inc.

Mishler, E.G. (1986). *Research interviewing: Context and narrative.* Cambridge, MS: Harvard University Press.

Mitchell, C., & Kumar, R. (2001). The development of administrative moral discourse in a pluralistic society. *The Journal of Educational Administration and Foundations, 15*(2), 47-67.

Moffett, J. (1994). *The Universal schoolhouse: Spiritual awakening through education.* San Francisco, CA: Jossey-Bass.

Morris, M. (1997). *An Excursion into creative sociology.* New York: Columbia University Press.

Morrisseau, C. (1998). *Into the daylight: A wholistic approach to healing.* Toronto: University of Toronto Press.

Morse, M. (2000). *Where God lives: The science of the paranormal and how our brains are linked to the universe.* New York: Harper Collins Publishers.

Myss, C. (2001). *Sacred contracts: Awakening your divine potential.* New York: Harmony Books.

Nair, K. (1994). *A higher standard of leadership:Lessons from the life of Gandhi.* San Francisco, CA: Barrett-Koehler.

Newberg, A., D'Aquili, E., & Rause, V. (2001). *Why God won't go away: Brain science and the biology of belief.* New York: Random House.

Noddings, N. (1992). *The challenge to care in schools: An alternative approach to education.* New York: Teachers College Press.

Nouwen, H. (1975). *The three movements of the spiritual life: Reaching out.* Garden City NY: Doubleday & Company.

O'Murchu, D. (1997). *Reclaiming spirituality.* New York: Crossroad Publishing Company.

Ocker, R. (1999). A heart-centred journey: An educational vision for paradigm pioneers. In L.Carroll & J. Tober (Eds.), *The Indigo children: The new kids have arrived* (pp. 74-76). Carlsbad, CA: Hay House.

Omery, A. (1983). Phenomenology: The method. In P. Munhall & C. Oiler (Eds.), *Advances in Nursing Science, 5,* 101-115.

Ornish, D. (1998). *Love and survival: 8 pathways to intimacy and health.* New York: Harper Collins Publishers.

Palmer, P. (1998) *To know as we are known: A spirituality of education.* San Francisco, CA: Harper and Row.

Palmer, P. (1999a). The grace of great things: Reclaiming the sacred in knowing, teaching, and learning. In S. Glazer (Ed.), *The heart of learning: Spirituality in education* (pp. 15-32). New York: Jeremy P. Tarcher/Putnam.

Palmer, P. (1999b). *The courage to teach: Exploring the inner landscape of a teacher's life.* San Francisco, CA: Jossey-Bass Publishers.

Palmer P. (2000). *Let your life speak: Listening to the voice of vocation.* San Francisco, CA: Jossey-Bass.

Park, P. (2001). Knowledge and participatory research: Appreciative Inquiry: The power of the unconditional positive question In P. Reason & H. Bradbury (Eds.), *Handbook of action research.* (pp. 81-88). Thousand Oaks, CA: Sage Publications.

Parker, J. (2000). *Dialogues with emerging teachers.* Fort Collins, CO: Sagewood Press.

Pearce, J. (2002). *The Biology of transcendence: A blueprint of the human spirit.* Rochester, VT: Park Street Press.

Pearsall, P. (1998). *The heart's code.* New York: Random House.

Peters, T. (1990, September). The best new managers will listen, motivate, support: Isn't that just like a woman? *Working Women, 1,* 142-147.

Porat, K. (1985). *The woman in the principal's chair.* The A.T.A. Magazine, 65, 10-15.

Postman, N. (1993). *Typology: The surrender of culture to technology.* New York, NY: Vintage.

Postman, N. (1995, May). *What does the future hold in public education?* Paper prepared for the Canadian Teachers' Federation National Conference Public Education: Meeting the Challenges, New York.

Psathas, G. (1973). *Phenomenological sociology: Issues and applications.* New York, NY: Wiley.

Purpel, D. E. (1989). *The moral and spiritual crisis in education: A curriculum for justice and compassion in education.* Granaby, MA: Bergin & Gravey.

Pyrch, T. (1998a). *Mapmakers on mapmaking. Systemic Practice and Action Research*, 11(6), 651-668.

Pyrch, T. (1998b). Introduction to the action research family. *Studies in Cultures, Organizations and Societies, 4*(2), v-x.

Rajagopal, D. (1989). *Krishnamurti: Think on these things.* Ujai, CA: Harper & Row.

Reason, P. (1998), Political, epistemological, ecological and spiritual dimensions of participation. *Studies in Cultures, Organizations and Societies 4*(2), 147-167.

Reason, P., & Bradbury, H. (2001). The practise of cooperative inquiry and participation in search of a world worthy of human aspiration. In P. Reason & H. Bradbury (Eds.), *Handbook of action research* (pp. 1-12), Thousand Oaks, CA: Sage Publications.

Reinhartz, S. (1985). *On becoming a social scientist.* San Francisco, CA: Jossey-Bass.

Reynolds, C., & Young, B. (1995) *Women and leadership in Canadian education.* Calgary, AB: Detselig Enterprises Ltd.

Restine, L. *(1993).* *Women in administration: Facilitators for change.* Newbury Park, CA: Corwin Press.

Richmon, M., & Allison, D. (2000, May 25). *Toward a conceptual framework for leadership inquiry.* Paper presented at the Canadian Federation for the Humanities and Social Sciences Canadian Association of Educational Administration annual congress, University of Alberta, Edmonton.

Robertson, J.,& Webber, C. (2000). Cross-cultural leadership development. *International Journal Leadership in Education,3*(4), 315-330.

Rockford, J. (2003). Reflection on action research. In G. Mills (Ed.) *Action Research: A guide for the teacher researcher* (pp. 47-73). Saddle River, NJ: Pearson Education.

Roels, S. (2000). Dealing with vulnerability. In R. Banks,. & K. Powell (Eds.), *Faith in leadership: How leaders live out their faith in their work and why it matters* (pp. 123- 139). San Francisco, CA: Jossey-Bass.

Rolheiser, R. (1999). *The holy longing: The search for Christian spirituality.* New York: Random House.

Ryan, J. (1999). Beyond the veil: Moral educational administration and inquiry in a postmodern world. In P. Begley (Ed.), *Values and educational leadership* (pp. 75-94). New York: State University Press.

Salas, M., & Tillmann, T. (1998). About people's dreams and visions and how to return our perceptions: Convergence of PAR and PRA. *Studies in Cultures, Organizations and Societies, 4* (2), 169-195.

Salzberg, S., (1995). *Loving-kindness: The revolutionary art of happiness.* Boston, MA: Random House.

Sandelowski, N. (1986, April). The problem of rigor in qualitative research. *Advances in nursing science, 8* (3), 27-37.

Schmidt, A., (2001). *Under the influence: How Christianity transformed civilization.* Grand Rapids, MI: Library of Congress.

Schoemperlen, D. (2001). *Our lady of the lost and found.* Toronto, ON: HarperCollins Canada.

Schratz, M., & Walker, R. (1998). Towards an ethnography of learning: Reflection on action as an experience of experience. In B. Rusted, B. Czarniawsk-Joerges & T. Pyrch (Eds.), *Studies in Cultures, Organizations and Societies 4* (2), 197-209, Overseas Publishers Association.

Schutz, A., Wagner, H. (1970a). *On phenomenology and social relations.* Chicago, IL: University of Chicago Press.

Schutz, A., Zaner, R. (1970b). *Reflections on the problem of relevance:* New Haven CT: Yale University Press.

Schutz, A. (1973). *Collected papers: Studies of the life world.* Martinus Nijhoff, NE: The Hague Press.

Seale, C. (1998). *Researching society and culture.* Thousand Oaks, CA: Sage Publications.

Secretan, L. (1999). Inspirational leadership. San Francisco, CA: University of California Press.

Senge, P. (2000). Give me a lever long enough and single-handed so I can move the world. In *The Jossey-Bass reader on educational leadership* (pp. 18-20). San Francisco, CA: Jossey-Bass.

Sennett, R. (1998). *The corrosion of character: The personal consequences of work in the new capitalism.* New York: Norton.

Sergiovanni, T. (1996). *Leadership for the schoolhouse: How is it different? Why is it important.* San Francisco, CA: Jossey-Bass.

Sergiovanni, T.(2000). *The lifeworld of leadership: Creating culture, community and personal meaning in our schools.* San Francisco, CA: Jossey-Bass.

Shakotko, D. & Walker, K. (1999). In P. Begley, & P. Leonard (Eds.), *The values of educational administration* (pp. 201-220), New York: Falmer Press.

Shank, G. (2002). *Qualitative research: A personal skills approach.* Saddle River, NJ: Pearson Education.

Simington, J. (2003). *Journey to the sacred: Mending a fractured soul.* Edmonton, AB: Taking Flight Books.

Smith, D. E. (1979). A sociology for women. In J. Sherman, & C. Beck, (Eds.), *Prism of sex: Essays in the sociology of knowledge* (pp. 25-31). Madison, WI: University of Wisconsin Press.

Smith, D. E., (1990). *The conceptual practices of power: A feminist sociology of knowledge.* Toronto, ON: University of Toronto Press.

Smith, D. (1992). Feminist reflections on political economy. In D. Connelly & P. Armstrong (Eds.), *Feminism in Action: Studies in Action* (pp. 3-21). Toronto, ON: Canadian Scholars' Press.

Snow, C. (2000). Rebuilding trust in the fractured workplace. In R. Banks & K. Powell (Eds.), *Faith in leadership: How leaders live out their faith in their work and why it matters* (pp. 35-45). San Francisco, CA: Jossey-Bass.

Solomon, R. (2002). *Spirituality for the skeptic: The thoughtful love of life.* New York: Oxford University Press.

Somerville, M. (2000). *The ethical canary: Science, society and the human spirit.* Toronto, ON: Penguin Books.

Spears, L. (1995). *Reflections on leadership: How Robert K. Greenleaf's theory of servant leadership influenced today's top management thinkers.* New York: John Wiley & Sons.

Spears, L. (1998). Robert K. Greenleaf: *The Power of Servant Leadership.* San Francisco, CA: Berrett-Koehler Publishers.

Spink, K. (1997). *Mother Teresa: A complete authored biography.* San Francisco, CA: Harper Collins.

Stamp, R. (1982). *The schools of Ontario, 1876-1976.* Toronto, ON: University of Toronto Press.

Stanley, L. (1990). Feminist praxis and academic mode of production: An editorial introduction. In L. Stanley (ed.), *Feminist praxis research, theory, and epistemology in feminist sociology* (pp. 3-19). London, UK: Routledge.

Starratt, R. (1993). *The drama of leadership.* Great Britian, UK: Burgess Science Press.

Starratt, R. (2001, Nov. 9). *Building a learning community.* Paper presented at a University of Calgary, Educational Leadership Symposium, Calgary, AB.

Stewart, D. (2000). *Philospbers of education on spirituality.* Paper presented at the Canadian Federation for the Humanities and Social Sciences, Canadian Association of Educational Administration annual congress, at the University of Alberta, Edmonton, AB.

Stringer, E. T. (1993). Socially responsive educational research: Linking theory and practice. In E. Flinders & G. Mills (Eds.), *Theory and concepts in qualitative research: Perspectives from the field* (pp. 141-162). New York: Teachers College Press.

Stringer, E. (1996). *Action research: A handbook for practitioners.* Thousand Oaks, CA: Sage.

Sullivan, E. & Decker, P, (1992). *Effective management in nursing.* Toronto, ON: Addison-Wesley.

Sweet, L. (1997). *God in the classroom: The controversial issue of religion in Canada's schools.* Toronto, ON: McClelland & Stewart.

Talbot, M. (1991). *The Holographic universe.* New York: HarperCollins.

Thom, D. (1993). *Educational management and leadership: word, spirit and deed for a just society.* Calgary, AB: Detselig.

Thom, D. (2001). *The world leadership opportunity: Resolved Christianity and one education system.* Thunder Bay, ON: Lakehead University Faculty of Education.

Thurston, M. (1998). *Discovering your soul's purpose.* Virginia Beach, VA: Association for Research and Enlightenment (ARE) Press.

Tisdell, E. (2003). *Exploring spirituality and culture in adult and higher education.* San Francisco, CA: Jossey-Bass.

Toulmin, S. (1990). *Cosmopolis: The hidden agenda of modernity.* New York, NY: The Free Press.

Toulmin, S. (1995). Forward. In R. Goodman & W. Fisher (Eds.), *Rethinking knowledge: Reflections across the disciplines* (pp. x-xv). New York: State of New York Press.

Toulmin, S. (1996). Concluding methodological reflections: Elitism and democracy among the sciences. In S. Toulmin & B. Gustavsen (Eds.), *Beyond theory: Changing organizations through participation* (pp. 203-225). Amsterdam PH: John Benjamins.

Toulmin, S. (1997). Forward. In S. Toulmin & B. Gustavsen (Eds.), *Beyound theory: Changing organizations through participation.* (pp. 1-4). Amsterdam PH: John Benjamins.

Ulich, R. (1945). *History of educational thought.* New York, NY: American Book Company.

Urantia Foundation. (1999). *The Urantia Book.* (12th ed.) Chicago, IL: Urantia Foundation.

Vaill, P. (1996). *Learning as a way of being.* San Francisco, CA: Jossey Bass.

Vaill, P. (1998). *Spirited leading and learning.* San Francisco, CA: Jossey Bass.

Valle, R. & Halling, S. (1989). *Existential phenomenological perspectives in psychology: Exploring the breadth of human experience.* New York: Plenum Press.

Vanier, J. (1998). *Becoming human.* Toronto, ON: House of Anansi Press.

Van Dusen, W. (1996). *Returning to the source: The way to the experience of God.* Moab, UT: Real People Press.

van Manen, M., (1990). *Researching lived experiences: Human science for an action sensitive pedagogy.* London, ON: University of Western Ontario.

van Manen, M. (2002). *Writing in the dark: Phenomenological studies in interpretive inquiry.* London, ON: Althouse Press.

Wadsworth, Y. (2001). The mirror, the magnifying glass, the compass and the map: Facilitating participatory action research. In P. Reason & H. Bradbury (Eds.), *Handbook of action research* (pp. 421-431). Thousand Oaks, CA: Sage Publications.

Walker, S. (2002, Apr. 27). The role of education in shaping community values. Paper presented at the Sheldon Chumir Foundation Community Values in an age of Globalization Symposium, April 26-28, Calgary, AB.

Walter, J. D. (1990). *The essence of self-realization: The wisdom of Paramhansa* Yogananda. Nevada City, CA: Crystal Clarity.

Wallace, R., & Wolf, A. (1995). *Contemporary sociological theory: Continuing the classical tradition.* New Jersey, NY: Prentice & Hall.

Walsch, N. (1995). *Conversations with God: An uncommon dialogue.* New York, NY: G. P. Putnam & Sons.

Watkinson, A. (1999). *Education, student rights and the charter.* Saskatoon, SK: Purich Publishing.

Webber, C., & Robertson, J. (1998). Boundary breaking: An emergent model for leadership development. In *Educational Policy Analysis, 6* (21). Retrieved July 5, 1999, from htpp://olam.ed.asu.edu/epaa/v6n21.html

Weber, M. (1947). *The theory of social and economic organization.* New York: Oxford University Press.

Weber, M. (1968). *Charisma and institutional building.* Chicago, IL: University of Chicago Press.

Weber, M. (1978). *Economy and society: An outline of interpretive sociology.* G. Rough & C. Wittich (Eds.), Berkeley, CA: University of California Press.

Weingarten, H. (2002, April). *The role of education in shaping community values.* Paper presented at the Sheldon Chumir Foundation Community Values in an Age of Globalization, symposium, April 28, Calgary, AB.

Wheatcroft, D. (2003, June 21). *The Virtues project.* Paper presented to Calgary educators at an Educational Leadership workshop held in the Garden studio, Calgary AB. Also retrieved January 10, 2004 from www.virtuesproject.com

Wilber, K. (1996). *A brief history of everything.* Boston, MA: Shambhala.

Williams, B. (2000). Humility and vision in the life of the effective leader. In R Banks. & K. Powell (Eds.), *Faith in leadership: How leaders live out their faith in their work and why it matters.* (pp. 63-76). San Francisco, CA: Jossey-Bass.

Williamson, K. (2001, Dec. 12). Differences put aside to remember Sept.11. *Calgary Herald*, pp. B4.

Wilson, J.D., Stamp, R., & Audet, L. (1970). *Canadian education: A history*. Scarborough, ON: Prentice-Hall of Canada.

Wilson, H. (1985). *Introducing research in nursing*. San Francisco, CA: Addison-Wesley.

Woods, G., & Woods, P. (2002, Jan.). Creativity in educational policy: Sociological and spiritual perspectives. Paper presented at a seminar at Open University, Walton Hall in Milton Keynes, U.K., January 8, 2002.

Woods, N., Lentz, M. & Mitchell, E. (1993). The new woman: health promoting and health damaging behaviors. *Health Care for Women International, 14* (5), 389-417.

Yancey, P. (1997). *What's so amazing about grace?* Grand Rapids, MI: Zondervan.

Yancey, P. (2000). *Reaching for the invisible God*. Grand Rapids, MI: Zondervan.

Yob, I. (1994). Spiritual education: A public school dialogue with religious interpretations. *Philosophy of Education, 1.* Retrieved March 1, 2000, from htpp:/www.ed.uiuc.edu/PES/94docs/YOB.HTM

Young, J. & Levin B. (1998). *Understanding Canadian schools: An introduction to educational administration* Toronto, ON: Harcourt Brace & Company.

Young, M. (1999). Multifocal educational policy research: Toward a method for enhancing traditional educational policy studies. *American Educational Research Journal, 36*(4), 677-714.

Zohar, D. & Marshall, I. (2000). *Spiritual intelligence: The ultimate intelligence*. New York: Bloomsbury.

Biography

Dr. Nancy Doetzel is an international speaker and an awarding winning scholar, journalist and musician. She received a PhD from the University of Calgary Graduate Division Education Research in 2004. From Lakehead University, she received an MA, HBA, HBSW and BA, and a International Certified Alcoholism and Drug Abuse Counsellor Certification from the Canadian Council of Professional Certification.

For her doctorate research, she won the Canadian Association of Educational Administration Distinguished Dissertation Award. At the University of Calgary, she designed and is teaching the graduate courses: 1. Leading with Heart and Mind, and 2. Cultivating Spirituality within Leadership.